ह्रीं – *Hrīṃ*

Śrī Tripura Sundarī Devī

*

Dr. Ramamurthy N.

M.Sc., B.G.L., CA‖ B, CCP, DSADP, CISA, PMP, CGBL, Ph.D.

*

Title: *Śrī Tripura Sundarī Devī*

Series: Three of Ten

First Edition: 2022

Author: **Dr. Ramamurthy N**, Chennai.
http://ramamurthy.jaagruti.co.in/

Number of pages: 182

Price: ₹ 300.00

ISBN (13):   978-93-82237-94-5

Printed at:

Published by:

*****

Table of Contents

Blessings...4

Introduction 6

Daśa Mahā Vidyā Devis 10

Śrī Tripura Sundarī Devī 13

Form(s) of *Śrī Tripura Sundarī Devī* 19

Śrī Tripura Sundarī Devī Mantras 23

Śrī Tripura Sundarī Devī Yantram 26

Śrī Tripura Sundarī Suprabhātam 34

Śrī Tripura Sundarī Prātaḥ Śloka Pañcakam 40

Śrī Tripura Sundarī Pañcaratna Stotram 42

Śrī Tripura Sundarī Aṣṭakam 44

Śrī Tripura Sundarī Stotram 47

Śrī Tripura Sundarī Hṛdaya Stotram 49

Śrī Tripura-Sundarī Kavacam 84

Śrī Tripura Sundaryaṣṭottara Śatanāmā Stotram 92

Śrī Tripura Sundaryaṣṭottara Śatanāmāvalī 97

Śrī Tripura Sundarī Cakrarāja Stotram 102

Śrī Tripura Sundarī Sahasranāma Stotram 109

Śrī Tripura Sundarī Sahasranāmāvaliḥ 143

Śrī Tripura Sundary Aparādha Kṣamāpaṇa Stotram 176

About the Author 179

Blessings

Date : 05/08/2022

ஹ்ரீங்காராங்கித-மந்த்ர-ராஜ-நிலயம் ஸ்ரீ ஸர்வ-ஸங்க்ஷோபி⁴ணீ

முக்²யாபி⁴ஶ்சல-குந்தலாபி⁴ருஷிதம் மன்வஸ்ர-சக்ரே ஶுபே⁴.

யத்ர ஸ்ரீ-புர-வாஸினீ விஜயதே ஸ்ரீ-ஸர்வ-ஸௌபா⁴க்³யதே³

ஸ்ரீ-சக்ரம் ஶரணம் வ்ரஜாமி ஸததம் ஸர்வேஷ்ட-ஸித்³தி⁴-ப்ரத³ம்

ஸகல தேவதா ஸ்வரூபிணியாய் மணித்வீபத்தில் வஸித்துக் கொண்டு தன் லீலையால் ப்ரஹ்மாண்டங்களை படைத்தும், காத்தும், அழித்தும், மறைத்தும், அருளியும் கொண்டிருக்கும் ஸ்ரீ புவனேச்வரி தேவியின் பரிபூர்ண கடாக்ஷத்தினால், நமது சிஷ்யர் ஸ்ரீ ராமமூர்த்தி அவர்கள் தசமஹாவித்யா வரிசையில் மூன்றாவது வித்யையான ஸ்ரீத்ரிபுர ஸுந்தரி தேவி குறித்த நூலினை வெளியிடப்போகிறார்.

ஆத்மவித்யா, மஹாவித்யா, ஸ்ரீவித்யா என்கிறது லலிதா ஸஹஸ்ரநாமம். ஆத்ம வித்யையும் ஸ்ரீவித்யையும் வேறு வேறல்ல ! ஸ்ரீ லலிதா த்ரிபுரஸுந்தரி ஸ்ரீபுரத்தில் வசிப்பதாக லலிதோபாக்யானம் கூறுகிறது. அந்த ஸ்ரீபுரத்தில் திவ்யமான சிந்தாமணி க்ருஹத்தின் நடுவில் நவரத்ந மயமான சபையில் கோடி சூர்ய பிரகாசத்துடன் கூடிய, ஒப்புயர்வற்ற, அழகிய சிம்ஹாஸனத்தில் அம்பிகை மஹாகாமேச்வருடன் அமர்ந்திருக்கிறாள். அந்த ஸ்ரீபுரமே ஸ்ரீவித்யா உபாஸகர்களால் ஸ்ரீசக்ரவடிவில் பூஜிக்கப்படுகிறது. அதன் நடுவில் பிந்து ஸ்தானத்தில் ஸ்ரீலலிதாம்பிகா அமர்ந்து, படைத்தல், காத்தல், அழித்தல், மறைத்தல், அருளல் என்ற ஐந்தொழிலையும் செய்து வருகிறாள்.

அந்த ஸ்ரீசக்ரமே நம் உடல். 9 ஆவரணங்களும் நம் உடலிலேயே உள்ளன என பாவித்து . ஸ்ரீமாதா நம்மிலேயே உறைகிறாள் என்று அம்பிகையை ஸஹஸ்ரார கமலத்தில் தியானிக்க, அந்த தியானத்தின் முதிர்ச்சியில் சரீரம் முழுவதும் அம்ருதம் பரவி எல்லையற்ற பேரானந்தம் உண்டாகிறது.

இதையே பாவனோபநிஷத்,
தயோ: காமேச்வரீ ஸதானந்த கநா பரிபூர்ண ஸ்வாத்மைக்ய ரூபா தேவதா லலிதா என்கிறது.

எத்தனையோ உபாஸனை இருந்தாலும் ஸ்ரீவித்யை தனிச்சிறப்பு வாய்ந்தது !

மஹேச-மாதவ-விதாத்ரு-மன்மத-ஸ்கந்த-நந்தி-இந்த்ர-மனு-சந்த்ர-குபேர-அகஸ்த்ய-க்ரோதபட்டாரக- வித்யாத்மிகே எனும்படி ப்ரம்ம விஷ்ணு மஹேசர் துவங்கி அத்துணை பேரும் உபாஸிப்பது லலிதா த்ரிபுரஸுந்தரியைத் தான்.

அந்த அம்பிகையை உபாஸிப்பது எல்லோருக்கும் கிட்டும் பாக்யமல்ல ! ஸுந்தரி உபாஸக புங்கவானாம் போகஸ்ய மோக்ஷஸ்ய கரஸ்ய ஏவ என்று சொல்லும்படி ஸ்ரீவித்யையை உபாஸிப்பவர் இகலோகத்திலும் ஸகல ஸௌக்யத்துடன் வாழ்ந்து பரலோகத்திலும் மோக்ஷத்தை அடையும் பேறுபெற்றவர்கள்.

யாருக்கு இது கடைசி பிறவியோ அவனுக்கே ஸ்ரீவித்யோபாஸனை லபிக்கும் என்கிறார்கள் மஹானீயர்கள்.

இந்நூலில் ஸ்ரீத்ரிபுரஸுந்தரியின் மந்த்ரங்கள், கவசம், யந்த்ரம், அஷ்டோத்திரம், ஸஹஸ்ரநாமம் என உபாஸனைக்குரிய அனைத்தும் உள்ளடக்கி இருப்பது பெரிதும் போற்றத்தக்க அம்சமாகும். இதனால் இந்நூல் ஸ்ரீவித்யோபாஸகர்களுக்கு ஒரு கையேடு போல உபயோகப்படும் !

இந்நூலை தொகுத்த முனைவர். N.ராமமூர்த்தி அவர்களுக்கு ஜகன்மாதா ஸ்ரீ புவனேச்வரி தேவியின் பரமானுக்ரஹம் கிடைக்கட்டும் என்று நாமும் ஆசியளிக்கிறோம்.

ஆனந்தம் சுபம் மங்களம் !

ஜய புவனேச்வரி!

ஸ்ரீ ப்ரணவாநந்த ஸ்வாமின:
ஸ்ரீ புவனேச்வரி அவதூத வித்யா பீடம்
புதுக்கோட்டை

*****

Introduction

ॐ श्री गुरुभ्यो नम: । *Oṃ Śrī Gurubhyo Namaḥ* ।

गुरुर्ब्रह्मा गुरुर्विष्णु गुरुर्देवो महेश्वर: । गुरु साक्षात् परं ब्रह्म तस्मै श्रीगुरवे नम:॥

Gururbrahma Gururviṣṇuḥ Gururdevo Maheśvaraḥ ।

Guru Sākśāt Parabrahma Tasmai Śrīgurave Namaḥ ॥

गुरुवे सर्वलोकानां भिषजे भवरोगिनां। निधये सर्व विद्यानां दक्षिणा मूर्तये नम:॥

Guruve Sarvloksansam Bhiṣaje Bhavaroginām ।

Nidhaye Sarva Vidhyānām Dakśiṇa Mūrtaye Namaḥ ॥

सदाशिव समारंभां शङ्कराचार्य मध्यमां अस्मद आचार्य पर्यन्तां वन्दे गुरु परंपराम्॥

Sadāshiva Samārambām Śankarāchārya Madhyamām ।

Asmad Achārya Paranthām Vande Guru Paramparām ॥

श्रुति स्मृति पुराणानामालयं करुणालयम्। नमामि भगवत्पादंशंकरं लोकशंकरम्॥

Śruti Smruti Purānānām Ālayam Karunālayam ।

Namāmi Bhagavatapādam Śankaram Lokaśankaram ॥

वागर्थाविव सम्प्रुक्तौ वागर्थ प्रतिपत्तये। जगत: पितरौ वन्दे पार्वती परमेश्वरौ ॥

Vāgarthāviva Sampruktakou Vāgartha Pratipaye ।

Jagataḥ Pitarou Vande Pārvati Parameśwarou ॥

We all originated from *Brahmam*[1]. We reach that *Brahmam* – merge with that *Brahmam*. That is actually *lia-samāti*. This rhythm cannot be exercised without the use or support of an appropriate instructor. The *Upasana* is aimed at an idol. It is both *Suguna* (with qualities) and (without qualities) *Nirguna*. A person is capable of doing *Nirguna Upasana* only after he has attained *Sagunopasana*. Suddenly, it is impossible for one to get involved in *Nirgunobasana* straight away.

As mentioned in *Brahadāranyaka Upanishat* the *Ādhi Moolam*, also called as *Parabrahmam*, does not have any form or qualities. It does not fit within any limitations. However, in order to realise that *Brahmam* without any form, a sort of image worship is suggested. Once the maturity (*Sāloka, Sāmeepya* and *Sāyujya*) is reached, there is no need for any prescriptions

---

[1] *Brahmam* is different *Brahma*. *Brahma* is the head of all Devas. On the other hand *Brahmam* is *Parabrahmam*, the supreme.

and/ or restrictions to worship gods with different images, fasting, etc. Various *karmas* have to be performed to take us to this *yogic* position.

Shiva, Shakti and *Vishnu* are all one and the same. These three Gods are without origin. For all other Gods we could read the origin and for some even the end could also be seen in one or other *Purana* or stories.

In the form of *Arddhanāreeshwara* the left half of Lord *Shiva* is *Shakti*. Again, in the form of *Shankara Nārāyana*, the left half of Lord *Shiva* is *Vishnu*. This clearly evidences that *Shakti* and *Vishnu* are one and the same and naturally *Shiva* also.

Brahadāranyaka Upanishat verses (I–3, I–4), starting from "*Ātmaivetamagra Āseet*" till "*Sa Imamevātmānam Tvetāpātayat Tataḥ*" describes in this manner – the *Parabrahmam* seems to be two as husband and wife.

The energy of the *Parabrahmam* is *Sri Devi – Shakti*. Even when the power of that object is within it, the power cannot exist without the entity. Hence, the *Parabrahmam* is the *Shakti* and the *Shakti* is the *Parabrahmam*. Both cannot be different.

In the same manner, if *Eswaran* is considered as *Brahmam*, Goddess Ambika is merged with that *Eswaran*. Can the fragrant and the flower be separate? How about whiteness and the milk? *Ambika* is thus unsplittable from *Eswaran*. *Parameswara* and *Parāshakti* are the earliest/ first couple to be inseparable; They are the mother and father of all living beings. Yet they are one and the same.

Chāndogya Upanishat (6:2:1) says "*Ekam Evātvetīyam*" – That is, all the Gods are the same – there is only one God, no two. *Brahma Sootram* says "*Ekam Brahma Dvitīya Nāste Neha Naye Nāste Naya Kinchana*" – there is only one God – no two – not at all two. *Yajur Veda* (32-3) utters – "*Na Tasya Pratimāsti Śutāma Pāpvitam*" – He is so holy and does not have any image.

Jagadguru Sri Adi Shankara Bhagavat Pada divided our *Sanatana* Hindu religion into six branches – sub-religions and established *Shanmathas* – *Gānapatyam, Koumaram, Shaivam, Vaishnavam, Shaktam* and Souram. *Adi Shankara*, though equally treated all these six sub-religions, he had a distinct admiration for Shaktam-Shakti. She is *Jaganmata* – the mother of this universe – the mother of all living beings.

We are not yet mature enough to realise the formless *Parabrahmam* (no need of writing/ reading this book, if we are that much mature).

Someone has to hold back or attach side wheels until one learns to drive a bicycle. Once he becomes expert these are not needed. We need a boat to cross a river. Once we have reached the other shore, what is the need of a boat.

Therefore, until we all mature enough, we need to worship a God with form – why can't it be the holy mother – is it not that we get that much pleasure when we call mother as '*Amma*'?

When we think of incarnation of God – immediately the 10 incarnations of Lord *Vishnu* (*Dasha avatar*) only come to our mind. If we think a little bit deep, one may be reminded of the 24 incarnations of Lord *Vishnu* as described in *Shrimad Vishnu Bhagavatam* (1.3.6-25).

However, the *Shakta* texts, more importantly *Sri Devi Bhagavatam*, describe many an incarnation of *Sri Devi*, who is a sister of Lord *Vishnu*. Among them are the ten cosmic forms of the Divine Mother, called the "*Dasha Maha Vidya*"[2], are the most special. He later wrote and published a book on the various forms of *Sri Devi* entitled "Incarnations of Ambika".

The author's Sri Vidya Guru, Head of Pudukkottai Bhuvaneshwari Mutt, Pujyasri Pranavananda Saraswathi Avadutha Swamiji, has led the way in writing many books. He asked the author to write a separate book detailing each of the ten goddesses of "*Dasha Maha Vidya*". In defiance of that order, this third book is written about *Sri Tripura Sundarī Devī*.

A few related mantras are also indicated wherever possible. In general, all the *mantras* are supposed to be secretive. All the more about *Shakti* related *mantras*. Hence, they are to be got initiated by an appropriate teacher (*guru*) only, before trying to chant of to do *japam*.

Primarily, the aim of this book is to explain in detail, the incarnation of Sri Devi as *Tripura Sundarī*, to explain her form and purpose and to explain some of the mantras. It is believed that the devotees will get benefitted by reading and understanding this and worshiping *Sri Tripura Sundarī Devī* in the right and appropriate way.

---

[2] This author of this book wrote and published a book in 2011, entitled " *Dasha Maha Vidya* " about the ten incarnations in general.

Devotees are advised to consult a qualified scholar or guru, if they have any doubts about any mantras or worshipping methods mentioned in this book. It is highly suggested not to start recitation/ puja with half-knowledge and assuming the rest. Books can only be a reference guide, but cannot act as a teacher (*guru*).

Generally, it is very difficult to read Samskruta words in English with proper pronunciation. It is apt to read them in Samskruta script itself. But to benefit those who cannot read Samskruta script the *mantras* have been given in English also. The Samskruta words, when transliterated in English are given in *italics*. Also, whenever She denotes Goddess *Sri Devi*, it is written as **She** or **Her**. Normally diacritical marks will be used for transliteration of Samskruta words into English. But general readers are not fully conversant with diacritical marks and hence they find it difficult to read. Hence, it not been used in this book in normal texts. But for proper pronunciation it has been completely used in *mantras*.

This book is simultaneously written in Tamil also.

My humble *pranāms* to *Śrīśrī Pranavānanda Saraswathi Swamiji*, for his blessings and some pleasantries about this edition. To enjoy his own wordings, the blessings have been given in Tamil itself.

My sincere thanks are due to all those who supported in this noble cause of bring out this book. Attempts have been made to give this book as much error free as possible. Still if there are any errors, apologies are sought. If the errors are given as feedback, it will the next edition to be fault free. Hope the readers would be benefitted by the contents of this book. The readers are requested to feel free to send their feedback and comments.

There is no doubt that *Sri Tripura Sundarī Devī* will shower her compassion and blessings to all those who read this book.

Our humble *Praṇāms* to all our *Gurus*.
Om Tat Sat

Chennai
2022   *Dr. Ramamurthy N.*

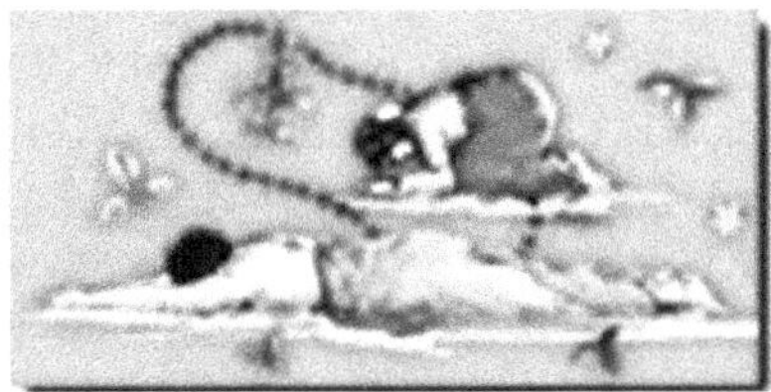

Daśa Mahā Vidyā Devis

There are 'n' number of images of *Devi*-s worshipped by sages for quite a long time. The most significant ten among them are being discussed in this chapter.

Each of these ten *vidya*-s, itself called as *Brahma Vidya*. *Tantra sastras* describe in detail the worshipping methods of these *Devis*.

Out of these 10 *vidya*-s, the *Tripura Sundari Vidya* also called as *Sri Vidya* is more famous in South India.

The *mantras, yantra, dhyana*, worshipping methods, results, forms, etc., of these ten *vidya*-s can be read in the tantra texts in Samskrutam. Sir Arthur Avalon, has also explained in detail in English.

There are different types, in the worship of *Sri Devi* – like *Vāmāchāra, Dakshināchāra, Samayāchāra* and *Koulachāra*. *Sri Lalita Sahasranāma* (*Sri Lalitā Sahasranāma* – 98th name – *Samayāchāratatparā*, 441st name – *Koulamārga Tatpara Sevitā*) accepts all these methods.

The destruction of *Daksha's yagna* by *Sati Devi* has been described in the 4th *Skanda* of *Shrimad Bhagavatam*. This has also been described in detail in *Bruhat Dharma Purana*. Once when *Daksha Prajapati* was proceeding towards the *yagna-Shala* (the place where the holy fire was being conducted), Lord *Shiva* (his son-in-law), who was in meditation did not get up as a respect. On account of this *Daksha* got wild and gave a curse that Lord Shiva will not get any share from the *yagna*. From that moment onwards, Lord Shiva does not even see Daksha.

In another instance, Daksha Prajapati himself started a *yagna*. All his daughters were invited with their husbands excepting *Sati Devi*. Knowing this, **she** asked permission from her husband Lord Shiva to attend the *yagna*, executed by her father. When Lord Shiva did not permit her, **she** took the form of *Mahā Kālī*, the first of Dasha Maha Vidya.

Surprised by the most terrified form of peaceful *Sati Devi*, Lord *Shiva* started running from that place. But in whichever direction he ran, *Devi* was before him with the terrified form. The ten forms **She** took in all the ten directions (8 directions + upward + downward) are *Dasha Maha Vidyas* of *Sri Devi*.

Surprised by this Lord Shiva stood stunned. Though *Devi* tried to console him stating that **She** is *Sati Devi* only, Lord *Shiva* could not get away from the fear immediately. Then *Devi* explained the specialties and purposes of all the ten *Vidya*-s to her husband.

Further **She** mentioned – "the *Vedas* and sacred writings (*Agamas*) told by you to this world are my two hands. I wear moveable and immoveable things of this world with those two hands. These ten forms will help to bless the worshippers. People should reach me by secretly following the *mantra*, *yantra*, verses, *kavacha*, etc., as taught by the teacher (Guru). I am telling you with the affection on you. Please permit me to attend the *yagna*" – **She** requested.

After getting his permission, **she** reached the *yagna* place of Daksha, which was protected by Nandi, Brungi and others. **She** could not tolerate the reprimands on Lord Shiva and hence disappeared in the fire of *yoga*. Knowing this Lord Shiva created *Veerabhadra* from his entangled locks of hair and sent him to destroy the *yagna* of Daksha. *Devi* also took the form of *Bhadrakālī* and with the help of *Veerabhadra* destroyed Daksha and all the opponents of Lord Shiva. This is the origin of *Dasha Maha Vidyas*.

The directions in which the ten *Mahavidyas* originated are described in the below diagram.

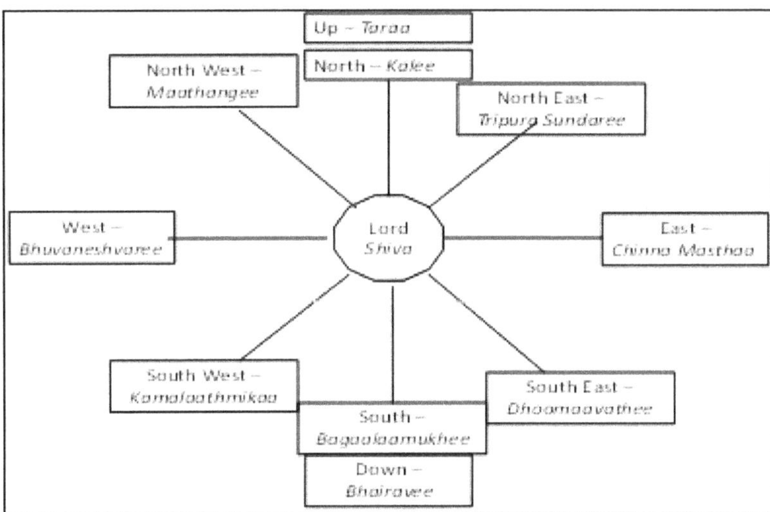

Out of the three qualities of illusion, the pure *sattva* quality related with *Brahmam* (the Supreme Being) is called *Vidya*. Sir Arthur Avalon feels that even in this the fourth and which is beyond any *tattva* is the blissful form of *Devi* is called *Maha Vidya*.

The relation of *Brahmam* to the pure Sattva quality, of the three qualities of *Maya*, is called *Vidya*. The fourth (transcendental) philosophy is the blissful form of the Goddess, which is called *Maha Vidya*. *Chamuṇḍa Tattva* splits these ten *Mahavidyas* into *Mahavidyas*, *Siddhavidyas* and *Vidyas*. But the text *Shyāmā Rahasya* mentions all these as *Mahavidyas* only. We also follow this and call all the ten as *Mahavidyas*.

The presiding deity(ies) of the 10th Chapter of *Sri Devi Mahatmyam* is said to be these *Dasha Maha Vidyas*.

Let us try to understand a little more about each of these 10 Devis. Books about the first Two *Devis* viz. Sri *Bhadra Kālī* and *Sri Tara Devi* have already been written. Now this is about the third *Sri Tripura Sundari Devi*. We will try to know about other Devis in forthcoming books.

*****

Śrī Tripura Sundarī Devī

Adiparasakti, Paradevata, Sarva Loka Jaganmata, Sri Devi creates, preserves and destroys all the worlds. In addition, she performs the tasks of Anugraham and Tirodanam also, in accordance with one of the names in Sri Lalita Sahasranama *"Pancha Krutya Parayana"*. As a *Parabrahma Mahishi*, she, after creating lives, has taken many divine incarnations for the state and has been regularly doing sishta maintenance and evil discipline.

Among the various incarnations of Sriman Narayana described by Sri Vishnu Bhagavatam, ten avatars are prominent. Similarly, to protect the entire world, Sri Devi has manifested herself in ten different forms known as Dasha Maha Vidyas, as described in the previous chapter. Among those ten, Sri Tripura Sundari Devi Vidya is the third among the ten. Though these ten names are not much popular, the name "Tripura Sundari" alone is much known and heard off by all.

Maha Tripura Sundari, is the Eeshvari ruling the world but is none other than the indwelling spirit (atman) within us and which pervades us all that exists. This introduction deals with the background on the name of Tripurasundari. This is one of the best epithets to describe the Devi meaning that she is the belle of all the three worlds. The Word tripura can be interpreted variously. The Kalika Purana says that by the will of Pradhana, the body of lord Shiva became triple; The upper part became Brahma, the middle part became Vishnu and the lower part became Rudra. As these three pura-s (bodies) are in lord Shiva, he is called Tripura (three bodied) and his wife is known as Tripura. In the Kamakala Vilasa (13,14), the honoured sage, Abhiyukta, mentions that Devi created all the three forms and She is before all (Purobhava), because She is in the form of all the three (Trayeemayee) and exists even after the dissolution of the three worlds and recreates them again.

The word Tripura (त्रिपुर) means three cities or three worlds, Sundari (सुन्दरी) means beautiful woman. Tripura Sundari means the most beautiful woman in the three worlds. She is called Tripura because it is similar to the triangle that symbolizes the yoni and forms her circle. She is also known as Tripura as her mantra has three clusters of letters. She is called Tripura because she is manifested in Brahma, Vishnu and Shiva as the creator, preserver and destroyer of the universe.

Tripura Sundari is most often mentioned in the Lalitopakhyana of Brahmanda Purana and Tripura Rahasya.

She alone is supreme atman. She alone is the greatest destination. She alone is the greatest holy place of pilgrimage. She alone is the great fruit and result.

Brahmanda Purana – Lalita Mahatmya, Chapter 38, Verse 75 – The Tripura Upanishad places the goddess Tripura Sundari as the ultimate Shakti (energy, power) of the universe. She is described as the supreme consciousness, above Brahma, Vishnu and Shiva. She rules over three cities, three paths' children of the universe. 'a', 'ka' and 'tha', fully present – She is present in these letters. She is ageless, birth less, the greatest and she is the glory of all gods.

Tripura Upanishad Verse 01 – The Bahuvrihi Upanishad is notable for asserting that the Self (soul, Atman) is a Goddess who alone existed before the creation of the universe.

Bahuvrihi Upanishad, Verse 05 – She alone is Atman. Other than She is untruth, non-self. She is Brahman-Consciousness. She is the Vidya of Consciousness, non-dual Brahman Consciousness, a wave of Being-Consciousness-Bliss. The Beauty of the three-great-cities, penetrating without and within, is resplendent, nondual, self-subsisting. What is, is pure Being; what shines, is pure Consciousness; what is dear, is Bliss. So here is the Maha-Tripura Sundari who assumes all forms. You and I and all the world and all divinities and all besides are the Maha Tripura Sundari. The sole Truth is the thing named "the Beautiful". It is the nondual, integral, supreme Brahman.

According to the Patala Khanda of Padma purana, God Krishna is the male form of the goddess Lalita. I am Goddess Lalita and that Radhika who is celebrated in songs. I am called Vasudeva, who always is of the nature of the art of love. I am truly of a feminine form, and I am the ancient woman, and I am goddess Lalita, and in a manly form I have Krishna's body.

Padma purana, Patala-Khanda, Verses 46:47 – Role in creation – According to the Tripura Rahasya, only goddess Tripura Sundari existed before the beginning of the universe. She created the Trimurti and began the creation of the universe.

Long ago, at the time of creation, Tripura the Universal Consciousness was all alone. There was nothing other than her. She, the embodiment of

Power, who is Self-independent wanted to create; the desire developed. From desire, knowledge was born and then action. From Her three glances the three gods were born. Pasupathi represented desire, Hari knowledge and Brahma action. They were looked at by Sankari and became naturally powerful and Truth abiding.

Shri Tripura Rahasya (Mahatmya Khanda), Chapter 10, Verses 18 to 22 – Those who are deluded by my maya, don't know me completely. I alone, worshipped by all, give the desired fruit. Other than me, there is none who is to be worshipped or who grants the fruits.

In the Brahmanda-purana, it is mentioned that the Goddess Tripura Sundari rules over the entire universe and She is the supreme empress and Brahma, Vishnu and Shiva are mere functionaries in her empire. The Lalita Sahasranama portrays Her as being attended by Lakshmi and Saraswati on either side. Shankaracharya, in his Soundrayalahari, mentions that Brahma, Vishnu and Shiva started their cosmic processes when the Supreme shakti knitted her brow for a split second.

We have all heard of Sri Vidya, Sri Vidya upasaka, etc. But what is Sri Vidya? Who is a Sri Vidya upasaka? The *Shree Vidyaa* is the famous *Tripura Sundaree vidya* only. In Sri Lalita Sahasranama, 585th name is "Sri Vidya" – that means Sri Lalita is Sri Vidya and Sri Vidya is Sri Lalita. There is no difference between Sri Devi and Sri Vidya. The devi mantra consisting of fifteen letters called, *Panchadashakshari* is the Sri Vidya. One who got initiated in this mantra from an appropriate guru and continue chanting the japam is the Sri Vidya upasaka. Anything in the form of triplets is Sri Tripura Devi only;

- This *Panchadashakshari* mantra composed of three koota-s (peaks).
- She resides in three nadi-s (nerve channels), namely sushumna, pingala and ida.
- She is the ruler of the three shaktis – ichcha (will), kriya (action) and jnana (knowledge).
- She pervades all the three worlds – heaven, earth and the nether world.
- She is the controller of all the three bodies – sthula (gross), sookshma (subtle) and kaarana (causal).
- She is the self which is present through the three states of existence – Jagrat (awaking), Svapna (dream) and Sushupti (deep sleep).
- Though she is above all guna-s (Nirguna), she pervades the three modes of energy – sattva (purity), rajas (mobility) and tamas (inertia).

Love and joy are the inherent qualities of beauty. Sundari means belle and beauty. Shankaracharya, in his bhaashyam for Chandogya upanishat (7, 31:1), mentions that all longing and desires is a source of pain and in what is finite there is no Bliss. He mentions that the infinite alone can produce bliss. When bliss takes on a form, it is Sundari – sarvaanga sundari (Sri Lalita Trishati – 130) and Shankara comments on this name of the Devi as the one who possesses all the marks of beauty and has all the qualities of perfection and is thus the source of bliss.

Tripura Sundaree is the *Icchaa Shakti* (wish energy) of the Supreme Being. The *tantras* do not distinguish the energy and the person who has that energy. Hence *Tripura Sundaree*, who is the *Icchaa Shakti* is the Supreme Being. *Upanishads* mention that the knowledge called *Pragnaanam* is energy and hence that is a character of the Supreme Being. The transcendental form of this *Devee* resides in our forehead between the two eye-brows – the place of *Aagnaa chakra*. This is being conveyed by *Bhaalasthaa, Indradhanu: prabhaa* (*Lalita Sahasranaama* 593, 594). The second place is the *Vishuddhi chakra* or *Shanginee Naadi*, the place of dreams, the neck. This is also conveyed by the names *Shira: sthitaa, Chandranibhaa* (*L.S.* 591, 592). Thirdly **She** has a place in our hearts – *Hrudayasthaa, Raviprakhyaa* (*L.S.* 595, 596) – indicating that **She** is in the form of the intellectual who is fond of sleep.

All the three states of a soul (*Jaagrath, Swapna* and *Sushupti* – awakened, sleep and deep sleep states) and the fourth one (*tureeyam* – swoon), which is beyond all these, are all *Tripurasundaree's* only. This *Devee* shines in our body in three places Sun, Moon and fire *mandalas* alongwith the corresponding illumination and hence **She** is called as *Tripurasundaree*. Because of her light the Sun, Moon, fire, stars and lightning get illuminated (Kat. Up. 2-15).

Vedas convey that only the knowledge of the form of this *Devee* characters the form of Supreme Being – *Satyam* (truth), *Gnaanam* (knowledge) and *Anantam* (endless) *Brahma* (*Tai. Up.* 2.1) – so also *Vignaanam* (science) and *Aanandam* (bliss) *Brahma* (*Br. Up.* 39.25).

The description of the gross form of *Devee* has been described in the meditation verses. In addition, the *mantra* with 15 letters is her subtle form. *Kaamakalaa bheeja* (root letter) thought as further subtle form (*paraaroopa*) is another form. Learned secretly mention only this as a fourth form. *Vaamakeshvara tantra* (1.8) advises as – *Tāmīkārākṣara Uddhāram Sārātsārām Parātparām*. We read in *Vedas* as – *taam padmineemeem sharanamaham prabadye* (*R.V.* 4-4-34). It seems this is what has been advised by *Hayagreeva*.

Only this *vidyaa* is mentioned by the word '*aham*'. If the first letter '*a*' and the last letter '*ha*' are united, then the *mantra* of *Devee* is obtained. The meaning of the word *aham* is 'I' (self). This is announced by the great sentence "*aham brahmaasmi*" (*Br. Up.* 2-5-16).

Tripurasundaree has a name as *Maatrukaavarnaroopinee* (*L.S.* 577). The meaning of this name is that **She** is in the form of letters. Whichever language or word anyone utters in this world, it all becomes only the name of the mother.

Those who worship *Shakti* are called *Shaaktaas* – *Shree Vidyaa Upaasakas* are sub-set of *Shaaktaas*. Worshiping *Shakti* comes along the *guru parampara*.

The method of worshipping male Gods is with *mantras*. The method of worshipping female Goddesses is called *Vidyaa*. *Shree Vidyaa* is worshipping the unison of *Shiva* and *Shakti*. Hence this comes under the *mantra* group also. *Shree Vidyaa* is said to be the greatest among the *mantras*.

One *Shree Lalita Sahasranaama* describes *Shree Vidyaa* through various names;
- 587 – *Shree Shodashaaksharee Vidyaa* – sixteen lettered mantra.
- 583 – *Aatma Vidyaa* – One who is the doctrine to help understand the self.
- 584 – *Mahaa Vidyaa* – One who is in the form of a great doctrine
- 585 – *Shree Vidyaa* - One who is in the form of *Panchadashee Vidya*.
     Shree Vidyaa is of four types. They are;
     a. *Yagna Vidyaa* – about actions
     b. *Mahaa Vidyaa* – devotion to deities
     c. *Guhya Vidyaa* – secret science of *mantras*
     d. *Atma Vidyaa* – *Brahma Vidyaa* the science of *Brahmam*

Vishnu Puraana says that *Shree Devee* is in the form of all the above *Vidyaas*.
- who is in the form of the *mantra* with 16 letters. By suffixing one seed at the end of the *Panchadashee mantra*, we get the *Vidyaa* with 16 letters. (According to the rule since the *mantras* are to be learnt through appropriate *gurus*, they have not been detailed here).
- The above four names indicate;
     o *Karmavidyaa* teaching the action methods.

- o *Vishvaroopavidyaa* teaching the *Viraat* form (*mahat*) taken to show the *Brahmam* as this world – the *Vishvaroopa* view in the 11th chapter of *Shreemad Bhagavad Geeta* may be referred.
- o Instructing the *mantra* form of *Shree Devee*.
- o Some schools say that this is the *Brahmavidyaa* instructing the *Parabrahma* form of *Shree Devee*.

Tripura Sundari is also known as Rajarajeshwari, Shodashi, Kamakshi and Lalita. She is also a prominent Mahavidya. She is glorified in many Shakta texts, with Lalita Sahasranama, Soundarya Lahari being the most popular one. She is known as Adi Parashakti in Lalitopakhyana of Brahmanda Purana.

According to the Srikula tradition in Shaktism, Tripura Sundari is the foremost of the Mahavidyas, the supreme divinity of Hinduism and also the primary goddess of Sri Vidya. The Tripura Upanishad places her as the ultimate Shakti (energy, power) of the universe. She is described as the supreme consciousness, ruling from above Brahma, Vishnu, and Shiva.

May the divine mother guide us in our every action and thought and may she confer upon us the greatest gift of all, moksha (liberation) by removing the veil of maya which she weaves.

*****

Form(s) of *Śrī Tripura Sundarī Devī*

Usually meditative hymns (*dhyana shlokas*) about the gods are figurative of the concerned God or Goddess.

The meditation hymn of *Śrī Tripura Sundarī Devī*;

बालार्कायुततेजसं त्रिनयनं रक्ताम्बरोल्लासिनीं
नानालंकृति राजमानवपुषं बालोडुराट्शेखरम् ।
हस्तैरिक्षु धनुः सृणिं सुमशरं पाशं मुदा
बिभ्रतीं श्रीचक्रस्थितसुन्दरीं त्रिजगतामाधारभूतां स्मरेत् ॥

Bālārkāyutatejasam Trinayanam Raktāmbarollāsinīm

Nānālamkruti Rājamānavapuṣam Bālodurātśekharam |

Hastairikṣudhanuḥ Sruṇim Sumaśaram Pāśam Mudā

Bibhratīm Śrīcakrasthitasundarīm Trijagatāmādhārabhūtām Smaret ||

The meaning of this verses is;

Devee has thousand times powerful light like a rising Sun. **She** has three eyes and four hands. **She** is sitting on a cot, which has Brahma, Vishnu, Rudra and *Eeshaana* as four legs and *Sadaashiva* as plank. **She** has weapons like noose and goad in two hands and a bow made of sugar cane and an arrow made of five flowers (lotus, Red Lotus, Red Lily, Red Jasmine and Mango flower) in other two hands. These five flowers indicate five self-characteristics (*Tanmaatras*)

Among these the noose indicates *Icchaa Shakti* (the wish energy); the goad *jnaana Shakti* (knowledge energy); bow and arrows indicate *kriyaa Shakti* (energy of action). There are three halls in the *mantra* of *Shreedevee* – viz. *Vaagbhava koota, Kaamaraaja koota* and *Shakti koota*. This *vidyaa* is being worshipped through various maargas (methods) by different upaasakas (worshippers). The 12 major *upaasakas* and the name of the vidyaas prescribed by them are;

* *Khaadividyaa* followed by Manu, Lopaamudra, Manmata and Dhoorvaasa
* *Haadividyaa* followed by Kubera, Agastya, Sun, Vishnu and Shiva.
* *Saadividyaa* followed by Moon, Nandi and Skanda.

Brahmaanda Puranaa mentions that *Khaadividyaa* is the best among *Shree Vidyaas*.

The dwelling place of *Shreedevee* is *Shree chakra*. This has nine *Aavarnas*. At *Bindu*, the center place of it, **she** shines without parting with Lord *Parameshvara*. From this place **She** does the five tasks like creation, protection, destruction, concealing and blessing.

Her form is described in another Dhyana Stotra as follows;

ॐ अरुणां करुणा तरङ्गिताक्षीं धृत पाशाङ्कुश पुष्प बाणचापाम् ।
अणिमादिभि रावृतां मयूखैरहमित्येव विभावये भवानीम् ॥

Om Aruṇām Karuṇa Tharangitakshīm Dhrutha Paśānguśa Puśpabaṇa
Cāpām ।
Aṇimādhibhi-Rāvruthām Mayukhai – Raha Mityeva Vibhāvaye Bhavānīm ॥

I imagine of my goddess Bhavani, who has a colour of the rising sun. Who has eyes which are waves of mercy, who has bow made of sweet sugar-cane, Arrows made of soft flowers, and pasha and Ankush in her hands, and who is surrounded by her devotees with great powers great, as personification of the concept of 'I'?

Also details of her appearance are found in the famous hymn in her praise, the Lalita Sahasranama, where she is said to be;

Seated on a throne like a queen (names 2 and 3), to wear jewels (names 13 and 14), to have the auspicious marks of a married woman (names 16–25), and to have heavy breasts and a thin waist (name 36); the crescent moon adorns her forehead and her smile overwhelms Kameshwara, the lord of desire (name 28). She has as her throne with its legs being Pancha Brahmas (five Brahmas) (name 249).

She is often depicted ichnographically as a 16-year-old girl (hence the appellation "*Shodashi*") seated on a lotus that rests on the supine body of Sadashiva, which in turn lies on a throne whose legs are the gods Brahma, Vishnu, Ishvara and Rudra. In some cases, the lotus is growing out of Shiva's navel. In other more common cases, the lotus is grown directly from the *Sri Chakra*.

In the Jnana Khanda of Tripura Rahasya, Chapter 20, Verses 36:37, goddess herself describes her eternal form;

In the island of jewels, encircled by the ocean of nectar, beyond the universe, there is a mansion made of Chintamani (wish giving jewel) in the grove Kadamba (Burflower) trees. There is a platform with four legs representing Brahma, Vishnu, Mahesha and Ishwara, and the platform itself represent the back Sadashiva. On it, is installed my non-transcendent form as Tripura Sundari in the form of eternal consciousness.

The Vamakeshvara tantra says that Tripura-sundari dwells on the peaks of the Himalayas; is worshipped by sages and heavenly nymphs; has a body like pure crystal; wears a tiger skin, a snake as a garland around her neck, and her hair tied in a jata; holds a trident and drum; is decorated with jewels, flowers, and ashes; and has a large bull as a vehicle.

The Tantrasara describes her in detail from her hair to her feet. The Tantrasara dhyana mantra says that she is illuminated by the jewels of the crowns of Brahma and Vishnu, who when bowed down to worship her, their crowns are sharpened with the nails of her toes. It is also mentioned that "In Soundarya Lahari and Tantrasara she is not associated with Shiva in any obvious way as she is in other depictions".

Vaishnavism traditions have a similar set of complementary parallels between Vishnu and Lakshmi. The Tantric Vaishnava Pancharatra texts associates Lalita with Lakshmi. Author Douglas Renfrew Brooks says, "Lalita, like the Pancharatra conception of Lakshmi, acts independently by taking over the cosmic functions of the male deity; yet she does not defy the god's wishes". Brooks also says, "In contrast to most Vaishnava conceptions of Lakshmi, however, Lalita destabilizes temporarily for the purpose of reasserting order".

Sri Vidya, then, can be understood as one of the premier instances of Hindu Shakta Tantrism. Specifically, it is the tradition (sampradaya) which deals with worship of Tripurasundari, "the most beautiful Tantric form of Sri/Lakshmi, [who is] ... the most benign, beautiful and youthful yet motherly manifestation of the Supreme Shakti.

Tripura Sundari – Tripuram = three worlds, Sundari = beautiful. In all three worlds, her beauty is unmatched. In Soundaryalahari, Sri Adi Shankara Bhagavat Badal, devotes 58 (42-100) shlokas entirely to describe the beauty of Sri Devi. This passage describes the Shakti of the Supreme Mother from head to toe (*kesadi padam*).

He tries to describe Sri Devi from the top of the head, or above it, from the crown, to the feet, or below it, to the soles of the feet. It should be noted that it is mentioned that he tries to describe, not that he describes. Try as he might, he never seemed satisfied with describing her beauty.

Sri Devi emerged little by little from Cidagni Kunda (Sri Lalita Sahasranamam 4th name – *Cidagnikuṇḍasambhūtā*). Hence, first her crown appeared, then her hair, her forehead and so on. So, her parts are described in that order.

If anyone wants to describe the facial beauty of any women, it can be compared to the Moon. The Moon himself, is an eye on Sri Devi's face. Moon is one of the breasts in her body. The Moon is not even one hundredth of her beauty.

Similarly, if we want to describe the beauty of the walk of other women, we can say that the walk is like a swan's. But here it is said that the swan itself learned how to walk from Sri Devi. Sri Adi Shankar chokes on every shloka – No simile/ parables can describe her beauty. Still, he enjoys being stuck like that.

He grabs Ambika's legs and screams. Kanchi Paramacharya would say – for Gods, we see many heads and many hands in different places. But everywhere only two legs are shown. He would say that they are meant for us to hold them with our two hands and scream.

This *Devee* should be meditated upon in the 1,000 petalled lotus in the *Sahasraara chakra* at the top head of the human body. Let us hold her legs and yell.

*****

Śrī Tripura Sundarī Devī Mantras

Chanting *Mantras* create vibrations in the human body, which can only be felt by the individuals and cannot be explained in words. For instance, if anyone asks how sugar will taste, it can be said that it is sweet. On the other hand, is someone asks how will be sweet, no one can explain. It has to be enjoyed individually. In the same way the vibrations of the mantras can be only be felt. However, to get complete result, it should be chant with proper pronunciation with clear words entirely focusing on the deity and not as a routine. Lalita Sahasranama (206th name) is *Sarvamantra Svaroopinee. Sri Lalita Devi* is in the form of all the mantras.

Tripura Sundaree Vidyaa

In Samskrutam, in general *Vidyā* means mantra. Vidya means knowledge. Here is a very powerful *Srī Tripura Sundaree Devī Mantra*.

Om Asya Shree Tripura Sundaree Mahaa Mantrasya Dakshinaa Moorti Rishi: I Panktee Chanda: I Sreemad Tripura Sundaree Devataa I Im Beejam, Sou: Shakti: Kleem Keelakam I

Shreem Hreem Kleem Im Sou: Angushtābhyām Namaḥ I
Om Hreem Shreem   Darjaneebhyām Namaḥ I
Ka A E La Hreem   Madhymābhyām Namaḥ I
Ha Sa Ka Ha La Hreem   Anāmikābhyām Namaḥ I
Sa Ka La Hreem   Kanishtikābhyām Namaḥ I
Sou: Im Kleem Hreem Shreem Karatala Karabrushtābhyām Namaḥ I I

Shreem Hreem Kleem Im Sou: Hrudayāya Namaḥ I
Om Hreem Shreem   Sirase Svāhā I
Ka A E La Hreem   Shikāyai Vashat I
Ha Sa Ka Ha La Hreem   Kavachāya Hoom I
Sa Ka La Hreem   Netratrayāya Voushat I
Sou: Im Kleem Hreem Shreem Astrāyapaṭ I
Bhurbhuvasvarom Iti Dig Bandaḥ I I

Tripura Sundaree (Shodashee) **Dhyaanam**

बालार्कायुततेजसं त्रिनयनं रक्ताम्बरोल्लासिनीं
                    नानालंकृति राजमानवपुषं बालोडुराट्शेखरम्।
हस्तैरिक्षु धनुः सृणिं सुमशरं पाशं मुदा
                    बिभ्रतीं श्रीचक्रस्थितसुन्दरीं त्रिजगतामाधारभूतां स्मरेत् ॥

Bālārkāyutatejasam Trinayanam Raktāmbarollāsinīm

Nānālamkruti Rājamānavapuṣam Bālodurātśekharam |

Hastairikṣudhanuḥ Sruṇim Sumaśaram Pāśam Mudā

Bibhratīm Śrīcakrasthitasundarīm Trijagatāmādhārabhūtām Smaret ||

Lam Pritviyātmikāyai Gandham Samarpayāmi |

Ham Ākashātmikāyai Pushpaiḥ Poojayāmi |

Yam Vaivātmikāyai Dhoopam Agrāpayāmi |

Ram Vahniyātmikāyai Dheepam Dharshayāmi |

Vam Amrutātmikāyai Amrutam Mahāneivedhyam Nivedayāmi |

Sam Sarvātmikāyai Sarvopachāra Poojām Samarpayāmi ||

Tripura Sundaree Moola mantra

The famous *pancadashaaksharee* (15 lettered) *mantra* is the *moola mantra* of *Tripura Sundaree*;

ॐ ऐं क ए ई ल ह्रीं क्लीं हसकहल ह्रीं सौः सकलह्रीम् (स्वाहा) |

Om aim ka Aa Ee la hreem kleem hasakahala hreem sou: sakalahreem
(svaahaa) |

Prescribed process;

One should be interested in the words of the teacher. The four – self, teacher, *mantra* and the God should be treated as same. One should not reprimand other religions. One should always think of himself as Lord Shiva. One should not rebuke ladies.

Shaakta ideologies affirm – *Shree Devee* in the form of, *kundalinee* energy has to be brought from *Moolaadhaara Chakra* to *Sahasraara Chakra* through *Brahma Granti, Svaadhishtaana Chakra, Manipooraka Chakra, Vishnu Granti, Anaahata Chakra, Vishuddhi Chakra, Rudra Granti and Agnaa Chakra*. At the *Sahasraaraa Chakra*, in a *Sahasradala Padma* (1000 petalled lotus), the unison of *Shiva-Shakti* has to be inwardly looked (*antharmukha* – inwardly imagined) into and the devotee should be soaked in the rain of nectar (*Amruta Tara*).

Important tesults of worshipping *Tripura Sundaree*;

By worshipping this *Devee*, the devotee can obtain the art of speech, clear knowledge of *shaastras*, wealth like Kubera, energy to win anything in this world and at last liberation.

Progress is the only in the life, if the grace of Devī is given to a devotee. Motivation comes naturally in the actions that are done. There is nothing he cannot achieve by her grace. She is interested in removing the sins of her devotees and showing him the right way. She lovingly bestows grace on those who are active, solid, and engaged in worship.

Let us all get initiated with these mantras from an appropriate guru and reap all the benefits.

*****

Śrī Tripura Sundarī Devī Yantram

It is usual to worship Gods through *mantras, tantras* and *yantras*. Worshipping through *mantras* is called *Māntrīka* method. Worshipping through *tantras* is called *Tāntrīca* method. Worshipping through *yantras* is called *Vaidhīka* method. Whichever be the method *mantras* are definitely used to worship. But which is predominant is to be considered.

Mantras, the sound form of deities, are integral to *Sādhanas* (worship). *Mantra* pertaining to each God/ Goddess will have different number of letters called *chandas*. Similarly, each God/ Goddess will have various *mantras* – probably each one for a particular purpose/ satiating a desire.

Tantras (Looms or Weavings) refer to numerous and varied scriptures pertaining to any of several esoteric traditions rooted in philosophy of the religion. The religious culture of the *Tantras* is essentially *Tāntric* material can be shown to have been derived from earlier *Vedic* sources. And although *Tantras* of different religions have many similarities from the outside, internally they do have some clear distinctions.

Yantras are some mathematical drawings/ patterns used for worship. There are mathematical construction methods explaining the drawing of *yantras*. *Yantras* mean originally the mechanical, mnemonic and musical contraption in the macrocosm. It is a graphic symbol of the contemplative meditation in the tradition, which was intended to be unified with the Gods/ goddesses. *Yantras* area also called as *cakras*. In a human body itself we have seven cakras thought to be an energy point or node in the subtle body viz., *Mūlādhārā, Swādhiṣṭānā, Maṇipūrakā, Anāhatā, Viśuddha, Agjnā* and *Sahasrārā*.

Sri Lalita Sahasranama, names 204, 205 and 206, *Sarvamantra Svarūpiṇī, Sarvayantrātmikā* and *Sarva Tantrarūpā*. That is, Sri Lalita herself is in the form of all the mantras, yantras and Tantras.

Usually when consecrating an idol of a deity, it is customary to place the *yantras* of the respective deities beneath the respective idols, duly drawn on copper, five-metals, silver, gold, etc. Properly drawn *yantras* emit micro-vibrations. Those vibrations are not feelable by human beings. However, they have a huge impact on our body, mainly positive impact. It is customary to worship the concerned deity alongwith the respective *chakras/ yantras*.

Yantras are great cosmic conductors of energy, an antenna of Nature, a powerful tool for harmony, prosperity, success, good health, yoga and meditation. *Yantras* are usually made out of copper and consist of a series of geometric patterns. The eyes and mind concentrate at the center of the yantra to achieve higher levels of consciousness.

Tripura Sundaree Yantra

The famous Sri Chakra[3] itself is the yantra pertaining to Sri *Tripura Sundaree Devi.* This Yantra is also called as 'Chakraraja' – meaning king of all the chakras/ yantras.

The architecture of *Śrī Chakra* is a complicated wizard. It has a series of nine triangles along with a center point. Before we delve into the details of the structure of *Śrī Chakra*, let us know something in general about *Śrī Chakra* – definition and meaning of it;

बिंदु त्रिकोण वसु कोण दशारयुग्मं, मन्वस्र नागदल संयुत षोडशारम्।
वृत्तत्रयं च धरणीं सदनत्रयं च, श्री चक्रमेवमुदितं पर देवताया:॥

Bindu Trikoṇa Vasu Koṇa Daśārayugmam,
Manvasra Nāgadala Samyuta Ṣoḍaśāram |
Vruttatrayam Ca Dharaṇīm Sadanatrayam Ca,
Śrī Chakramevamuditam Para Devatāyā: | |

The *Śrī Chakram* belonging to the highest *Devī* (*Paradevatai*) contains, one dot, one triangle, one octagon, two decagons (ten-sided shape), one 14-sided figure, eight petals, 16 petals, three circles and on all the four sides

---

[3] This author has written separate books on "Mathematical construction to draw Sri Chakra" and also "Sri Chakra Navavarnam"

three lined squares. The midpoint *Bindu* indicates the unison of *Śiva* and *Śakti*. A method of worshipping a *yantra* through mantras is *Śrī Chakram*.

Among the herbs only some can cure some diseases. Among the words only the word of *Veda mantras* only has some potency. In this manner, only some lines drawn in a particular fashion/ design have bounteous divine power. They are the *yantras/ Chakras*. Serious devotees would like to do *pooja* in a *yantra* instead of a statute. In any pooja, the worshipper has to meditate upon self, his *guru, mantra* and the concerned deity and imagine that they are all one and the same. To make a place worthy of pooja, it has to be made ready with *mantras, tantras* and *yantras*.

Similar to *Śrī Chakra* is mapped to *Śrī Devī*, there are various *Chakras* pertaining to different Gods. When any God is installed in a temple, the corresponding *Chakra* would be placed beneath the statue. These *Chakras* emanate some vibrations, of course not feelable by human beings. Since the sanctum sanctorum is filled with these vibrations, the devotees, moving across, are cleansed, are able to concentrate on the deity and get their legal prayers satiated. It has been told that 27 such *Chakras* are kept beneath the statue of the main deity at Tirumala and hence even if a devotee passes through for a micro/ Nano second, he gets peace and happiness and all his wishes are satisfied.

A *yantra* is also called as *Chakra*. Among all the *Chakras* pertaining to various deities, *Śrī Chakra* is called as *Chakra Raja* (king of all *Chakras*). *Śrī Chakra* is also called as *Śrī Maṇḍalam*. This is considered the god of wisdom or supreme knowledge. That is *Śrī Vidyā*.

The *yantras* pertaining to most of other Gods are kept beneath or in front of the deities in temples. But with regard to *Śrī Chakra*, *Śrī Devī* herself is iconized in the *yantra* and worshipped. Hence this *Chakra* has a special status among the *Chakras*.

Śrī Chakra or *Śrī Yantra* is a beautiful, complex and sacred geometrical diagram used for devotion and meditation. This has been in use for 1000s of years. Its origin is not yet known to the world. It is a mathematical marvelous/ miracle. It consists of multiple inter-connected triangles meeting at particular points. That is the reason drawing[4] this figure is a very difficult task.

---

[4] The author of this book has drawn *Śrī Cakra* in a computer using Auto-cad and has authored a book titled "*Śrī Cakra*, An Esoteric Approach" using the computer images and explaining the mathematical construction. He has also talked about this in Internation conferences/ symposiums.

Śrī Chakra is a symbol of standardized movement from ancient days. *Śrī Chakra* is a;

- A device or tool. It is a go down of energy.
- This has a capacity to convert one type of energy into other one.
- The unrestricted form of omnipotence is within a controlled form
- A shape, defining unlimited measurements through lines, triangles, squares and circles.
- Indicates the dynamics of divinity.
- Transfers divine enthusiasm.

Śrī Chakra is a particular form containing different squares and triangles connected to the package in the cutting points at various edges. The word '*Śrī*' is used as a perfect adventure – a tool to make a good mind. It is a geometric representation of the cosmic energies. A complete clear description of the structure of *Śrī Chakra* has been provided in the 11th verse of Soundaryalahari;

चतुर्भिः श्रीकण्ठैः शिवयुवतिभिः पञ्चभिरपिप्रभिन्नाभिः शम्भोर्नवभिरपि

मूलप्रकृतिभिः ।

चतुश्चत्वारिंशद्वसुदल-कलाश्च-त्रिवलय- त्रिरेखाभिः सार्धं तव शरणकोणाः

परिणताः ॥

Chaturbhih Śrīkaṇṭhaih Śivayuvatibhih Pañchabhirapi
Prabhinnābhih Śambhōrnavabhirapi Mūlaprakṛtibhih ।
Chatuśchatvāriṃsad-Vasudala-Kalāśch-Trivalaya-
Trirēkhābhih Sārdham Tava Śaraṇakōṇāh Pariṇatāh ॥

Its translation goes – these nine *Chakras* form the basis of this world with;

- Four triangles having the characters of *Śiva* (*Majjā, Śuklam, Prāṇan,* and *Jīvan*)
- Five triangles having the characters of *Śakti* (*tvak, aśruk, māmsam, metas* and *asti*)
- *Śiva-Śakti Chakras* without touching each other

Your (*Devī's*) representation can be split into four parts;

- One eight petalled
- One 16 petalled
- One three circled
- Gapped lines in all the four sides
- Totaling 44 triangles.

Another book on *Śrī Devī*, called *Yāmalā*, describes *Śrī Chakra* in a different way – it is a shape containing one dot, triangle, hexagon, two decagons and one 14-sided figure. It has one eight petalled lotus, one 16 petalled lotus and squares around called as *Bhūpuras*. This is the *Chakra* of the uppermost *Devī*.

Śrī Chakra is a combination of lines, circles, squares and triangles. These are all integrated with the center point called *Bindu*. Such a design only can bring the energy pertaining to a particular deity. Actually, it is a storehouse of infinite energy. Hence, it can be called as fictional design. This design collects and accept the divine vigor. Further they have more energy to supply energy.

One *yantra* is a drawing of lines or circles or angles drawn in a prescribed measurements and ratios. There cannot be any deviation plus or minus. If a *mantra* is wrongly chant, it can result in negative impact or even end up with destruction. In the same manner, if there is an error in drawing of a *yantra*, it may end up in devastation.

If the vertex of the middle triangle in *Śrī Chakra* is kept towards West instead of East the result will be negated. Hence when a worshipper sits in front of a *Śrī Chakra* the vertex of the middle triangle should be near him and not towards opposite side. During worship of *yantras*, the worshipper has to follow the prescribed procedures/ rules more strictly than worshipping an idol. He should be more careful in this regard.

In modern days, lot many worship *Śrī Chakra* in their houses. In general, this is very good. But many do it as a pride, some do it as a style and some with ignorance. But the customs are not strictly followed. Resultantly, they suffer for want of peace.

It is not enough if one wants to follow the bigger things. Exact rules prescribed by *Śāstras* have to be clearly understood, absorbed and followed. These are time tested and handed over to us by our ancestors. It is our duty to stringently follow the same and get benefited. Definitely *Śrī Chakra* has been raised upto the sky by the *Śāstras*. But the same *Śāstras* have recommended lots of dos and don'ts, lots of processes. The approach that "I will do the pooja in my way" is not acceptable, the expected fruits will be missed. Sometimes that may result in negative angle.

One *yantra* is not a place of dwelling for the deity; It is the deity her/himself. It is not an alternative to the deity. It is not a representation – it the deity. It is all the more apt in the case of *Śrī Devī*. Her divine presence

Śrī Chakra is very special. That is because, importance is given to the *Yantra* than her idol.

Lord *Hayagrīva*, advised the details about *Śrī Chakra* to Agastya, even before he asked about it;

Na Teṣām Siddhidā Vidyā Kalpakoṭi Śatairapi |
Caturbhiḥ Śiva Chakraiśca Śakti Chakraiśca Pancabhiḥ ||
Nava Chakraśca Samsiddham Śrī Chakram Śivayor Vapuḥ |
Trikoṇa Maṣṭa Koṇañca Daśakoṇa Dvayam Tatā |
Catur Daśārañcai Tāni Śakti Cakrāṇi Panca Ca ||

The *Śrī Chakra* has the following components;

- At the center the '*Bindu*', a dot. This is an embodiment of the *Brahmānanda* or Supreme bliss that is the result of the union of male and female aspects of *Brahmam*, ready to create the Universe.
- The *Trikoṇa* (the small triangle) around the *Bindu*.
- *Aśtakoṇa* or *Vasukoṇa* – the group of eight triangles surrounding the *Trikoṇa*.
- *Antadaśara* – the inner group of ten triangles – around the inner triangles.
- *Bahirdaśara* – the outer group of ten triangles – around the inner triangles.
- *Caturdaśara* – the fourteen triangles surrounding the *Bahirdaśara*.
- The eight-petalled lotus or *aśtadala* around *Caturdaśara*
- The sixteen-petalled lotus encircling the *aśtadala*.
- The three girdles like circles around the sixteen-petalled lotus.
- The *Bhūpura* – the three quadrangular lines with gate like openings on all the four sides.

The mathematical shapes in *Śrī Chakra* has some deep philosophies;

- Circle – None can identify the beginning nor the end. This indicates the divinity, which does not have a birth nor an end.
- Triangle – Any triplets like – creation, maintenance and destruction – satva, *rajas* and *tamas* and so on. These triple energies are the three vertices of a triangle. The upward triangle indicates high goal. If it is downward it indicates the feature of a *Śakti*. One triangle being upward and the other downward – being a hexagon – indicate high goal and refers the lord coming towards the devotee.

- Lotus petals – Lotus blooms when Sun rises and closes when Sun sets. The lotus petals in *Śrī Chakra* indicates the blooming inner energy of the devotee. When it closes, the worshippers mind also concentrates on the deity.
- Square – The squares in a *Śrī Chakra* encloses all the shapes. The powers, energies and the meanings are controlled so that they do not spill over. Only in a controlled environment the required wishes are satiated.

The nine *aavarnas* in the *Sri Chakra* are called as *Navaavarnam*. These are comparable with six *chakras* and three *grantis* (knots) in the human body. – thus our body itself is the *Sri Chakra*. One should perform the Sri Chakra Navavarna Puja[5] and reach the point called Bindu, in the middle. Similarly, crossing the six chakras of our body, in addition to the three knots, should reach the Sahasrara Chakra at the scalp and be dipped in rain the nectar. Sahashara Chakra is balanced by worshipping this yantra. Chakra is seven centers of religious energy in the human body.

There is one *upanishat* called *Śrī Chakra Upaniṣat*. There are no *Veda Upaniṣats* available about *Chakras* pertaining to any other deities. This is another feather on the cap of *Śrī Chakra*.

The direct/ straight benefits of worshipping *Tripura Sundari Yantra – Śrī Chakra* is moksham (liberation) – no more birth. However, in this world the below benefits can be seen;

- For the divine grace of Maa Tripurasundari or Mata Shodashi.
- Increase Business as well as name and fame.
- For harmony, prosperity, beauty and blessings.
- For getting a right life partner and blissful marital life.
- For stability in personal and professional life.
- This Dus Mahavidya yantra also gives peace of mind.
- Tripura Sundari Yantra is for power, and happiness.
- For protection from evil spirits and malefic energies.

Sahashara Chakra is balanced by worshipping this yantra. Chakra is seven centers of religious energy in the human body.

Every yantra or chakra emanate some vibrations, which are not feelable by the normal human body. The radiations of the Yantra will bring the devotee and the Goddess into direct contact. The energy will soothe the inner peace

---

[3] This puja has to be got initiated from an appropriate guru.

and will gift with beauty, happiness and prosperity. These power lines attract the amiability of the Goddess opening doors for harmony and success.

This Yantra is a great cosmic conductors of energy, an antenna of Nature, a powerful tool for harmony, prosperity, success, good health, yoga and meditation! Yantras consist of a series of geometric patterns. The eyes and mind concentrate at the center of the yantra to achieve higher levels of consciousness. Yantras are usually made out of copper.

Let us all choose an appropriate guru, get initiated and worship this yantra to exploit maximum benefits.

*****

Śrī Tripura Sundarī Suprabhātam

Generally, it is customary to sing *Suprabhatam* early in the morning to propitiate the deities in the temple. Such a *Suprabhatam*, on *Sri Tripura Sundari Devi*;

Oṃ Uttiṣṭottiṣṭha Deveśī Uttiṣṭha Śivasundarī |
Uttiṣṭhaśrī Mahārājñī Trailokya'ṃ Maṅgala'ṃ Kuru ‖ 1

Nīrājanena Jagadīśvari Bhaktasaṅghaiḥ
Nīrājyase Bhuvanamaṅgala Siddhihetoḥ |
Bhaktyā Prabhātasamaye Sahavādyaghoṣaiḥ
Samstūyase Jahihi Kaitava Yoganidrām ‖ 2

Nidrā Na Te Trijagadīśvari Viṣṇumāye
Sṛṣṭisthitipralaya Keliṣu Sa'ṃsthitāyāḥ |
Manmohapāśa Nigaḍasya Vimokṣaṇāya
Sa'mprārthyase Janani Maṅgalasūktibhistvam ‖ 3

Kalyāṇaśailanilaye Karuṇārṇave Śrī
Kāmeśvarāṅkanihite Kalidoṣahantrī |
Kālāmbudhābhakacabandhabare Manojñe
Śrīmanmahātripurasundari Suprabhātam ‖ 4

Eṇāṅkakhaṇḍayutaratnalasatkirīṭe
Śoṇācaleśa Sahadharmiṇi Bāṇahaste |
Vīṇādhareṇa Muninā Parigīyamāne
Śrīmanmahātripurasundari Suprabhātam ‖ 5

Īśānamukhyasuramauḷilasatpadābje
Śrīmatsadāśiva Mahāphalakāḍhyamañce |
Īśatsmitena Vikasatsumanoharāsye
Śrīmanmahātripurasundari Suprabhātam ‖ 6

Lajjanatena Nayanena Vilokamāne
Trailokyasundaratanu'ṃ Paraśambhunātham |
Mandasmitollasita Cāru Mukhāravinde
Śrīmanmahātripurasundari Suprabhātam ‖ 7

Hrīṅkārajāpasuhite Hṛdayāmbujasthe
Hārdāndhakāravinihantri Haritpatīḍhye |
Haryakṣavāhini Halāyudha Sevitāṅghre
Śrīmanmahātripurasundari Suprabhātam || 8

Hastena Devi Phaṇipāśamathekṣucāpam
Puṣpāstramaṅkuśavara' ṃ Satata' ṃ Dadhāne |
Hemādrituṅgataraśṛṅga Kṛtādhivāse
Śrīmanmahātripurasundari Suprabhātam || 9

Sarvāgamopaniṣadīḍhya Mahāprabhāve
Sāmābhigānavinute Sarasīruhākṣi |
Saccitsukhaikarasike Sakaleṣṭadātrī
Śrīmanmahātripurasundari Suprabhātam || 10

Kalyāṇadātri Kamanīyaguṇārṇave Śrī
Kalmāṣapādaparipūjita Pādapadme |
Kaivalyade Kalimalāpaha Citsvarūpe
Śrīmanmahātripurasundari Suprabhātam || 11

Hatvā' surendramatibāhubalāvaliptam
Bhaṇḍa' ṃ Pracaṇḍasamarodyatamāttaśastram |
Samrakṣita Trijagati Tripurādhivāse
Śrīmanmahātripurasundari Suprabhātam || 12

Labdhu' ṃ Tava Tripurasundari Satkaṭākṣam
Kāruṇyapūrṇamamareśamukhādigīśāḥ |
Kakṣyāntametya Nivasanti Tava Prabodhe
Śrīmanmahātripurasundari Suprabhātam || 13

Hrīmityajasramapi Te Manumādareṇa
Hṛtpaṅkajcnukalayan Prajapāmi Nityam |
Harṣaprade Hṛdayasantamasāpahantrī
Śrīmanmahātripurasundari Suprabhātam || 14

Satyātmike Sakalalokahitaprade' mba
Sampatkarī Kiṭamukhī Parisevitāṅghre |
Sarvānavadyacarite Sukumāragātri
Śrīmanmahātripurasundari Suprabhātam || 15

Kāmohi Te'mba Karuṇālavameva Labdhvā
Puṣpāyudho'pi Bhavati Trijagadvijetā |
Kāmeśvareṇa Parikāṅkṣita Satkaṭākṣe
Śrīmanmahātripurasundari Suprabhātam || 16

Lajjāpadāṅkita Manupratipādyarūpe
Līlāvilokana Visṛṣṭajagatsahasre |
Lāvaṇyapūrṇavadane Lalitābhidhāne
Śrīmanmahātripurasundari Suprabhātam || 17

Hrīṅkāramantranilaye Hṛdibhāvanīye
Hrīṅkāragarbhamanujāpaka Siddhidātri |
Hrīṅkāramantramahanīya Nijasvarūpe
Śrīmanmahātripurasundari Suprabhātam || 18

Śrīśaṅkarārcitapade Śivabhāgadheye
Śrīkāmarājamahiṣi Śritakāmadheno |
Śrīśaṅkarasyakulamaṅgaladevate'mba
Śrīmanmahātripurasundari Suprabhātam || 19

Śrī Suprabhātamahita Stavamambikāyāḥ
Bhaktyā Prabhātasamaye Bhuvi Ye Paṭhanti |
Śrī Mātranugrahanirastasamasta Khedāḥ
Saccitsukhātmaka Pada'ṃ Praviśanti Satyam || 20

Munīndranāradāgastya Mānyāyai Jaya Maṅgalam |
Praṇatārtinivāriṇyai Pūrṇāyai Śubhamaṅgalam || 21

Vividhopaniṣadvetṛ Vedyāyai Jaya Maṅgalam |
Śuddhabuddhasadānanda Brahmaṇe Śubha Maṅgalam || 22

Natalokeṣṭadāyinyai Nityāyai Nitya Maṅgalam |
Sarvamaṅgalayuktāyai Satyāyai Sarva Maṅgalam || 23

Sarvabrahmāṇḍasandoha Jananyai Jaya Maṅgalam |
Śaṅkarārcitapādāyai Śivāṇyai Śubhamaṅgalam || 24

Śrīcakrarājanilayāyai Śrīmātre Jaya Maṅgalam |
Mahātripurasundaryai Śivāyai Śubhamaṅgalam || 25

|| Iti Śrī Śaṅkarānandanātha Viracita'ṃ Śrī Tripura Sundarī Suprabhātam
Samāptam || Oṃ||

श्रीमहात्रिपुरसुन्दरी सुप्रभातम्

ॐ उत्तिष्ठोत्तिष्ठ देवेशी उत्तिष्ठ शिवसुन्दरी।
उत्तिष्ठश्री महाराज्ञी त्रैलोक्यꣳ मङ्गलꣳ कुरु॥ 1

नीराजनेन जगदीश्वरि भक्तसङ्घैः नीराज्यसे भुवनमङ्गल सिद्धिहेतोः।
भक्त्या प्रभातसमये सहवाद्यघोषैः सम्स्तूयसे जहिहि कैतव योगनिद्राम्॥ 2

निद्रा न ते त्रिजगदीश्वरि विष्णुमाये सृष्टिस्थितिप्रलय केलिषु सꣳस्थितायाः।
मन्मोहपाश निगडस्य विमोक्षणाय सꣳप्रार्थ्यसे जननि मङ्गलसूक्तिभिस्त्वम्॥ 3

कल्याणशैलनिलये करुणार्णवे श्री कामेश्वराङ्कनिहिते कलिदोषहन्त्री।
कालाम्बुधाभकचबन्धबरे मनोज्ञे श्रीमन्महात्रिपुरसुन्दरि सुप्रभातम्॥ 4

एणाङ्ककखण्डयुतरत्नलसत्किरीटे शोणाचलेश सहधर्मिणि बाणहस्ते।
वीणाधरेण मुनिना परिगीयमाने श्रीमन्महात्रिपुरसुन्दरि सुप्रभातम्॥ 5

ईशानमुख्यसुरमौलिलसत्पदाब्जे श्रीमत्सदाशिव महाफलकाद्यमञ्चे।
ईशत्स्मितेन विकसत्सुमनोहरास्ये श्रीमन्महात्रिपुरसुन्दरि सुप्रभातम्॥ 6

लज्जनतेन नयनेन विलोकमाने त्रैलोक्यसुन्दरतनुꣳ परशम्भुनाथम्।
मन्दस्मितोल्लसित चारु मुखारविन्दे श्रीमन्महात्रिपुरसुन्दरि सुप्रभातम्॥ 7

ह्रीङ्कारजापसुहिते हृदयाम्बुजस्थेहार्दान्धकारविनिहन्त्रि हरित्पतीड्ये।
हर्यक्षवाहिनि हलायुध सेविताङ्घ्रे श्रीमन्महात्रिपुरसुन्दरि सुप्रभातम्॥ 8

हस्तेन देवि फणिपाशमथेक्षु चापम् पुष्पास्त्रमङ्कुशवरꣳ सततꣳ दधाने।
हेमाद्रितुङ्गतरशृङ्ग कृताधिवासे श्रीमन्महात्रिपुरसुन्दरि सुप्रभातम्॥ 9

सर्वागमोपनिषदीड्य महाप्रभावे सामाभिगानविनुते सरसीरुहाक्षि।
सच्चित्सुखैकरसिके सकलेष्टदात्री श्रीमन्महात्रिपुरसुन्दरि सुप्रभातम्॥ 10

कल्याणदात्रि कमनीयगुणार्णवे श्री कल्माषपादपरिपूजित पादपद्मे।
कैवल्यदे कलिमलापह चित्स्वरूपे श्रीमन्महात्रिपुरसुन्दरि सुप्रभातम्॥ 11

हत्वाऽसुरेन्द्रमतिबाहुबलाविलिप्तम् भण्डꣳ प्रचण्डसमरोद्यतमात्तशस्त्रम्।
सम्रक्षित त्रिजगति त्रिपुराधिवासे श्रीमन्महात्रिपुरसुन्दरि सुप्रभातम्॥ 12

लब्धुऽ तव त्रिपुरसुन्दरि सत्कटाक्षम्कारुण्यपूर्णममरेशमुखादिगीशाः।
कक्ष्यान्तमेत्य निवसन्ति तव प्रबोधे श्रीमन्महात्रिपुरसुन्दरि सुप्रभातम्॥ 13

ह्रीमित्यजस्त्रमपि ते मनुमादरेण हृत्पङ्कजेनुकलयन् प्रजपामि नित्यम्।
हर्षप्रदे हृदयसन्तमसापहन्त्री श्रीमन्महात्रिपुरसुन्दरि सुप्रभातम्॥ 14

सत्यात्मिके सकललोकहितप्रदेऽम्ब सम्पत्करी किटमुखी परिसेविताङ्घ्रे।
सर्वानवद्यचरिते सुकुमारगात्रि श्रीमन्महात्रिपुरसुन्दरि सुप्रभातम्॥ 15

कामोहि तेऽम्ब करुणालवमेव लब्ध्वा पुष्पायुधोऽपि भवति त्रिजगद्विजेता।
कामेश्वरेण परिकाङ्क्षित सत्कटाक्षे श्रीमन्महात्रिपुरसुन्दरि सुप्रभातम्॥ 16

लज्जापदाङ्कित मनुप्रतिपाद्यरूपे लीलाविलोकन विसृष्टजगत्सहस्त्रे।
लावण्यपूर्णवदने ललिताभिधाने श्रीमन्महात्रिपुरसुन्दरि सुप्रभातम्॥ 17

ह्रीङ्कारमन्त्रनिलये हृदिभावनीये ह्रीङ्कारगर्भमनुजापक सिद्धिदात्रि।
ह्रीङ्कारमन्त्रमहनीय निजस्वरूपे श्रीमन्महात्रिपुरसुन्दरि सुप्रभातम्॥ 18

श्रीशङ्करार्चितपदे शिवभागधेये श्रीकामराजमहिषि श्रितकामधेनो।
श्रीशङ्करस्यकुलमङ्गलदेवतेऽम्ब श्रीमन्महात्रिपुरसुन्दरि सुप्रभातम्॥ 19

श्री सुप्रभातमहित स्तवमम्बिकायाः भक्त्या प्रभातसमये भुवि ये पठन्ति।
श्री मात्रनुग्रहनिरस्तसमस्त खेदाः सच्चित्सुखात्मक पदऽ प्रविशन्ति सत्यम्॥ 20

मुनीन्द्रनारदागस्त्य मान्यायै जय मङ्गलम्।
प्रणतार्तिनिवारिण्यै पूर्णायै शुभमङ्गलम्॥ 21

विविधोपनिषद्वेत्तृ वेद्यायै जय मङ्गलम्।
शुद्धबुद्धसदानन्द ब्रह्मणे शुभ मङ्गलम्॥ 22

नतलोकेष्टदायिन्यै नित्यायै नित्य मङ्गलम्।
सर्वमङ्गलयुक्तायै सत्यायै सर्व मङ्गलम्॥ 23

सर्वब्रह्माण्डसन्दोह जनन्यै जय मङ्गलम्।
शङ्करार्चितपादायै शिवाण्यै शुभमङ्गलम्॥ 24

श्रीचक्रराजनिलयायै श्रीमात्रे जय मङ्गलम् ।
महात्रिपुरसुन्दर्यै शिवायै शुभमङ्गलम् ॥ 25

॥ इति श्री शङ्करानन्दनाथ विरचितः श्री महात्रिपुरसुन्दरी सुप्रभातम् समाप्तम् ॥

*****

Śrī Tripura Sundarī Prātaḥ Śloka Pañcakam

Five versess on *Sri Tripura Sundari Devi* – usually for morning prayers.

Prātarnamāmi Jagatāṃ Jananyāścaraṇāmbujam |

Śrīmattripurasundaryā Namitā Yā Harādibhiḥ ‖ 1

Prātastripurasundaryā Namāmi Padapaṅkajam |

Harirharo Viriñciśca Sṛṣṭyādīn Kurute Yathā ‖ 2

Prātastripurasundaryā Namāmi Caraṇāmbujam |

Yatpādamambu Śirasi Bhāti Gaṅgā Maheśituḥ ‖ 3

Prātaḥ Pāśāṅkuśaśarāñcāpahastāṃ Namāmyaham |

Udayādityasaṅkāśāṃ Śrīmattripurasundarīm ‖ 4

Prātarnamāmi Pādābjaṃ Yayedaṃ Dhāryate Jagat |

Tasyāstripurasundaryā Yatprasādānnivartate ‖ 5

Yaḥ Ślokapañcakamidaṃ Prātarnityaṃ Paṭhennaraḥ |

Tasmai Dadātyātmapadaṃ Śrīmattripurasundarī ‖ 6

Iti Śrī Tripura Sundarī Prātaḥ Śloka Pañcakaṃ Sampūrṇam |

श्री त्रिपुरसुन्दरी प्रातःश्लोकपञ्चकम्

प्रातर्नमामि जगतां जनन्याश्चरणाम्बुजम्।
श्रीमत्त्रिपुरसुन्दर्या नमिता या हरादिभिः॥ १

प्रातस्त्रिपुरसुन्दर्या नमामि पदपङ्कजम्।
हरिर्हरो विरिञ्चिश्च सृष्ट्यादीन् कुरुते यथा॥ २

प्रातस्त्रिपुरसुन्दर्या नमामि चरणाम्बुजम्।
यत्पादमम्बु शिरसि भाति गङ्गा महेशितुः॥ ३

प्रातः पाशाङ्कुशशराञ्चापहस्तां नमाम्यहम्।
उदयादित्यसङ्काशां श्रीमत्त्रिपुरसुन्दरीम्॥ ४

प्रातर्नमामि पादाब्जं ययेदं धार्यते जगत्।
तस्यास्त्रिपुरसुन्दर्या यत्प्रसादान्निवर्तते॥ ५

यः श्लोकपञ्चकमिदं प्रातर्नित्यं पठेन्नरः।
तस्मै ददात्यात्मपदं श्रीमत्त्रिपुरसुन्दरी॥ ६

इति श्रीत्रिपुरसुन्दरीप्रातःश्लोकपञ्चकं सम्पूर्णम्।

*****

Śrī Tripura Sundarī Pañcaratna Stotram

Five gems like powerful verses on *Sri Devi.*

Nīlālakāṃ Śaśimukhīṃ Navapallavoṣṭhīṃ
   Cāmpeyapuṣpasuṣamojjvaladivyanāsām |
Padmekṣaṇāṃ Mukurasundaragaṇḍabhāgāṃ
   Tvāṃ Sāmprataṃ Tripurasundari! Devi! Vande ‖ 1

Śrīkundakuḍmalaśilojjvaladantavṛndāṃ
   Mandasmitadyutitirāhitacāruvāṇīm |
Nānāmaṇisthagitahārasucārukaṇṭhīṃ
   Tvāṃ Sāmprataṃ Tripurasundari! Devi! Vande ‖ 2

Pīnastanīṃ Ghanabhujāṃ Vipulābjahastāṃ
   Bhṛṅgāvalījitasuśobhitaromarājim |
Mattebhakumbhakucabhārasunamramaddhyāṃ
   Tvāṃ Sāmprataṃ Tripurasundari! Devi! Vande ‖ 3

Rambhojjvaloruyugalāṃ Mṛgarājapatrā-
   Mindrādidevamakuṭojjvalapādapadmām |
Hemāmbarāṃ Karadhṛtāñcitakhaḍgavallīṃ
   Tvāṃ Sāmprataṃ Tripurasundari! Devi! Vande ‖ 4

Mattebhavaktrajananīṃ Mṛḍadehayuktāṃ
   Śailāgramaddhyanilayāṃ Varasundarāṅgīm |
Koṭīśvarākhyahṛdisaṃsthitapādapadmām
   Tvāṃ Sāmprataṃ Tripurasundari! Devi! Vande ‖ 5

Bāle! Tvatpādayugalaṃ Dhyātvā Samprati Nirmitam |
Navīnaṃ Pañcaratnaṃ Ca Dhāryatāṃ Caraṇadvaye ‖ 6

   Iti Śrī Tripura Sundarī Pañcaratna Stotraṃ Sampūrṇam |

श्री त्रिपुर सुन्दरी पञ्चरत्न स्तोत्रम्

नीलालकां शशिमुखीं नवपल्लवोष्ठीं
चाम्पेयपुष्पसुषमोज्ज्वलदिव्यनासाम्।
पद्मेक्षणां मुकुरसुन्दरगण्डभागां
त्वां साम्प्रतं त्रिपुरसुन्दरि! देवि! वन्दे॥ १

श्रीकुन्दकुड्मलशिलोज्ज्वलदन्तवृन्दां
मन्दस्मितद्युतितिराहितचारुवाणीम्।
नानामणिस्थगितहारसुचारुकण्ठीं
त्वां साम्प्रतं त्रिपुरसुन्दरि! देवि! वन्दे॥ २

पीनस्तनीं घनभुजां विपुलाब्जहस्तां
भृङ्गावलीजितसुशोभितरोमराजिम्।
मत्तेभकुम्भकुचभारसुनम्रमद्ध्यां
त्वां साम्प्रतं त्रिपुरसुन्दरि! देवि! वन्दे॥ ३

रम्भोज्ज्वलोरुयुगलां मृगराजपत्रा-
मिन्द्रादिदेवमकुटोज्ज्वलपादपद्माम्।
हेमाम्बरां करधृताञ्चितखड्गवल्लीं
त्वां साम्प्रतं त्रिपुरसुन्दरि! देवि! वन्दे ॥ ४

मत्तेभवक्त्रजननीं मृडदेहयुक्तां
शैलाग्रमद्ध्यनिलयां वरसुन्दराङ्गीम्।
कोटीश्वराख्यहृदिसंस्थितपादपद्मां
त्वां साम्प्रतं त्रिपुरसुन्दरि! देवि! वन्दे॥ ५

बाले! त्वत्पादयुगलं ध्यात्वा संप्रति निर्मितम्।
नवीनं पञ्चरत्नं च धार्यतां चरणद्वये॥ ६

इति श्री त्रिपुरसुन्दरीपञ्चरत्न स्तोत्रं सम्पूर्णम्।

*****

Śrī Tripura Sundarī Aṣṭakam

This is one of the foremost stotrams in eight verses (octal) composed by Sri Adi Shankara.

Kadambavanacāriṇīṃ Munikadambakādambinīṃ

    Nitambajita Bhūdharāṃ Suranitambinīsevitām |

Navāmburuhalocanāmabhinavāmbudaśyāmalāṃ

    Trilocanakuṭumbinīṃ Tripurasundarīmāśraye ‖ 1

Kadambavanavāsinīṃ Kanakavallakīdhāriṇīṃ

    Mahārhamaṇihāriṇīṃ Mukhasamullasadvāruṇīm |

Dayāvibhavakāriṇīṃ Viśadalocanīṃ Cāriṇīṃ

    Trilocanakuṭumbinīṃ Tripurasundarīmāśraye ‖ 2

Kadambavanaśālayā Kucabharollasanmālayā

    Kucopamitaśailayā Gurukṛpālasadvelayā |

Madāruṇakapolayā Madhuragītavācālayā

    Kayā'pi Ghananīlayā Kavacitā Vayaṃ Līlayā ‖ 3

Kadambavanamadhyagāṃ Kanakamaṇḍalopasthitāṃ

    Ṣaḍamburuhavāsinīṃ Satatasiddhasaudāminīm |

Viḍambitajapāruciṃ Vikacacaṃdracūḍāmaṇiṃ

    Trilocanakuṭumbinīṃ Tripurasundarīmāśraye ‖ 4

Kucāñcitavipañcikāṃ Kuṭilakuntalālaṃkṛtāṃ

    Kuśeśayanivāsinīṃ Kuṭilacittavidveṣiṇīm |

Madāruṇavilocanāṃ Manasijārisammohinīṃ

    Mataṅgamunikanyakāṃ Madhurabhāṣiṇīmāśraye ‖ 5

Smaraprathamapuṣpiṇīṃ Rudhirabindunīlāmbarāṃ

    Gṛhītamadhupātrikāṃ Madavighūrṇanetrāñcalāṃ |

Ghanastanabharonnatāṃ Galitacūlikāṃ Śyāmalāṃ

    Trilocanakuṭuṃbinīṃ Tripurasundarīmāśraye ‖ 6

Sakuṅkumavilepanāmalakacuṃbikastūrikāṃ

    Samandahasitekṣaṇāṃ Saśaracāpapāśāṅkuśām |

Aśeṣajanamohinīmaruṇamālya Bhūṣāmbarāṃ

    Japākusumabhāsurāṃ Japavidhau Smarāmyambikām ‖ 7

Puraṃdarapuraṃdhrikāṃ Cikurabandhasairaṃdhrikāṃ

Pitāmahapativratāṃ Paṭapaṭīracarcāratām |

Mukundaramaṇīmaṇīlasadalaṃkriyākāriṇīṃ

Bhajāmi Bhuvanāṃbikāṃ Suravadhūṭikāceṭikām || 8

|| Iti Śrīmad Śaṃkarācāryaviracitaṃ Tripurasundaryaṣṭakaṃ Samāptaṃ ||

त्रिपुरसुन्दरी अष्टकम्।

कदम्बवनचारिणीं मुनिकदम्बकादम्बिनीं
नितम्बजित भूधरां सुरनितम्बिनीसेविताम्।
नवाम्बुरुहलोचनामभिनवाम्बुदश्यामलां
त्रिलोचनकुटुम्बिनीं त्रिपुरसुन्दरीमाश्रये॥ १

कदम्बवनवासिनीं कनकवल्लकीधारिणीं
महार्हमणिहारिणीं मुखसमुल्लसद्धारुणीम्।
दयाविभवकारिणीं विशदलोचनीं चारिणीं
त्रिलोचनकुटुम्बिनीं त्रिपुरसुन्दरीमाश्रये॥ २

कदम्बवनशालया कुचभरोल्लसन्मालया
कुचोपमितशैलया गुरुकृपालसद्वेलया।
मदारुणकपोलया मधुरगीतवाचालया
कयाऽपि घननीलया कवचिता वयं लीलया॥ ३

कदम्बवनमध्यगां कनकमण्डलोपस्थितां
षडम्बुरुहवासिनीं सततसिद्धसौदामिनीम्।
विडम्बितजपारुचिं विकचचंद्रचूडामणिं
त्रिलोचनकुटुम्बिनीं त्रिपुरसुन्दरीमाश्रये॥ ४

कुचाञ्चितविपञ्चिकां कुटिलकुन्तलालंकृतां
कुशेशयनिवासिनीं कुटिलचित्तविद्वेषिणीम्।
मदारुणविलोचनां मनसिजारिसंमोहिनीं
मतङ्गमुनिकन्यकां मधुरभाषिणीमाश्रये॥ ५

स्मरप्रथमपुष्पिणीं रुधिरबिन्दुनीलाम्बरां
गृहीतमधुपात्रिकां मदविघूर्णनेत्राञ्चलां।
घनस्तनभरोन्नतां गलितचूलिकां श्यामलां
त्रिलोचनकुटुंबिनीं त्रिपुरसुन्दरीमाश्रये॥ ६

सकुङ्कुमविलेपनामलकचुंबिकस्तूरिकां
समन्दहसितेक्षणां सशरचापपाशाङ्कुशाम्।
अशेषजनमोहिनीमरुणमाल्य भूषाम्बरां
जपाकुसुमभासुरां जपविधौ स्मराम्यम्बिकाम्॥ ७

पुरंदरपुरंध्रिकां चिकुरबन्धसैरंध्रिकां
पितामहपतिव्रतां पटपटीरचर्चरिताम्।
मुकुन्दरमणीमणीलसदलंक्रियाकारिणीं
भजामि भुवनांबिकां सुरवधूटिकाचेटिकाम्॥ ८

॥ इति श्रीमद् शंकराचार्यविरचितं त्रिपुरसुन्दर्यष्टकं समाप्तं॥

*****

Śrī Tripura Sundarī Stotram

A short and powerful *mantra* offered to Sri Devi.

Śvetapadmāsanārūḍhāṃ Śuddhasphaṭikasannibhām |

Vande Vāgdevatāṃ Dhyātvā Devīṃ Tripurasundarīm || 1

Śailādhirājatanayāṃ Śaṅkarapriyavallabhām |

Taruṇendunibhāṃ Vande Devīṃ Tripurasundarīm || 2

Sarvabhūtamanoramyāṃ Sarvabhūteṣu Saṃsthitām |

Sarvasampatkarīṃ Vande Devīṃ Tripurasundarīm || 3

Padmālayāṃ Padmahastāṃ Padmasambhavasevitām |

Padmarāganibhāṃ Vande Devī Tripurasundarīm || 4

Pañcabāṇadhanurbāṇapāśāṅkuśadharāṃ Śubhām |

Pañcabrahmamayīṃ Vande Devīṃ Tripurasundarīm || 5

Ṣaṭpuṇḍarīkanilayāṃ Ṣaḍānanasutāmimām |

Ṣaṭkoṇāntaḥsthitāṃ Vande Devīṃ Tripurasundarīm || 6

Harārdhabhāganilayāmambāmadrisutāṃ Mṛḍām |

Haripriyānujāṃ Vande Devīṃ Tripurasundarīm || 7

Aṣṭaiśvaryapradāmambāmaṣṭadikpālasevitām |

Aṣṭamūrtimayīṃ Vande Devīṃ Tripurasundarīm || 8

Navamāṇikyamakuṭāṃ Navanāthasupūjitām |

Navayauvanaśobhāḍhyāṃ Vande Tripurasundarīm || 9

Kāñcīvāsamanoramyāṃ Kāñcīdāmavibhūṣitām |

Kāñcīpurīśvarīṃ Vande Devīṃ Tripurasundarīm || 10

Iti Śrī Tripura Sundarī Stotram Sampūrṇam |

*****

श्री त्रिपुर सुन्दरी स्तोत्रम्

श्वेतपद्मासनारूढां शुद्धस्फटिकसन्निभाम्।
वन्दे वाग्देवतां ध्यात्वा देवीं त्रिपुरसुन्दरीम्॥ १

शैलाधिराजतनयां शङ्करप्रियवल्लभाम्।
तरुणेन्दुनिभां वन्दे देवीं त्रिपुरसुन्दरीम्॥ २

सर्वभूतमनोरम्यां सर्वभूतेषु संस्थिताम्।
सर्वसम्पत्करीं वन्दे देवीं त्रिपुरसुन्दरीम्॥ ३

पद्मालयां पद्महस्तां पद्मसम्भवसेविताम्।
पद्मरागनिभां वन्दे देवीं त्रिपुरसुन्दरीम्॥ ४

पञ्चबाणधनुर्बाणपाशाङ्कुशधरां शुभाम्।
पञ्चब्रह्ममयीं वन्दे देवीं त्रिपुरसुन्दरीम्॥ ५

षट्पुण्डरीकनिलयां षडाननसुतामिमाम्।
षट्कोणान्तःस्थितां वन्दे देवीं त्रिपुरसुन्दरीम्॥ ६

हरार्धभागनिलयामम्बामद्रिसुतां मृडम्।
हरिप्रियानुजां वन्दे देवीं त्रिपुरसुन्दरीम्॥ ७

अष्टैश्वर्यप्रदामम्बामष्टदिक्पालसेविताम्।
अष्टमूर्तिमयीं वन्दे देवीं त्रिपुरसुन्दरीम्॥ ८

नवमाणिक्यमकुटां नवनाथसुपूजिताम्।
नवयौवनशोभाढ्यां वन्दे त्रिपुरसुन्दरीम्॥ ९

काञ्चीवासमनोरम्यां काञ्चीदामविभूषिताम्।
काञ्चीपुरीश्वरीं वन्दे देवीं त्रिपुरसुन्दरीम्॥ १०

इति श्री त्रिपुर सुन्दरी स्तोत्रं सम्पूर्णम्।

*****

Śrī Tripura Sundarī Hṛdaya Stotram

These prayers are offered to Sri Devi, who dwells in every heart – the devotee should imagine her in the heart.

Oṃ Śuddhasphaṭikasaṅkāśaṃ Dvinetraṃ Karuṇānidhim |
Varābhayakaraṃ Vande Śrīguruṃ Śivarūpiṇam || 1

Bhaktājñānatamobhānuṃ Mūrdhni Paṅkajasaṃsthitam |
Sadāśivamayaṃ Nityaṃ Śrīguruṃ Praṇamāmyaham || 2

Śrīvidyāṃ Jagatāṃ Dhātrīṃ Sargasthitilayeśvarīm |
Namāmi Lalitāṃ Nityaṃ Mahātripurasundarīm || 3

Bindutrikoṇasaṃyuktaṃ Vasukoṇasamanvitam |
Daśakoṇadvayopetaṃ Bhuvanārasamanvitam || 4

Dalāṣṭakasamopetaṃ Dalaṣoḍaśakānvitam |
Vṛttatrayānvitaṃ Bhūmisadanatrayabhūṣitam || 5

Namāmi Lalitācakraṃ Bhaktānāmetadiṣṭadam |
Amṛtāmbhonidhau Tatra Ratnadvīpaṃ Namāmyaham || 6

Nānāvṛkṣamahodyānaṃ Vande'haṃ Kalpavāṭikām |
Santānavāṭikāṃ Vande Haricandanavāṭikām || 7

Mandāravāṭikāṃ Vande Pārijātākhyavāṭikām |
Namāmi Tava Deveśi Kadambavanavāṭikām || 8

Puṣparāgamahāratnaprākāraṃ Praṇamāmyaham |
Padmarāgākhyamaṇibhiḥ Prākāraṃ Sarvadā Bhaje || 9

Gomedaratnaprākāraṃ Vajraprākāramāśraye |
Vaiḍūryaratnaprākāraṃ Praṇamāmi Taveśvari || 10

Indranīlākhyaratnānāṃ Prākāraṃ Praṇamāmyaham |
Muktāratnamayaṃ Caiva Prākāraṃ Sarvadā Bhaje || 11

Marakatākhyamahāratnaprākārāya Namastava |
Vidrumākhyamahāratnaprākāraṃ Tu Tavāśraye || 12

Māṇikyamaṇḍapaṃ Vande Sahasrastambhamaṇḍapam |
Lalite Tava Deveśi Bhajāmyamṛtavāpikām || 13

Ānandavāpikāṃ Vande Bhaje Caiva Vimarśikām |
Bhaje Bālātapodgāraṃ Candrikodgāramāśraye || 14

Mahāśṛṅgāraparikhāṃ Mahāpadmāṭavīṃ Bhaje |
Cintāmaṇimahāratnagṛharājaṃ Namāmyaham || 15

Pūrvāmnāyamayaṃ Pūrvadvāraṃ Devi Bhajāmi Te |
Dakṣiṇāmnāya Rūpaṃ Te Dakṣiṇadvāramāśraye || 16

Namāmi Te Paraṃ Dvāraṃ Paścimāmnāyarūpakam |
Vande'hamuttaraṃ Dvāramuttarāmnāyarūpakam || 17

Ūrdhvāmnāyama'haṃ Vande Ūrdhvadvāraṃ Kuleśvari |
Lalite Tava Deveśi Mahāsiṃhāsanaṃ Bhaje || 18

Brahmātmakamañcapādamekaṃ Tava Namāmyaham |
Ekaṃ Viṣṇumayaṃ Mañcapādaṃ Tava Namāmyaham || 19

Ekaṃ Rudramayaṃ Mañcapādaṃ Tava Namāmyaham |
Mañcapādaṃ Namāmyekaṃ Tava Devīśvarātmakam || 20

Mañcaikaphalakaṃ Vande Sadāśivamayaṃ Śubham |
Namāmi Te Haṃsatūlatalimāṃ Parameśvari || 21

Bhajāmi Te Haṃsatūla Mahopādhānamuttamam |
Kausumbhāstaraṇaṃ Devi Tava Nityaṃ Namāmyaham || 22

Mānasapūjā |

Mahāvitānakaṃ Vande Mahājavanikāṃ Bhaje |
Evaṃ Pūjāgṛhaṃ Dhyātvā Śrīcakrasya Śivapriye || 23

Maddakṣiṇe Sthāpayāmi Bhāge Puṣpākṣatādikam |
Abhitaste Mahādevi Dīpāṃstān Darśayāmyaham || 24

Mūlena Tripurācakraṃ Tava Sampūjayāmyaham |
Tribhiḥkhaṇḍaistava Tryastraṃ Pūjayāmi Śivapriye || 25

Vāyvagnijalasaṃyuktaprāṇāyāmairahaṃ Śive |
Śoṣaṇaṃ Dāhanaṃ Devi Karomyāplāvanaṃ Tathā || 26

Trivāraṃ Mūlamantreṇa Prāṇāyāmaṃ Karomyaham |
Apasarpantu Te Bhūtā Ye Bhūtā Bhūmisaṃsthitāḥ || 27

Ye Bhūtā Vighnakartāraste Naśyantu Śivājñayā |
Karomyanena Mantreṇa Tālatrayamahaṃ Śive || 28

Nārāyaṇo'haṃ Brahmā'haṃ Bhairavo'haṃ Śivo'smyaham |
Devo'haṃ Paramātmā'haṃ Mahātripurasundari || 29

Dhyātvaivaṃ Vajrakavacaṃ Nyāsaṃ Tava Karomyaham |
Kumārībījasaṃyuktaṃ Mahātripurasundari || 30

Māṃ Rakṣa Rakṣeti Hṛdi Karomyañjalimīśvari |
Namo Devyāsanāyeti Te Karomyāsanaṃ Śive || 31

Cakrāsanaṃ Namasyāmi Sarvamantrāsanam Bhaje |
Sādhyasiddhāsanaṃ Vande Mantrairebhirmaheśvari || 32

Karomyasmiṃścakramantradevatāsanamuttamam |
Karomyatha Ṣaḍaṅgākhyaṃ Mātṛkāśca Karomyaham || 33

Vaśinyādyaṣṭakaṃ Nyāsaṃ Śoḍhānyāsaṃ Karomyaham |
Mahāṣoḍhāṃ Tataḥ Kurve Navayonyākhyamuttamam || 34

Cakranyāsaṃ Tataḥ Kurve Śrīkaṇṭhanyāsamuttamam |
Keśavādi Mahānyāsaṃ Kāmanyāsaṃ Karomyaham || 35

Kalānyāsaṃ Tataḥ Kurve Kurve Kāmakalāhvayam |
Pīṭhanyāsaṃ Tataḥ Kurve Tattvanyāsaṃ Karomyaham || 36

Tataḥ Karomi Sthityādinyāsaṃ Tat Tripureśvari |
Tataḥ Śuddhodakenāhaṃ Vāmabhāge Maheśvari || 37

Karomi Maṇḍalaṃ Vṛttaṃ Caturasraṃ Śivapriye |
Puṣpairabhyarcya Sādhāraṃ Śaṅkhaṃ Saṃsthāpayāmyaham || 38

Arcayāmi Ṣaḍaṅgena Jalamāpūrayāmyaham |
Dadāmi Cādimaṃ Binduṃ Kurve Mūlābhimantritam || 39

Tajjalena Jaganmātastrikoṇaṃ Vṛttasaṃyutam |
Ṣaṭkoṇaṃ Caturastraṃ Ca Maṇḍalaṃ Prakaromyaham || 40

Vidyayā Pūjanaṃ Madhye Khaṇḍaistryastrābhipūjanam |
Bījāvṛtyā Koṇaṣaṭkaṃ Pūjayāmi Śivapriye || 41

Tasmin Daśakalāyuktamagnimaṇḍalamāśraye |
Dhūmārciṣaṃ Namasyāmi Ūṣmāṃ Ca Jvalinīṃ Bhaje || 42

Jvalinīṃ Ca Namasyāmi Vande'haṃ Visphulliṅginīm |
Suśriyaṃ Ca Surūpāṃ Ca Kapilāṃ Praṇamāmyaham || 43

Naumi Havyavahāṃ Nityaṃ Bhaje Kavyavahāṃ Kalām |
Yādibhiḥ Sahitā Vahneḥ Kalā Daśa Tathā Bhaje || 44

Sūryasya Maṇḍalaṃ Tatra Kalādvādaśakātmakam |
Arghyapātre Tva'haṃ Vande Tapinīṃ Tāpinīṃ Bhaje || 45

Dhūmrāṃ Marīciṃ Vande'haṃ Jvālinīṃ Ca Ruciṃ Bhaje |
Suṣumṇāṃ Bhogadāṃ Vande Bhaje Viśvāṃ Ca Bodhinīm || 46

Dhāriṇīṃ Ca Kṣamāṃ Vande Saurā Etāḥ Kalā Bhaje |
Somasya Maṇḍalaṃ Tatra Kalāḥ Ṣoḍaśakātmakāḥ || 47

Arghyāmṛtātmakaṃ Vande'mṛtāṃ Mānadāṃ Stuve |
Pūṣāṃ Tuṣṭiṃ Bhaje Puṣṭiṃ Ratiṃ Dhṛtimahaṃ Bhaje || 48

Śaśinīṃ Candrikāṃ Vande Kāntiṃ Jyotsnāṃ Śriyaṃ Bhaje |
Naumi Prītiṃ Cāṅgadāṃ Ca Pūrṇāṃ Pūrṇāmṛtāṃ Bhaje || 49

Svaraiḥ Ṣoḍaśabhiryuktā Bhaje Somasya Vai Kalāḥ |
Trikoṇalekhanaṃ Kurve Akathādisurekhakam || 50

Haḷakṣavarṇasaṃyuktaṃ Sthitāntarhaṃsabhāsvaram |
Vākkāmaśaktisaṃyuktaṃ Haṃsenārādhayāmyaham || 51

Vṛttādbahiḥ Ṣaḍasre Ca Lekhanaṃ Prakaromyaham |
Purobhāgādi Ṣaṭkoṇaṃ Ṣaḍaṅgenārcayāmyaham || 52

Śrīvidyāyāḥ Saptavāraṃ Karomyatrābhimantraṇam |
Samarpayāmi Viśveśi Tasmin Gandhākṣatādikam || 53

Dhyāyāmi Pūjādravyaṃ Te Sarvaṃ Vidyāmayaṃ Śubham |
Caturnavati Sanmantrān Spṛṣṭvā Tatprajapāmyaham || 54

Vahnerdaśakalāḥ Sūryakalādvādaśakaṃ Bhaje |
Āśraye Ṣoḍaśakalāstatra Somasya Kāmadāḥ || 55

Sṛṣṭimṛddhiṃ Smṛtiṃ Vande Medhāṃ Kāntiṃ Namāmyaham |
Lakṣmīṃ Dhṛtiṃ Sthirāṃvande Sthitiṃ Siddhiṃ Bhajāmyaham || 56

Etāṃ Brahmakalāṃ Vande Jarāṃ Tāṃ Pālinīṃ Bhaje |
Śāntiṃ Namāmīśvarīṃ Ca Ratiṃ Vande Ca Kāmikām || 57

Varadāṃ Hlādinīṃ Vande Prītiṃ Dīrghāṃ Bhajāmyaham |
Ṭādibhiḥ Sahitā Viṣṇoḥ Kalā Daśa Tathā Bhaje || 58

Etā Viṣṇoḥ Kalā Vande Tīkṣṇāṃ Raudrīṃ Bhayāṃ Tathā |
Nidrāṃ Tandrāṃ Kṣudhāṃ Vande Namāmi Krodhinīṃ Kriyām || 59

Udgārīṃ Ca Bhaje Mṛtyumetā Rudrakalā Bhaje |
Pītāṃ Śvetāṃ Bhaje Nityamaruṇāṃ Ca Tathā Bhaje || 60

Bhaje'sitāṃ Tathā'nantāṃ Ṣādibhiḥ Sahitāstathā |
Īśvarasya Kalā Hyetā Vande Nityamabhīṣṭadāḥ || 61

Nivṛttiṃ Ca Pratiṣṭhāṃ Ca Vidyāṃ Śāntiṃ Namāmyaham |
Indhikāṃ Dīpikāṃ Caiva Recikāṃ Mocikāṃ Tathā || 62

Parāṃ Sūkṣmāṃ Namasyāmi Naumi Sūkṣmāmṛtāṃ Kalām |
Vande Jñānāṃ Kalāṃ Caiva Tathā Jñānāmṛtāṃ Kalāṃ || 63

Āpyāyinīṃ Vyāpinīṃ Ca Vyomarūpāṃ Namāmyaham |
Kalāḥ Sadāśivasyaitāḥ Ṣoḍaśa Praṇamāmyaham || 64

Hāṃsākhyaṃ Ca Mahāmantraṃ Jyotiṣaṃ Haṃsamāśraye |
Pratatprathamaviśvāntaṃ Mantraṃ Jyotiṣamāśraye || 65

Tryambakaṃ Ca Namasyāmi Tadviṣṇoḥ Praṇamāmyaham |
Viṣṇuryoniṃ Mūlavidyāṃ Mantrairebhiranuttamaiḥ || 66

Amṛtaṃ Mantritaṃ Vande Caturnavatibhistava |
Akhaṇḍaikarasānandakare'parasudhātmani || 67

Svacchandasphuraṇāmatra Nidhehyakularūpiṇi |
Akulasthāmṛtākāre Śuddhajñānakare Pare ‖ 68

Amṛtatvaṃ Nidhehyasmin Vastuni Klinnarūpiṇi |
Tadrūpiṇyaikarasyatvaṃ Kṛtvā Hyetatsvarūpiṇi ‖ 69

Bhūtvā Parāmṛtā"kārā Mayi Citsphuraṇaṃ Kuru |
Amṛteśīṃ Namasyāmi Sarvadāmṛtavarṣiṇīm ‖ 70

Vāgvādinīṃ Namasyāmi Śrīvidyāṃ Praṇamāmyaham |
Ebhirmanūttamairvande Mantritaṃ Paramāmṛtam ‖ 71

Jyotirmayamidaṃ Kurve Paramarghyaṃ Maheśvari |
Tadbindubhirme Śirasi Trigurūn Pūjayāmyaham ‖ 72

Brahmā'hamasmi Tadbinduṃ Kuṇḍalinyā Juhomyaham |
Hṛccakrasthā Mahādevīṃ Mahātripurasundarīm ‖ 73

Nirastamohatimirāṃ Sākṣāt Saṃvitsvarūpiṇīm |
Nāsāpuṭe Parakalāmatha Nirgamayāmyaham ‖ 74

Samānayāmi Tāṃ Haste Trikhaṇḍakusumāñjalau |
Jaganmātarmahādevi Mahātripurasundari ‖ 75

Sudhācaitanyamūrtiṃ Te Kalpayāmi Namaḥ Śive |
Anena Manunā Devi Yantre Tvāṃ Sthāpayāmyaham ‖ 76

Mahāpadmavanāntaḥsthe Kāraṇānandavigrahe |
Sarvabhūtahite Mātarehyehi Parameśvari ‖ 77

Deveśi Bhaktisulabhe Sarvāvaraṇasaṃyute |
Yāvat Tvāṃ Pūjayiṣyāmi Tāvat Tvaṃ Susthirā Bhava ‖ 78

Anena Mantrayugmena Tvāmatrāvāhayāmyaham |
Kalpayāmi Namaḥ Pādyamarghyaṃ Te Kalpayāmyaham ‖ 79

Sugandhatailābhyaṅgaṃ Ca Majjaśālāpraveśanam |
Kalpayāmi Namastasmin Maṇipīṭhopaveśanam ‖ 80

Divyasnānīyamīśāni Gṛhāṇodvartanaṃ Śubham |
Gṛhāṇoṣṇodakasnānaṃ Kalpayāmi Namastava ‖ 81

Hemakumbhacyutaistīrthaiḥ Kalpayāmyabhiṣecanam |
Kalpayāmi Namastubhyaṃ Dhautena Parimārjanam || 82

Bālabhānupratīkāśaṃ Dukūlaparidhānakam |
Aruṇena Dukūlenottarīyaṃ Kalpayāmi Te || 83

Praveśanaṃ Kalpayāmi Tavālepanamaṇḍapam |
Namaste Kalpayāmyatra Maṇipīṭhopaveśanam || 84

Aṣṭagandhaiḥ Kalpayāmi Sarvāṅgeṣu Vilepanam |
Kālāgaru Mahādhūpastava Keśabharasya Hi || 85

Mallikāmālatījātīcampakādimanoramaiḥ |
Racitāḥkusumairmālāḥ Kalpayāmi Namastava || 86

Praveśanaṃ Kalpayāmi Namo Bhūṣaṇamaṇḍapam |
Upaveśaṃ Ratnapīṭhe Tatra Te Kalpayāmyaham || 87

Navamāṇikyamukuṭaṃ Taccandraśakalaṃ Tataḥ |
Tataḥ Sīmantasindūraṃ Tatastilakamuttamam || 88

Kālāñjanaṃ Kalpayāmi Pālīyugalamuttamam |
Maṇikuṇḍalayugmaṃ Te Nāsābharaṇamīśvari || 89

Te Kalpayāmi Tripure Lalitā'dharayāvakam |
Athā''dyabhūṣaṇaṃ Kaṇṭhe Hemacintākamuttamam || 90

Padakaṃ Te Kalpayāmi Mahāpadakamuttamam |
Kalpayāmi Namo Muktāvalimekāvaliṃ Ca Te || 91

Channavīraṃ Ca Keyūrayugalānāṃ Catuṣṭayam |
Valayāvalimīśāni Ūrmikāvalimīśvari || 92

Kāñcīdāmakaṭīsūtraṃ Saubhāgyābharaṇaṃ Ca Te |
Tripure Pādakaṭakaṃ Kalpaye Ratnanūpuram || 93

Pādāṅgulīyakaṃ Tubhyaṃ Pāśamekakare Tava |
Anyasminnaṅkuśaṃ Devi Puṇḍrekṣudhanuṣaṃ Pare || 94

Apare Puṣpabāṇāṃśca Śrīmanmāṇikyapāduke |
Navāvaraṇadevībhirmahācakrādhirohaṇam || 95

Kāmeśvarāṅkaparyaṅka Upaveśanamuttamam |

Sudhāsavākhyaṃ Caṣakaṃ Tataḥ Ācamanīyakam || 96

Karpūravīṭikāṃ Tubhyaṃ Kalpayāmi Namaḥ Śive |

Ānandollāsavelāsahāsaṃ Te Kalpayāmyaham || 97

Maṅgalārārtikaṃ Devi Chatraṃ Te Kalpayāmyaham |

Tataścāmarayugmaṃ Te Darpaṇaṃ Kalpayāmyaham || 98

Tālavṛntaṃ Kalpayāmi Gandhaṃ Puṣpaṃ Maheśvari |

Dhūpaṃ Dīpaṃ Ca Naivedyaṃ Kalpayāmi Namastava || 99

Athā' haṃ Vaindave Cakre Sarvānandamayātmike |

Ratnasiṃhāsane Ramye Samāsīnāṃ Śivapriyām || 100

Dhyānam |

Udyadbhānusahasrābhyāṃ Japāpuṣpasamaprabhām |

Navaratnaprabhādīptamukuṭena Virājitām || 101

Candrarekhāsamopetāṃ Kastūrītilakāñcitām |

Kāmakodaṇḍasaundaryanirjitabhrūlatāyugām || 102

Añjanāñcitanetrāṃ Tāṃ Padmapatranibhekṣaṇām |

Maṇikuṇḍalasaṃyuktakarṇadvayavirājitām || 103

Muktāmāṇikyakhacitanāsikābharaṇānvitām |

Madapāṭalasaṃyuktakapolayugalānvitām || 104

Pakvabimbaphalābhāsādharadvayavirājitām |

Śuddhamuktāvaliprakhyadantapaṅktivirājitām || 105

Tāmbūlapūritamukhīṃ Susmitāsyavirājitām |

Ādyabhūṣaṇasaṃyuktāṃ Hemacintākasaṃyutām || 106

Padakena Samopetāṃ Mahāpadakasaṃyutām |

Muktāvalisamopetāmekāvalivirājitām || 107

Keyūrāṅgadasaṃyuktacaturbāhuvirājitām |

Aṣṭagandhasamopetāṃ Śrīcandanavilepanām || 108

Hemakumbhasamaprakhyastanadvayavirājitām |
Raktavastraparīdhānāṃ Raktakañcukasamyutām || 109

Sūkṣmaromāvalīyuktatanumadhyavirājitām |
Muktāmāṇikyakhacitakāñcīyutanitambinīm || 110
Sadāśivāṅkasthapṛthumahājaghanamaṇḍalām |
Kadalīstambhasaṅkāśaūruyugmavirājitām || 111

Kadalīkāntisaṅkāśajaṅghāyugalaśobhitām |
Gūḍhagulphadvayopetāṃ Raktapādayugānvitām || 112

Brahmāviṣṇumahādevaśiromukuṭajātayā |
Kāntyā Virājitapadāṃ Bhaktatrāṇaparāyaṇām || 113

Ikṣukārmukapuṣpeṣu Pāśāṅkuśadharāṃ Parām |
Saṃvitsvarūpiṇīṃ Devīṃ Dhyāyāmi Parameśvarīm || 114

Iti Dhyānam |

Pradarśayāmyatha Śive Navamudrā Varapradāḥ |
Tvāṃ Tarpayāmi Tripure Tridhā Mūlena Pārvati || 115

Āgneyyāmīśadigbhāge Nairṛtyāṃ Mārute Tathā |
Madhye Dikṣu Ṣaḍaṅgāni Kramādabhyarcayāmyaham || 116

Ādyāṃ Kāmeśvarīṃ Vande Namāmi Bhagamālinīm |
Nityaklinnāṃ Namasyāmi Bheruṇḍāṃ Praṇamāmyaham || 117

Vahnivāsāṃ Namasyāmi Mahāvajreśvarīṃ Stuve |
Śivadūtīṃ Namasyāmi Tvaritāṃ Kulasundarīm || 118

Nityāṃ Nīlapatākāṃ Ca Vijayāṃ Sarvamaṅgalām |
Jvālāmālāṃ Ca Citrāṃ Ca Mahānityāṃ Ca Saṃstuve || 119

Divyaughebhyo Namasyāmi Pareśaparameśvarīm |
Mitreśamatha Ṣaṣṭhīśamuḍḍīśaṃ Praṇamāmyaham || 120

Caryānāthaṃ Namasyāmi Lopāmudrāmahaṃ Bhaje |
Agastyaṃ Praṇamasyāmi Siddhaughe Kālatāpanam || 121

Dharmācāryaṃ Namasyāmi Muktakeśīśvaraṃ Bhaje |
Bhaje Dīpakalānāthaṃ Mānavaughe Tataḥ Param ǁ 122

Viṣṇudevaṃ Namasyāmi Prabhākaramahaṃ Bhaje |
Tejodevaṃ Namasyāmi Manojamatha Saṃstuve ǁ 123

Kalyāṇadevaṃ Kalaye Ratnadevaṃ Bhajāmyaham |
Vāsudevaṃ Namasyāmi Śrīrāmānandamāśraye ǁ 124

Parameṣṭhiguruṃ Vande Paramaṃ Gurumāśraye |
Śrīguruṃ Praṇamasyāmi Mūrdhni Brahmabile Sthitam ǁ 125

Kaṃ Bile'haṃ Namasyāmi Śrīguroḥ Pādukāṃ Tataḥ |
Atha Prāthamike Devi Caturasre Taveśvari ǁ 126

Aṇimāṃ Laghimāṃ Vande Mahimāṃ Praṇamāmyaham |
Īśitvasiddhiṃ Vande'haṃ Vaśitvaṃ Ca Namāmyaham ǁ 127

Prākāmyasiddhiṃ Vande'haṃ Bhuktimicchāmahaṃ Bhaje |
Prāptisiddhiṃ Sarvakāmapradāsiddhimahaṃ Bhaje ǁ 128

Madhyame Caturasre'haṃ Brāhmīṃ Māheśvarīṃ Bhaje |
Kaumārīṃ Vaiṣṇavīṃ Vande Vārāhīṃ Praṇamāmyaham ǁ 129

Māhendrīmapi Cāmuṇḍāṃ Mahālakṣmīmahaṃ Bhaje |
Tṛtīye Caturasre'haṃ Sarvasaṃkṣobhiṇīṃ Bhaje ǁ 130

Sarvavidrāviṇīṃ Mudrāṃ Sarvākarṣiṇikāṃ Bhaje |
Mudrāṃ Vaśaṅkarīṃ Vande Sarvonmādinikāṃ Bhaje ǁ 131

Bhaje Mahāṅkuśāṃ Mudrāṃ Khecarīṃ Praṇamāmyaham |
Bījamudrāṃ Yonimudrāṃ Bhaje Sarvatrikhaṇḍinīm ǁ 132

Trailokyamohanaṃ Cakraṃ Namāmi Lalite Tava |
Namāmi Yoginīṃ Tatra Prakaṭākhyāmabhīṣṭadām ǁ 133

Sudhārṇavāsanaṃ Vande Tatra Te Parameśvari |
Cakreśvarīṃ Tatra Vande Tripurāṃ Parameśvarīm ǁ 134

Sarvesaṃkṣobhiṇīṃ Mudrāṃ Tato'haṃ Kalaye Śive |
Athā'haṃ Ṣoḍaśadale Kāmākarṣaṇikāṃ Bhaje ǁ 135

Buddhyākarṣaṇikāṃ Vande'haṅkārākarṣaṇīṃ Bhaje |
Śabdākarṣaṇikāṃ Vande Sparśākarṣaṇikāṃ Bhaje || 136

Rūpākarṣaṇikāṃ Vande Rasākarṣaṇikāṃ Bhaje |
Gandhākarṣaṇikāṃ Vande Cittākarṣaṇikāṃ Bhaje || 137

Dhairyākarṣaṇikāṃ Vande Smṛtyākarṣaṇikāṃ Bhaje |
Nāmākarṣaṇikāṃ Vande Bījākarṣaṇikāṃ Bhaje || 138

Ātmākarṣaṇikāṃ Vande Hyamṛtākarṣaṇīṃ Bhaje |
Śarīrākarṣaṇīṃ Vande Nityāṃ Śrīparameśvarīm || 139

Sarvāśāpūrakaṃ Cakraṃ Kalaye'haṃ Taveśvari |
Guptākhyāṃ Yoginīṃ Vande Tatrā'haṃ Guptapūjitām || 140

Pītāmbujāsanaṃ Tatra Namāmi Lalite Tava |
Tripureśīṃ Mahādevīṃ Bhajāmīṣṭārthaṃsiddhidām || 141

Sarvaṃvidrāviṇīṃ Mudrāṃ Tatrā'haṃ Tāṃ Vicintaye |
Śive Tavāṣṭapatre'hamanaṅgakusumāṃ Bhaje || 142

Anaṅgamekhalāṃ Vande Hyanaṅgamadanāṃ Bhaje |
Tato'haṃ Praṇamasyāmi Hyanaṅgamadanāturām || 143

Anaṅgarekhāṃ Kalaye Bhaje Te'naṅgaveginīm |
Bhaje'naṅgāṅkuśāṃ Devi Tava Cānaṅgamālinīm || 144

Sarvasaṃkṣobhaṇaṃ Cakraṃ Tatrā'haṃ Kalaye Sadā |
Vande Guptatarākhyāṃ Tāṃ Yoginīṃ Sarvakāmadām || 145

Tatrā'haṃ Praṇamasyāmi Devyātmāsanamuttamam |
Namāmi Jagadīśānīma'haṃ Tripurasundarīm || 146

Sarvākarṣaṇikāṃ Mudrāṃ Tatrā'haṃ Kalayāmi Te |
Bhuvanāre Tava Śive Sarvasaṃkṣobhiṇīṃ Bhaje || 147

Sarvavidrāviṇīṃ Vande'haṃ Sarvākarṣiṇikāṃ Bhaje |
Sakalāhlādinīṃ Vande Sarvasammohinīṃ Bhaje || 148

Sakala Stambhinīṃ Vande Kalaye Sarvajṛrmbhinīm |
Vaśaṅkarīṃ Namasyāmi Sarvarañjanikāṃ Bhaje || 149

Sakalonmādinīṃ Vande Bhaje Sarvārthasādhinīm |
Sampattipūriṇīṃ Vande Sarvamantramayīṃ Bhaje || 150

Bhajāmyahaṃ Tataḥ Śaktiṃ Sarvadvandvakṣayaṅkarīm |
Tatrā' haṃ Kalaye Cakraṃ Sarvasaubhāgyadāyakam || 151

Namāmi Jagatāṃ Dhātrīṃ Sampradāyākhyayoginīm |
Śive Tava Namasyāmi Śrīcakrāsanamuttamam || 152

Namāmi Jagadīśānīmahaṃ Tripuravāsinīm |
Kalaye' haṃ Tava Śive Mudrāṃ Sarvavaśaṅkarīm || 153

Bahirdaśāre Te Devi Sarvasiddhipradāṃ Bhaje |
Sarvasampatpradāṃ Vande Bhaje Sarvapriyaṅkarīm || 154

Namāmyahaṃ Tato Devīṃ Sarvamaṅgalakāriṇīm |
Sarvakāmapradāṃ Vande Sarvaduḥkhavimocinīm || 155

Sarvamṛtyupraśamanīṃ Sarvavighnanivāriṇīm |
Sarvāṅgasundarīṃ Devīṃ Sarvasaubhāgyadāyinīm || 156

Sarvārthasādhakaṃ Cakraṃ Tathā' haṃ Kalaye Sadā |
Kalayāmi Tato Devīṃ Kulottīrṇākhyayoginīm || 157

Sarvamantrāsanaṃ Vande Tripurāśrīyamāśraye |
Kalayāmi Tato Mudrāṃ Sarvonmādanakāriṇīm || 158

Antardaśāre Te Devi Sarvajñāṃ Praṇamāmyaham |
Sarvaśaktiṃ Namasyāmi Sarvaiśvaryapradāṃ Bhaje || 159

Sarvajñānamayīṃ Vande Sarvavyādhivināśinīm |
Sarvādhārasvarūpāṃ Ca Sarvapāpaharāṃ Bhaje || 160

Sarvānandamayīṃ Vande Sarvarakṣāsvarūpiṇīm |
Praṇamāmi Mahādevīṃ Sarvepsitapradāṃ Bhaje || 161

Sarvarakṣākaraṃ Cakraṃ Tatrā' haṃ Kalaye Sadā |
Nigarbhayoginīṃ Vande Tatrā' haṃ Parameśvarīm || 162

Sādhyasiṃhāsanaṃ Vande Bhaje Tripuramālinīm |
Kalayāmi Tato Devi Mudrāṃ Sarvamahāṅkuśām || 163

Aṣṭāre Vaśinīṃ Vande Bhaje Kāmeśvarīṃ Sadā |
Modinīṃ Vimalāṃ Vande Hyaruṇāṃ Jayinīṃ Bhaje || 164

Sarveśvarīṃ Namasyāmi Kaulinīṃ Praṇamāmyaham |
Sarvarogaharaṃ Cakraṃ Tavā'haṃ Devi Cintaye || 165

Rahasyayoginīṃ Devīṃ Sadā'haṃ Kalayāmi Te |
Namāmi Tripurāsiddhāṃ Bhaje Mudrāṃ Ca Khecarīm || 166

Mahātrikoṇasya Bāhye Caturdikṣu Maheśvari |
Namāmi Jṛmbhṇān Bāṇān Cāpaṃ Sammohanaṃ Bhaje || 167

Pāśaṃ Vaśaṅkaraṃ Vande Bhaje Stambhanamaṅkuśam |
Trikoṇe'haṃ Jagaddhātrīṃ Mahākāmeśvarīṃ Bhaje || 168

Mahāvajreśvarīṃ Vande Mahāśrīmālinīṃ Bhaje |
Mahāśrīsundarīṃ Vande Sarvakāmaphalapradām || 169

Sarvasiddhipradaṃ Cakraṃ Tava Devi Namāmyaham |
Namāmyatirahasyākhyāṃ Yoginīṃ Tatra Kāmadām || 170

Tripurāmbāṃ Namasyāmi Bījamudrāṃ Namāmyaham |
Mūlamantreṇa Lalite Tvāṃ Bindau Pūjayāmyaham || 171

Sarvānandamayaṃ Cakraṃ Namāmi Lalite Tava |
Parāpararahasyākhyāṃ Yoginīṃ Kalaye Sadā || 172

Mahācakreśvarīṃ Vande Yonimudrāmahaṃ Bhaje |
Dhūpādikaṃ Sarvamayi Te Kalpayāmyaham || 173

Tvatprītaye Mahāmudrāṃ Darśayāmi Tataḥ Śive |
Tridhā Tvāṃ Mūlamantreṇa Tarpayami Iataḥ Śive || 174

Śālyannaṃ Madhusaṃyuktaṃ Pāyasāpūpasaṃyutam |
Ghṛtasūpasamāyuktaṃ Sarvabhakṣyasamanvitam || 175

Sasitaṃ Kṣīrasaṃyuktaṃ Bahuśākasamanvitam |
Nikṣipya Kāñcane Pātre Naivedyaṃ Kalpayāmi Te || 176

Saṅkalpya Bindunā Vaktraṃ Kucau Bindudvayena Ca |
Yoniṃ Tu Saparārdhena Kṛtvā Śrītripure Tava || 177

Etat Kāmakalārūpaṃ Bhaktānāṃ Sarvakāmadam |
Sarvasampatpradaṃ Vande Namaste Tripureśvari || 178

Vāmabhāge Trikoṇaṃ Ca Vṛttaṃ Ca Caturasrakam |
Kṛtvā Gandhākṣatādyaiśca Hyarcayāmi Maheśvari || 179

Vāgbhavādyaṃ Namasyāmi Tatra Vyāpakamaṇḍalam |
Jalayuktārdrānnayuktaṃ Makāratrayabhājanam || 180

Tatra Vinyasya Dāsyāmi Bhūtebhyo Balimuttamam |
Namaste Devadeveśi Namastrailokyavandite || 181

Namaḥ Paraśivāṅkasthe Namastripurasundari |
Pradakṣiṇāṃ Namaskāraṃ Manasā'haṃ Karomi Te || 182

Tataḥ Sakalamantrāṇāṃ Samrājñīṃ Parameśvarīm |
Prajapāmi Mahāvidyāṃ Tvatprītyārthamahaṃ Sadā |
Tava Vidyāṃ Prajaptvā'tha Staumi Tvāṃ Parameśvarīm || 183

Mahādevi Maheśāni Sadāśiva Mahāpriye |
Mahānitye Mahāsiddhe Tvāmahaṃ Śaraṇaṃ Vraje || 184

Jaya Tvaṃ Tripure Devi Lalite Jagadīśvari |
Sadāśivapriyakari Pāhi Māṃ Karuṇākari || 185

Jaganmātarjagadrūpe Jagadīśvaravallabhe |
Jaganmaye Jagastulye Gauri Tvāmahamāśraye || 186

Anādye Sarvalokānāmādye Bhakteṣṭadāyini |
Girirājasya Tanaye Namaste Tripureśvari || 187

Jayādidevadeveśi Brahmamātarnamo'stu Te |
Viṣṇumātaranādyante Haramātaḥ Sureśvari || 188

Brahmādisurasaṃstutye Lokatrayavaśaṅkari |
Sarvasampatprade Nitye Tvāmahaṃ Kalaye Sadā || 189

Nityānande Nirādhāre Cidrūpiṇi Śivapriye |
Aṇimādiguṇādhāre Tvāṃ Sadā Kalayāmyaham || 190

Brāhmyādimātṛsaṃstutye Sarvāvaraṇasaṃyute |
Jyotirmaye Mahārūpe Pāhi Māṃ Tripure Sadā || 191

Lakṣmīvāṇyādisampūjye Brahmaviṣṇuśivastute |
Bhajāmi Tava Pādābjaṃ Sarvakāmaphalapradam || 192

Sarvaśaktisamopetaṃ Sarvābhīṣṭaphalaprade |
Namāmi Tava Pādābjaṃ Devi Tripurasundari || 193

Tvatpriyārthaṃ Tataḥ Kāṃścicchaktiṃ Sampūjayāmyaham |
Mapañcakena Tāṃ Śaktiṃ Tarpayāmi Maheśvari || 194

Tayopetaṃ Haviḥśeṣaṃ Cidagnau Prajuhomyaham |
Tvatpriyārthaṃ Mahādevi Mamābhīṣṭārthasiddhaye || 195

Baddhvā Tāṃ Khecarīṃ Mudrāṃ Kṣamasvodvāsayāmyaham |
Tiṣṭha Me Hṛdaye Nityaṃ Tripure Parameśvari || 196

Jagadambe Mahārājñi Mahāśakti Śivapriye |
Hṛccakre Tiṣṭha Satataṃ Mahātripurasundari || 197

Sarvalokaikasampūjye Sakalāvaraṇairyute |
Hṛccakre Tiṣṭha Me Nityaṃ Mahātripurasundari || 198

|| Phalaśruti ||

Etat Tripurasundaryā Hṛdayaṃ Sarvakāmadam |
Mahārahasyaṃ Paramaṃ Durlabhaṃ Daivatairapi || 1

Sākṣāt Sadāśivenoktaṃ Guhyādguhyamanuttamam || 2

Yaḥ Paṭhennityamekāgraḥ Śṛṇuyād Vā Samāhitaḥ |
Nityapūjāphalaṃ Devyāḥ Sa Labhennātra Saṃśayaḥ || 3

Pāpaiḥ Sa Mucyate Sadyaḥ Kāyavākcittasambhavaiḥ |
Sarvajanmasamudbhūtairjñānakṛtairapi || 4

Sarvakratuṣu Yatpuṇyaṃ Sarvatīrtheṣu Yat Phalam |
Tatpuṇyaṃ Labhate Nityaṃ Mānavo Nātra Saṃśayaḥ || 5

Acalāṃ Labhate Lakṣmīṃ Trailokye Cāpi Durlabhām |
Sākṣād Viṣṇusamo Martyo Śīghrameva Bhavet Sadā || 6

Aṣṭaiśvaryamavāpnoti Sa Śīghraṃ Mānavottamaḥ |

Guṭikāpādukāsiddhyādyaṣṭakaṃ Śīghramaśnute || 7

Śaṅkhādyā Nidhyo Vā'pi Taṃ Nityaṃ Paryupāsate |

Vaśyādīnyaṣṭakarmāṇi Śīghraṃ Siddhyanti Sarvadā || 8

Bhūlokasthāḥ Sarvanāryaḥ Pātālasthāḥ Sadāṅganāḥ |

Sarvalokasthitāḥ Sarvā Yāścānyārūpagarvitāḥ || 9

Ramante Tena Satataṃ Śīghraṃ Vaśyā Na Saṃśayaḥ |

Rājādyāḥ Sakalā Martyāḥ Haraharyādayaḥ Surāḥ || 10

Anantādyā Mahānāgāḥ Siddhayogeśvarādayaḥ |

Ṛṣayo Munayo Yakṣāstaṃ Nityaṃ Paryupāsate || 11

Mahatīṃ Kīrtimāpnoti Śivaviṣṇusamaprabhām |

Paramaṃ Yogamāsādya Khecaro Jāyate Sadā || 12

Apamṛtyuvinirmuktaḥ Kālamṛtyuvivarjitaḥ |

Paramāyuṣyamāpnoti Haraharyādidurlabham || 13

Aśrutāni Ca Śāstrāṇi Vyācaṣṭe Vidhivat Sadā |

Mūḍho'pi Sarvavidyāvān Dakṣiṇāmūrtivadbhavet || 14

Grahabhūtapiśācādyā Yakṣagandharvarākṣasāḥ |

Etasya Smaraṇādeva Vinaśyanti Hi Sarvadā || 15

Tadgātraṃ Prāpya Sakalaṃ Viṣaṃ Sadyo Vinaśyati |

Sahasrakāmasaṅkāśaḥ Kāntyā Yaḥ Sarvadā Bhavet || 16

Tasmādetat Paṭhet Stotraṃ Tripurāhṛdayaṃ Śubham |

Japed Yaḥ Sarvadā Sākṣād Bhaved Devīsvarūpakaḥ || 17

Sāṅgaṃ Tripurasundaryā Nityapūjāphalaṃ Labhet |

Vimukto Rogasaṅghātairārogyaṃ Mahadaśnute || 18

Prāpnoti Mahadaiśvaryaṃ Sarvavidyānidhirbhavet |

Tatkarasparśamātreṇa Naro Brāhmaṇatāṃ Labhet || 19

Mucyate Sakalairvighnaiḥ Sa Nityaṃ Mānavottamaḥ |

Sa Bhuṅkte Sakalān Bhogān Durlabhāṃśca Dine Dine || 20

Labhate Putrapautrāṃśca Mahālakṣmīsamanvitān |
Paramāyuṣyasaṃyuktān Sākṣacchivasamān Guṇaiḥ || 21

Sṛṣṭipālanasaṃhārakartevāyaṃ Sadā Bhavet |
Yaste Kṛpāvān Bhavati Sa Trimūrtirna Saṃśayaḥ || 22

Tatsamīpasthitaḥ Śīghraṃ Sadā Jātismarobhavet |
Tasya Gehe Sadā Kāmadhenuḥ Kalpatarustathā || 23

Cintāmaṇiśca Satataṃ Tiṣṭhatyeva Na Saṃśayaḥ |
Mahājayamavāpnoti Sadā Sarvatra Mānavaḥ || 24

Vajrakāyasamo Bhūtvā Caratyeva Jagatyayam |
Mahāsukhī Bhavennityaṃ Paramātmā Bhavet Sadā || 25

Mucyate Sakalebhyo'pi Bandhanaiḥ Śṛṅkhalādibhiḥ |
Taṃ Pūjayanti Satataṃ Harirudrādayo'pi Ca || 26

Śubhameva Bhavennityaṃ Sadāpadbhirvimucyate |
Devagandharvarakṣādyairbrahmādyairapi Durlabhān || 27

Prāpnoti Sakalān Kāmān Śīghrameva Na Saṃśayaḥ |
Divyabhogayuto Divyakanyābhiḥ Saha Saṃyutaḥ || 28

Vimānaṃ Sa Samāsthāya Divyābharaṇabhūṣitaḥ |
Divyacandanaliptāṅgaḥ Sadā Viṃśativārṣikaḥ || 29

Sa Bhuṅkte Sakalān Bhogān Devaloke Naraḥ Sadā |
Tasmādetat Paṭhet Stotraṃ Tripurāhṛdayaṃ Śubham |
Japedyaḥ Satataṃ Bhaktyā Bhavet Sākṣāt Sadā Śivaḥ || 30

|| Iti Śrī Rudrayāmale Īśvarapārvatīsaṃvade Śrī Tripura Sundarī Hṛdaya
Stotram ||

श्री त्रिपुर सुन्दरी हृदय स्तोत्रम्

ॐ शुद्धस्फटिकसङ्काशं द्विनेत्रं करुणानिधिम्।
वराभयकरं वन्दे श्रीगुरुं शिवरूपिणम्॥ १

भक्ताज्ञानतमोभानुं मूर्ध्नि पङ्कजसंस्थितम्।
सदाशिवमयं नित्यं श्रीगुरुं प्रणमाम्यहम्॥ २

श्रीविद्यां जगतां धात्रीं सर्गस्थितिलयेश्वरीम्।
नमामि ललितां नित्यं महात्रिपुरसुन्दरीम्॥ ३

बिन्दुत्रिकोणसंयुक्तं वसुकोणसमन्वितम्।
दशकोणद्वयोपेतं भुवनारसमन्वितम्॥ ४

दलाष्टकसमोपेतं दलषोडशकान्वितम्।
वृत्तत्रयान्वितं भूमिसदनत्रयभूषितम्॥ ५

नमामि ललिताचक्रं भक्तानामेतदिष्टदम्।
अमृताम्भोनिधौ तत्र रत्नद्वीपं नमाम्यहम्॥ ६

नानावृक्षमहोद्यानं वन्देऽहं कल्पवाटिकाम्।
सन्तानवाटिकां वन्दे हरिचन्दनवाटिकाम्॥ ७

मन्दारवाटिकां वन्दे पारिजाताख्यवाटिकाम्।
नमामि तव देवेशि कदम्बवनवाटिकाम्॥ ८

पुष्परागमहारत्नप्राकारं प्रणमाम्यहम्।
पद्मरागाख्यमणिभिः प्राकारं सर्वदा भजे॥ ९

गोमेदरत्नप्राकारं वज्रप्राकारमाश्रये।
वैडूर्यरत्नप्राकारं प्रणमामि तवेश्वरि॥ १०

इन्द्रनीलाख्यरत्नानां प्राकारं प्रणमाम्यहम्।
मुक्तारत्नमयं चैव प्राकारं सर्वदा भजे॥ ११

मरकताख्यमहारत्नप्राकाराय नमस्तव।
विद्रुमाख्यमहारत्नप्राकारं तु तवाश्रये॥ १२

माणिक्यमण्डपं वन्दे सहस्रस्तम्भमण्डपम्।
ललिते तव देवेशि भजाम्यमृतवापिकाम्॥ १३

श्रीआनन्दवापिकां वन्दे भजे चैव विमर्शिकाम्।
भजे बालातिपोद्द्वारं चन्द्रिकोद्द्वारमाश्रये॥ १४

महाशृङ्गारपरिखां महापद्माटवीं भजे।
चिन्तामणिमहारत्नगृहराजं नमाम्यहम्॥ १५

पूर्वाम्नायमयं पूर्वद्वारं देवि भजामि ते।
दक्षिणाम्नाय रूपं ते दक्षिणद्वारमाश्रये॥ १६

नमामि ते परं द्वारं पश्चिमाम्नायरूपकम्।
वन्देऽहमुत्तरं द्वारमुत्तराम्नायरूपकम्॥ १७

ऊर्ध्वाम्नायमऽहं वन्दे ऊर्ध्वद्वारं कुलेश्वरि।
ललिते तव देवेशि महासिंहासनं भजे॥ १८

ब्रह्मात्मकमञ्चपादमेकं तव नमाम्यहम्।
एकं विष्णुमयं मञ्चपादं तव नमाम्यहम्॥ १९

एकं रुद्रमयं मञ्चपादं तव नमाम्यहम्।
मञ्चपादं नमाम्येकं तव देवीश्वरात्मकम्॥ २०

मञ्चैकफलकं वन्दे सदाशिवमयं शुभम्।
नमामि ते हंसतूलतलिमां परमेश्वरि॥ २१

भजामि ते हंसतूल महोपाधानमुत्तमम्।
कौसुम्भास्तरणं देवि तव नित्यं नमाम्यहम्॥ २२

मानसपूजा।

महावितानकं वन्दे महाजवनिकां भजे।
एवं पूजागृहं ध्यात्वा श्रीचक्रस्य शिवप्रिये॥ २३

मद्दक्षिणे स्थापयामि भागे पुष्पाक्षतादिकम्।
अभितस्ते महादेवि दीपाँस्तान् दर्शयाम्यहम्॥ २४

मूलेन त्रिपुराचक्रं तव सम्पूजयाम्यहम्।
त्रिभिःखण्डैस्तव त्र्यस्त्रं पूजयामि शिवप्रिये॥ २५

वाय्वग्निजलसंयुक्तप्राणायामैरहं शिवे।
शोषणं दाहनं देवि करोम्याप्लावनं तथा॥ २६

त्रिवारं मूलमन्त्रेण प्राणायामं करोम्यहम्।
अपसर्पन्तु ते भूता ये भूता भूमिसंस्थिताः॥ २७

ये भूता विघ्नकर्तारस्ते नश्यन्तु शिवाज्ञया ।
करोम्यनेन मन्त्रेण तालत्रयमहं शिवे ॥ २८

नारायणोऽहं ब्रह्माऽहं भैरवोऽहं शिवोऽस्म्यहम् ।
देवोऽहं परमात्माऽहं महात्रिपुरसुन्दरि ॥ २९

ध्यात्वैवं वज्रकवचं न्यासं तव करोम्यहम् ।
कुमारीबीजसंयुक्तं महात्रिपुरसुन्दरि ॥ ३०

मां रक्ष रक्षेति हृदि करोम्यञ्जलिमीश्वरि ।
नमो देव्यासनायेति ते करोम्यासनं शिवे ॥ ३१

चक्रासनं नमस्यामि सर्वमन्त्रासनं भजे ।
साध्यसिद्धासनं वन्दे मन्त्रैरेभिर्महेश्वरि ॥ ३२

करोम्यस्मिंश्चक्रमन्त्रदेवतासनमुत्तमम् ।
करोम्यथ षडङ्गाख्यं मातृकाश्च करोम्यहम् ॥ ३३

वशिन्याद्यष्टकं न्यासं षोढान्यासं करोम्यहम् ।
महाषोढां ततः कुर्वे नवयोन्याख्यमुत्तमम् ॥ ३४

चक्रन्यासं ततः कुर्वे श्रीकण्ठन्यासमुत्तमम् ।
केशवादि महान्यासं कामन्यासं करोम्यहम् ॥ ३५

कलान्यासं ततः कुर्वे कुर्वे कामकलाह्वयम् ।
पीठन्यासं ततः कुर्वे तत्त्वन्यासं करोम्यहम् ॥ ३६

ततः करोमि स्थित्यादिन्यासं तत् त्रिपुरेश्वरि ।
ततः शुद्धोदकेनाहं वामभागे महेश्वरि ॥ ३७

करोमि मण्डलं वृत्तं चतुरस्रं शिवप्रिये ।
पुष्पैरभ्यर्च्य साधारं शङ्खं संस्थापयाम्यहम् ॥ ३८

अर्चयामि षडङ्गेन जलमापूरयाम्यहम् ।
ददामि चादिमं बिन्दुं कुर्वे मूलाभिमन्त्रितम् ॥ ३९

तज्जलेन जगन्मातस्त्रिकोणं वृत्तसंयुतम् ।
षट्कोणं चतुरस्रं च मण्डलं प्रकरोम्यहम् ॥ ४०

विद्यया पूजनं मध्ये खण्डैस्त्र्यस्त्राभिपूजनम्।
बीजावृत्या कोणषट्कं पूजयामि शिवप्रिये॥ ४१

तस्मिन् दशकलायुक्तमग्निमण्डलमाश्रये।
धूमार्चिषं नमस्यामि ऊष्मां च ज्वलिनीं भजे॥ ४२

ज्वलिनीं च नमस्यामि वन्देऽहं विस्फुल्लिङ्गिनीम्।
सुश्रियं च सुरूपां च कपिलां प्रणमाम्यहम्॥ ४३

नौमि हव्यवहां नित्यं भजे कव्यवहां कलाम्।
यादिभिः सहिता वह्नेः कला दश तथा भजे॥ ४४

सूर्यस्य मण्डलं तत्र कलाद्वादशकात्मकम्।
अर्घ्यपात्रे त्वऽहं वन्दे तपिनीं तापिनीं भजे॥ ४५

धूम्रां मरीचिं वन्देऽहं ज्वालिनीं च रुचिं भजे।
सुषुम्णां भोगदां वन्दे भजे विश्वां च बोधिनीम्॥ ४६

धारिणीं च क्षमां वन्दे सौरा एताः कला भजे।
सोमस्य मण्डलं तत्र कलाः षोडशकात्मकाः॥ ४७

अर्घ्यामृतात्मकं वन्देऽमृतां मानदां स्तुवे।
पूषां तुष्टिं भजे पुष्टिं रतिं धृतिमहं भजे॥ ४८

शशिनीं चन्द्रिकां वन्दे कान्तिं ज्योत्स्नां श्रियं भजे।
नौमि प्रीतिं चाङ्गदां च पूर्णां पूर्णामृतां भजे॥ ४९

स्वरैः षोडशभिर्युक्ता भजे सोमस्य वै कलाः।
त्रिकोणलेखनं कुर्वे अकथादिसुरेखकम्॥ ५०

हळक्षवर्णसंयुक्तं स्थितान्तर्हंसभास्वरम्।
वाक्कामशक्तिसंयुक्तं हंसेनाराधयाम्यहम्॥ ५१

वृत्ताद्बहिः षडस्त्रे च लेखनं प्रकरोम्यहम्।
पुरोभागादि षट्कोणं षडङ्गेनार्चयाम्यहम्॥ ५२

श्रीविद्यायाः सप्तवारं करोम्यत्राभिमन्त्रणम्।
समर्पयामि विश्वेशि तस्मिन् गन्धाक्षतादिकम्॥ ५३

ध्यायामि पूजाद्रव्यं ते सर्वं विद्यामयं शुभम्।
चतुर्नवति सन्मन्त्रान् स्पृष्ट्वा तत्प्रजपाम्यहम्॥ ५४

वह्नेर्देशकलाः सूर्यकलाद्वादशकं भजे।
आश्रये षोडशकलास्तत्र सोमस्य कामदाः॥ ५५

सृष्टिमृद्धिं स्मृतिं वन्दे मेधां कान्तिं नमाम्यहम्।
लक्ष्मीं धृतिं स्थिरांवन्दे स्थितिं सिद्धिं भजाम्यहम्॥ ५६

एतां ब्रह्मकलां वन्दे जरां तां पालिनीं भजे।
शान्तिं नमामीश्वरीं च रतिं वन्दे च कामिकाम्॥ ५७

वरदां ह्लादिनीं वन्दे प्रीतिं दीर्घां भजाम्यहम्।
टादिभिः सहिता विष्णोः कला दश तथा भजे॥ ५८

एता विष्णोः कला वन्दे तीक्ष्णां रौद्रीं भयां तथा।
निद्रां तन्द्रां क्षुधां वन्दे नमामि क्रोधिनीं क्रियाम्॥ ५९

उद्धारीं च भजे मृत्युमेता रुद्रकला भजे।
पीतां श्वेतां भजे नित्यमरुणां च तथा भजे॥ ६०

भजेऽसितां तथाऽनन्तां षादिभिः सहितास्तथा।
ईश्वरस्य कला ह्येता वन्दे नित्यमभीष्टदाः॥ ६१

निवृत्तिं च प्रतिष्ठां च विद्यां शान्तिं नमाम्यहम्।
इन्धिकां दीपिकां चैव रेचिकां मोचिकां तथा॥ ६२

परां सूक्ष्मां नमस्यामि नौमि सूक्ष्मामृतां कलाम्।
वन्दे ज्ञानां कलां चैव तथा ज्ञानामृतां कलाम्॥ ६३

आप्यायिनीं व्यापिनीं च व्योमरूपां नमाम्यहम्।
कलाः सदाशिवस्यैताः षोडश प्रणमाम्यहम्॥ ६४

हांसाख्यं च महामन्त्रं ज्योतिषं हंसमाश्रये।
प्रतत्प्रथमविश्रान्तं मन्त्रं ज्योतिषमाश्रये॥ ६५

त्र्यम्बकं च नमस्यामि तद्विष्णोः प्रणमाम्यहम्।
विष्णुर्योनिं मूलविद्यांमन्त्रैरेभिरनुत्तमैः॥ ६६

अमृतं मन्त्रितं वन्दे चतुर्नवतिभिस्तव।
अखण्डैकरसानन्दकरेऽपरसुधात्मनि ॥ ६७

स्वच्छन्दस्फुरणामत्र निधेह्यकुलरूपिणि।
अकुलस्थामृताकारे शुद्धज्ञानकरे परे॥ ६८

अमृतत्वं निधेह्यस्मिन् वस्तुनि क्लिन्नरूपिणि।
तद्रूपिण्यैकरस्यत्वं कृत्वा ह्येतत्स्वरूपिणि ॥ ६९

भूत्वा परामृताऽऽङ्कारा मयि चित्स्फुरणं कुरु।
अमृतेशीं नमस्यामि सर्वदामृतवर्षिणीम् ॥ ७०

वाग्वादिनीं नमस्यामि श्रीविद्यां प्रणमाम्यहम्।
एभिर्मनूत्तमैर्वन्दे मन्त्रितं परमामृतम्॥ ७१

ज्योतिर्मयमिदं कुर्वे परमर्घ्यं महेश्वरि।
तद्विन्दुभिर्मे शिरसि त्रिगुरून् पूजयाम्यहम्॥ ७२

ब्रह्माऽहमस्मि तद्विन्दुं कुण्डलिन्या जुहोम्यहम्।
हच्चक्रस्था महादेवीं महात्रिपुरसुन्दरीम्॥ ७३

निरस्तमोहतिमिरां साक्षात् संवित्स्वरूपिणीम्।
नासापुटे परकलामथ निर्गमयाम्यहम्॥ ७४

समानयामि तां हस्ते त्रिखण्डकुसुमाञ्जलौ।
जगन्मातर्महादेवि महात्रिपुरसुन्दरि॥ ७५

सुधाचैतन्यमूर्तिं ते कल्पयामि नमः शिवे।
अनेन मनुना देवि यन्त्रे त्वां स्थापयाम्यहम्॥ ७६

महापद्मवनान्तःस्थे कारणानन्दविग्रहे।
सर्वभूतहिते मातरेह्येहि परमेश्वरि॥ ७७

देवेशि भक्तिसुलभे सर्वावरणसंयुते।
यावत् त्वां पूजयिष्यामि तावत् त्वं सुस्थिरा भव॥ ७८

अनेन मन्त्रयुग्मेन त्वामत्रावाहयाम्यहम्।
कल्पयामि नमः पाद्यमर्घ्यं ते कल्पयाम्यहम् ॥ ७९

सुगन्धतैलाभ्यङ्गं च मज्जशालाप्रवेशनम्।
कल्पयामि नमस्तस्मिन् मणिपीठोपवेशनम्॥ ८०

दिव्यस्नानीयमीशानि गृहाणोद्वर्तनं शुभम्।
गृहाणोष्णोदकस्नानं कल्पयामि नमस्तव॥ ८१

हेमकुम्भच्युतैस्तीर्थैः कल्पयाम्यभिषेचनम्।
कल्पयामि नमस्तुभ्यं धौतेन परिमार्जनम्॥ ८२

बालभानुप्रतीकाशं दुकूलपरिधानकम्।
अरुणेन दुकूलेनोत्तरीयं कल्पयामि ते॥ ८३

प्रवेशनं कल्पयामि तवालेपनमण्डपम्।
नमस्ते कल्पयाम्यत्र मणिपीठोपवेशनम्॥ ८४

अष्टगन्धैः कल्पयामि सर्वाङ्गेषु विलेपनम्।
कालागरु महाधूपस्तव केशभरस्य हि॥ ८५

मल्लिकामालतीजातीचम्पकादिमनोरमैः।
रचिताःकुसुमैर्मालाः कल्पयामि नमस्तव॥ ८६

प्रवेशनं कल्पयामि नमो भूषणमण्डपम्।
उपवेशं रत्नपीठे तत्र ते कल्पयाम्यहम्॥ ८७

नवमाणिक्यमुकुटं तच्चन्द्रशकलं ततः।
ततः सीमन्तसिन्दूरं ततस्तिलकमुत्तमम्॥ ८८

कालाञ्जनं कल्पयामि पालीयुगलमुत्तमम्।
मणिकुण्डलयुग्मं ते नासाभरणमीश्वरि॥ ८९

ते कल्पयामि त्रिपुरे ललिताऽधरयावकम्।
अथाऽऽद्यद्भूषणं कण्ठे हेमचिन्ताकमुत्तमम्॥ ९०

पदकं ते कल्पयामि महापदकमुत्तमम्।
कल्पयामि नमो मुक्तावलिमेकावलिं च ते॥ ९१

छन्नवीरं च केयूरयुगलानां चतुष्टयम्।
वलयावलिमीशानि ऊर्मिकावलिमीश्वरि॥ ९२

काञ्चीदामकटीसूत्रं सौभाग्याभरणं च ते।
त्रिपुरे पादकटकं कल्पये रत्ननूपुरम्॥ ९३

पादाङ्गुलीयकं तुभ्यं पाशमेककरे तव।
अन्यस्मिन्नङ्कुशं देवि पुण्द्रेक्षु धनुषं परे॥ ९४

अपरे पुष्पबाणाँश्च श्रीमन्माणिक्यपादुके ।
नवावरणदेवीभिर्महाचक्राधिरोहणम्॥ ९५

कामेश्वराङ्कपर्यङ्क उपवेशनमुत्तमम्।
सुधासवाख्यं चषकं ततः आचमनीयकम्॥ ९६

कर्पूरवीटिकां तुभ्यं कल्पयामि नमः शिवे।
आनन्दोल्लासवेलासहासं ते कल्पयाम्यहम्॥ ९७

मङ्गलारार्तिकं देवि छत्रं ते कल्पयाम्यहम्।
ततश्चामरयुग्मं ते दर्पणं कल्पयाम्यहम्॥ ९८

तालवृन्तं कल्पयामि गन्धं पुष्पं महेश्वरि।
धूपं दीपं च नैवेद्यं कल्पयामि नमस्तव॥ ९९

अथाऽहं वैन्दवे चक्रे सर्वानन्दमयात्मिके।
रत्नसिंहासने रम्ये समासीनां शिवप्रियाम्॥ १००

ध्यानम् ।

उद्यद्भानुसहस्राभ्यां जपापुष्पसमप्रभाम्।
नवरत्नप्रभादीप्तमुकुटेन विराजिताम्॥ १०१

चन्द्ररेखासमोपेतां कस्तूरीतिलकाञ्चिताम्।
कामकोदण्डसौन्दर्यनिर्जितभ्रूलतायुगाम्॥ १०२

अञ्जनाञ्चितनेत्रां तां पद्मपत्रनिभेक्षणाम्।
मणिकुण्डलसंयुक्तकर्णद्वयविराजिताम्॥ १०३

मुक्तामाणिक्यखचितनासिकाभरणान्विताम्।
मदपाटलसंयुक्तकपोलयुगलान्विताम्॥ १०४

पक्वबिम्बफलाभासाधरद्वयविराजिताम्।

शुद्धमुक्तावलिप्रख्यदन्तपङ्क्तिविराजिताम्॥ १०५

ताम्बूलपूरितमुखीं सुस्मितास्यविराजिताम्।

आद्यभूषणसंयुक्तां हेमचिन्ताकसंयुताम्॥ १०६

पदकेन समोपेतां महापदकसंयुताम्।

मुक्तावलिसमोपेतामेकावलिविराजिताम्॥ १०७

केयूराङ्गदसंयुक्तचतुर्बाहुविराजिताम्।

अष्टगन्धसमोपेतां श्रीचन्दनविलेपनाम्॥ १०८

हेमकुम्भसमप्रख्यस्तनद्वयविराजिताम्।

रक्तवस्त्रपरीधानां रक्तकञ्चुकसंयुताम्॥ १०९

सूक्ष्मरोमावलीयुक्ततनुमध्यविराजिताम्।

मुक्तामाणिक्यखचितकाञ्चीयुतनितम्बिनीम्॥ ११०

सदाशिवाङ्कस्थपृथुमहाजघनमण्डलाम्।

कदलीस्तम्भसङ्काशऊरुयुग्मविराजिताम्॥ १११

कदलीकान्तिसङ्काशजङ्घायुगलशोभिताम्।

गूढगुल्फद्वयोपेतां रक्तपादयुगान्विताम्॥ ११२

ब्रह्माविष्णुमहादेवशिरोमुकुटजातया।

कान्त्या विराजितपदां भक्तत्राणपरायणाम्॥ ११३

इक्षुकार्मुकपुष्पेषु पाशाङ्कुशधरां पराम्।

संवित्स्वरूपिणीं देवीं ध्यायामि परमेश्वरीम्॥ ११४

इति ध्यानम्।

प्रदर्शयाम्यथ शिवे नवमुद्रा वरप्रदाः।

त्वां तर्पयामि त्रिपुरे त्रिधा मूलेन पार्वति॥ ११५

आग्नेय्यामीशदिग्भागे नैरृत्यां मारुते तथा।

मध्ये दिक्षु षडङ्गानि क्रमादभ्यर्चयाम्यहम्॥ ११६

आद्यां कामेश्वरीं वन्दे नमामि भगमालिनीम्।
नित्यक्लिन्नां नमस्यामि भेरुण्डां प्रणमाम्यहम्॥ ११७

वह्निवासां नमस्यामि महावज्रेश्वरीं स्तुवे।
शिवदूतीं नमस्यामि त्वरितां कुलसुन्दरीम्॥ ११८

नित्यां नीलपताकां च विजयां सर्वमङ्गलाम्।
ज्वालामालां च चित्रां च महानित्यां च संस्तुवे॥ ११९

दिव्यौघेभ्यो नमस्यामि परेशपरमेश्वरीम्।
मित्रेशमथ षष्ठीशमुड्डीशं प्रणमाम्यहम्॥ १२०

चर्यानाथं नमस्यामि लोपामुद्रामहं भजे।
अगस्त्यं प्रणमस्यामि सिद्धौघे कालतापनम्॥ १२१

धर्माचार्यं नमस्यामि मुक्तकेशीश्वरं भजे।
भजे दीपकलानाथं मानवौघे ततः परम्॥ १२२

विष्णुदेवं नमस्यामि प्रभाकरमहं भजे।
तेजोदेवं नमस्यामि मनोजमथ संस्तुवे॥ १२३

कल्याणदेवं कलये रत्नदेवं भजाम्यहम्।
वासुदेवं नमस्यामि श्रीरामानन्दमाश्रये॥ १२४

परमेष्ठिगुरुं वन्दे परमं गुरुमाश्रये।
श्रीगुरुं प्रणमस्यामि मूर्ध्नि ब्रह्मबिले स्थितम्॥ १२५

कं बिलेऽहं नमस्यामि श्रीगुरोः पादुकां ततः।
अथ प्राथमिके देवि चतुरस्रे तवेश्वरि॥ १२६

अणिमां लघिमां वन्दे महिमां प्रणमाम्यहम्।
ईशित्वसिद्धिं वन्देऽहं वशित्वंच नमाम्यहम्॥ १२७

प्राकाम्यसिद्धिं वन्देऽहं भुक्तिमिच्छामिहं भजे।
प्राप्तिसिद्धिं सर्वकामप्रदासिद्धिमहं भजे॥ १२८

मध्यमे चतुरस्रेऽहं ब्राह्मीं माहेश्वरीं भजे।
कौमारीं वैष्णवीं वन्दे वाराहीं प्रणमाम्यहम्॥ १२९

माहेन्द्रीमपि चामुण्डां महालक्ष्मीमहं भजे।
तृतीये चतुरस्रेऽहं सर्वसंक्षोभिणीं भजे॥ १३०

सर्वविद्राविणीं मुद्रां सर्वाकर्षिणिकां भजे।
मुद्रां वशङ्करीं वन्दे सर्वोन्मादिनिकां भजे॥ १३१

भजे महाङ्कुशां मुद्रां खेचरीं प्रणमाम्यहम्।
बीजमुद्रां योनिमुद्रां भजे सर्वत्रिखण्डिनीम्॥ १३२

त्रैलोक्यमोहनं चक्रं नमामि ललिते तव।
नमामि योगिनीं तत्र प्रकटाख्यामभीष्टदाम्॥ १३३

सुधार्णवासनं वन्दे तत्र ते परमेश्वरि।
चक्रेश्वरीं तत्र वन्दे त्रिपुरां परमेश्वरीम्॥ १३४

सर्वसंक्षोभिणीं मुद्रां ततोऽहं कलये शिवे।
अथाऽहं षोडशदले कामाकर्षणिकां भजे॥ १३५

बुद्ध्याकर्षणिकां वन्देऽहङ्काराकर्षणीं भजे।
शब्दाकर्षणिकां वन्दे स्पर्शाकर्षणिकां भजे॥ १३६

रूपाकर्षणिकां वन्दे रसाकर्षणिकां भजे।
गन्धाकर्षणिकां वन्दे चित्ताकर्षणिकां भजे॥ १३७

धैर्याकर्षणिकां वन्दे स्मृत्याकर्षणिकां भजे।
नामाकर्षणिकां वन्दे बीजाकर्षणिकां भजे॥ १३८

आत्माकर्षणिकां वन्दे ह्यमृताकर्षणीं भजे।
शरीराकर्षणीं वन्दे नित्यां श्रीपरमेश्वरीम्॥ १३९

सर्वाशापूरकं चक्रं कलयेऽहं तवेश्वरि।
गुप्ताख्यां योगिनीं वन्दे तत्राऽहं गुप्तपूजिताम्॥ १४०

पीताम्बुजासनं तत्र नमामि ललिते तव।
त्रिपुरेशीं महादेवीं भजाम्यभीष्टार्थसिद्धिदाम्॥ १४१

सर्वविद्राविणीं मुद्रां तत्राऽहं तां विचिन्तये।
शिवे तवाष्टपत्रेऽहमनङ्गकुसुमां भजे॥ १४२

अनङ्गमेखलां वन्दे ह्यनङ्गमदनां भजे।
ततोऽहं प्रणमस्यामि ह्यनङ्गमदनातुराम्॥ १४३

अनङ्गरेखां कलये भजे तेऽनङ्गवेगिनीम्।
भजेऽनङ्गाङ्कुशां देवि तव चानङ्गमालिनीम्॥ १४४

सर्वसंक्षोभणं चक्रं तत्राऽहं कलये सदा।
वन्दे गुप्ततराख्यां तां योगिनीं सर्वकामदाम्॥ १४५

तत्राऽहं प्रणमस्यामि देव्यात्मासनमुत्तमम्।
नमामि जगदीशानीमऽहं त्रिपुरसुन्दरीम्॥ १४६

सर्वाकर्षणिकां मुद्रां तत्राऽहं कलयामि ते।
भुवनारे तव शिवे सर्वसंक्षोभिणीं भजे॥ १४७

सर्वविद्राविणीं वन्देऽहं सर्वाकर्षिणिकां भजे।
सकलाह्लादिनीं वन्दे सर्वसम्मोहिनीं भजे॥ १४८

सकल स्तम्भिनीं वन्दे कलये सर्वजृम्भिनीम्।
वशङ्करीं नमस्यामि सर्वरञ्जनिकां भजे॥ १४९

सकलोन्मादिनीं वन्दे भजे सर्वार्थसाधिनीम्।
सम्पत्तिपूरिणीं वन्दे सर्वमन्त्रमयीं भजे॥ १५०

भजाम्यहं ततः शक्तिं सर्वद्वन्द्वक्षयङ्करीम्।
तत्राऽहं कलये चक्रं सर्वसौभाग्यदायकम्॥ १५१

नमामि जगतां धात्रीं सम्प्रदायाख्ययोगिनीम्।
शिवे तव नमस्यामि श्रीचक्रासनमुत्तमम्॥ १५२

नमामि जगदीशानीमहं त्रिपुरवासिनीम्।
कलयेऽहं तव शिवे मुद्रां सर्ववशङ्करीम्॥ १५३

बहिर्दशारे ते देवि सर्वसिद्धिप्रदां भजे।
सर्वसम्पत्प्रदां वन्दे भजे सर्वप्रियङ्करीम्॥ १५४

नमाम्यहं ततो देवीं सर्वमङ्गलकारिणीम्।
सर्वकामप्रदां वन्दे सर्वदुःखविमोचिनीम्॥ १५५

सर्वमृत्युप्रशमनीं सर्वविघ्ननिवारिणीम् ।
सर्वाङ्गसुन्दरीं देवीं सर्वसौभाग्यदायिनीम् ॥ १५६

सर्वार्थसाधकं चक्रं तथाऽहं कलये सदा ।
कलयामि ततो देवीं कुलोत्तीर्णाख्ययोगिनीम् ॥ १५७

सर्वमन्त्रासनं वन्दे त्रिपुराश्रीयमाश्रये ।
कलयामि ततो मुद्रां सर्वोन्मादकारिणीम् ॥ १५८

अन्तर्दशारे ते देवि सर्वज्ञां प्रणमाम्यहम् ।
सर्वशक्तिं नमस्यामि सर्वैश्वर्यप्रदां भजे ॥ १५९

सर्वज्ञानमयीं वन्दे सर्वव्याधिविनाशिनीम् ।
सर्वाधारस्वरूपां च सर्वपापहरां भजे ॥ १६०

सर्वानन्दमयीं वन्दे सर्वरक्षास्वरूपिणीम् ।
प्रणमामि महादेवीं सर्वेप्सितप्रदां भजे ॥ १६१

सर्वरक्षाकरं चक्रं तत्राऽहं कलये सदा ।
निगर्भयोगिनीं वन्दे तत्राऽहं परमेश्वरीम् ॥ १६२

साध्यसिंहासनं वन्दे भजे त्रिपुरमालिनीम् ।
कलयामि ततो देवि मुद्रां सर्वमहाङ्कुशाम् ॥ १६३

अष्टारे वशिनीं वन्दे भजे कामेश्वरीं सदा ।
मोदिनीं विमलां वन्दे ह्यरुणां जयिनीं भजे ॥ १६४

सर्वेश्वरीं नमस्यामि कौलिनीं प्रणमाम्यहम् ।
सर्वरोगहरं चक्रं तवाऽहं देवि चिन्तये ॥ १६५

रहस्ययोगिनीं देवीं सदाऽहं कलयामि ते ।
नमामि त्रिपुरासिद्धां भजे मुद्रां च खेचरीम् ॥ १६६

महात्रिकोणस्य बाह्ये चतुर्दिक्षु महेश्वरि ।
नमामि जृम्भणान् बाणान् चापं सम्मोहनं भजे ॥ १६७

पाशं वशङ्करं वन्दे भजे स्तम्भनमङ्कुशम् ।
त्रिकोणेऽहं जगद्धात्रीं महाकामेश्वरीं भजे ॥ १६८

महावज्रेश्वरीं वन्दे महाश्रीमालिनीं भजे ।
महाश्रीसुन्दरीं वन्दे सर्वकामफलप्रदाम् ॥ १६९

सर्वसिद्धिप्रदं चक्रं तव देवि नमाम्यहम् ।
नमाम्यतिरहस्याख्यां योगिनीं तत्र कामदाम् ॥ १७०

त्रिपुराम्बां नमस्यामि बीजमुद्रां नमाम्यहम् ।
मूलमन्त्रेण ललिते त्वां बिन्दौ पूजयाम्यहम् ॥ १७१

सर्वानन्दमयं चक्रं नमामि ललिते तव ।
परापररहस्याख्यां योगिनीं कलये सदा ॥ १७२

महाचक्रेश्वरीं वन्दे योनिमुद्रामहं भजे ।
धूपादिकं सर्वमयि ते कल्पयाम्यहम् ॥ १७३

त्वत्प्रीतये महामुद्रां दर्शयामि ततः शिवे ।
त्रिधा त्वां मूलमन्त्रेण तर्पयामि ततः शिवे ॥ १७४

शाल्यन्नं मधुसंयुक्तं पायसापूपसंयुतम् ।
घृतसूपसमायुक्तं सर्वभक्ष्यसमन्वितम् ॥ १७५

ससितं क्षीरसंयुक्तं बहुशाकसमन्वितम् ।
निक्षिप्य काञ्चने पात्रे नैवेद्यं कल्पयामि ते ॥ १७६

सङ्कल्प्य बिन्दुना वक्त्रं कुचौ बिन्दुद्वयेन च ।
योनिं तु सपरार्धेन कृत्वा श्रीत्रिपुरे तव ॥ १७७

एतत् कामकलारूपं भक्तानां सर्वकामदम् ।
सर्वसम्पत्प्रदं वन्दे नमस्ते त्रिपुरेश्वरि ॥ १७८

वामभागे त्रिकोणं च वृत्तं च चतुरस्रकम् ।
कृत्वा गन्धाक्षतादैश्च ह्यर्चयामि महेश्वरि ॥ १७९

वाग्भवाद्यं नमस्यामि तत्र व्यापिकमण्डलम् ।
जलयुक्ताद्रन्नियुक्तं मकारत्रयभाजनम् ॥ १८०

तत्र विन्यस्य दास्यामि भूतेभ्यो बलिमुत्तमम् ।
नमस्ते देवदेवेशि नमस्त्रैलोक्यवन्दिते ॥ १८१

नमः परशिवाङ्कस्थे नमस्त्रिपुरसुन्दरि।
प्रदक्षिणां नमस्कारं मनसाऽहं करोमि ते॥ १८२

ततः सकलमन्त्राणां सम्राज्ञीं परमेश्वरीम्।
प्रजपामि महाविद्यां त्वत्प्रीत्यार्थमहं सदा।
तव विद्यां प्रजप्त्वाऽथ स्तौमि त्वां परमेश्वरीम्॥ १८३

महादेवि महेशानि सदाशिव महाप्रिये।
महानित्ये महासिद्धे त्वामहं शरणं व्रजे॥ १८४

जय त्वं त्रिपुरे देवि ललिते जगदीश्वरि।
सदाशिवप्रियकरि पाहि मां करुणाकरि॥ १८५

जगन्मातर्जगद्रूपे जगदीश्वरवल्लभे।
जगन्मये जगस्तुल्ये गौरि त्वामहमाश्रये॥ १८६

अनाद्ये सर्वलोकानामाद्ये भक्तेष्टदायिनि।
गिरिराजस्य तनये नमस्ते त्रिपुरेश्वरि॥ १८७

जयादिदेवदेवेशि ब्रह्ममातर्नमोऽस्तु ते।
विष्णुमातरनाद्यन्ते हरमातः सुरेश्वरि॥ १८८

ब्रह्मादिसुरसंस्तुत्ये लोकत्रयवशङ्करि।
सर्वसम्पत्प्रदे नित्ये त्वामहं कलये सदा॥ १८९

नित्यानन्दे निराधारे चिद्रूपिणि शिवप्रिये।
अणिमादिगुणाधारे त्वां सदा कलयाम्यहम्॥ १९०

ब्राह्म्यादिमातृसंस्तुत्ये सर्वावरणसंयुते।
ज्योतिर्मये महारूपे पाहि मां त्रिपुरे सदा॥ १९१

लक्ष्मीवाण्यादिसम्पूज्ये ब्रह्मविष्णुशिवस्तुते।
भजामि तव पादाब्जं सर्वकामफलप्रदम्॥ १९२

सर्वशक्तिसमोपेतं सर्वाभीष्टफलप्रदे।
नमामि तव पादाब्जं देवि त्रिपुरसुन्दरि॥ १९३

त्वत्प्रियार्थं ततः कांश्चिच्छक्तिं सम्पूजयाम्यहम्।
मपञ्चकेन तां शक्तिं तर्पयामि महेश्वरि॥ १९४

तयोपेतं हविःशेषं चिदग्नौ प्रजुहोम्यहम्।
त्वत्प्रियार्थं महादेवि ममाभीष्टार्थसिद्धये॥ १९५

बद्ध्वा तां खेचरीं मुद्रां क्षमस्वोद्वासयाम्यहम्।
तिष्ठ मे हृदये नित्यं त्रिपुरे परमेश्वरि॥ १९६

जगदम्बे महाराज्ञि महाशक्ति शिवप्रिये।
हृच्चक्रे तिष्ठ सततं महात्रिपुरसुन्दरि॥ १९७

सर्वलोकैकसम्पूज्ये सकलावरणैर्युते।
हृच्चक्रे तिष्ठ मे नित्यं महात्रिपुरसुन्दरि॥ १९८

॥ फलश्रुति ॥

एतत् त्रिपुरसुन्दर्या हृदयं सर्वकामदम्।
महारहस्यं परमं दुर्लभं दैवतैरपि॥ १

साक्षात् सदाशिवेनोक्तं गुह्याद् ह्यमनुत्तमम्॥ २

यः पठेन्नित्यमेकाग्रः शृणुयाद् वा समाहितः।
नित्यपूजाफलं देव्याः स लभेन्नात्र संशयः॥ ३

पापैः स मुच्यते सद्यः कायवाक्चित्तसम्भवैः।
सर्वजन्मसमुद्भूतैर्ज्ञानिकृतैरपि॥ ४

सर्वक्रतुषु यत्पुण्यं सर्वतीर्थेषु यत् फलम्।
तत्पुण्यं लभते नित्यं मानवो नात्र संशयः॥ ५

अचलां लभते लक्ष्मीं त्रैलोक्ये चापि दुर्लभाम्।
साक्षाद् विष्णुसमो मर्त्यो शीघ्रमेव भवेत् सदा॥ ६

अष्टैश्वर्यमवाप्नोति स शीघ्रं मानवोत्तमः।
गुटिकापादुकासिद्ध्याद्यष्टकं शीघ्रमश्नुते॥ ७

शङ्खाद्या निध्यो वाऽपि तं नित्यं पर्युपासते।
वश्यादीन्यष्टकर्माणि शीघ्रं सिद्ध्यन्ति सर्वदा॥ ८

भूलोकस्थाः सर्वनार्यः पातालस्थाः सदाङ्गनाः।
सर्वलोकस्थिताः सर्वा याश्चान्यारूपगर्विताः॥ ९

रमन्ते तेन सततं शीघ्रं वश्या न संशयः ।
राजाद्याः सकला मर्त्याः हरहर्यादयः सुराः ॥ १०

अनन्ताद्या महानागाः सिद्धयोगेश्वरादयः ।
ऋषयो मुनयो यक्षास्तं नित्यं पर्युपासते ॥ ११

महतीं कीर्तिमाप्नोति शिवविष्णुसमप्रभाम् ।
परमं योगमासाद्य खेचरो जायते सदा ॥ १२

अपमृत्युविनिर्मुक्तः कालमृत्युविवर्जितः ।
परमायुष्यमाप्नोति हरहर्यादिदुर्लभम् ॥ १३

अश्रुतानि च शास्त्राणि व्याचष्टे विधिवत् सदा ।
मूढोऽपि सर्वविद्यावान् दक्षिणामूर्तिवद्भवेत् ॥ १४

ग्रहभूतपिशाचाद्या यक्षगन्धर्वराक्षसाः ।
एतस्य स्मरणादेव विनश्यन्ति हि सर्वदा ॥ १५

तद्धात्रं प्राप्य सकलं विषं सद्यो विनश्यति ।
सहस्रकामसङ्काशः कान्त्या यः सर्वदा भवेत् ॥ १६

तस्मादेतत् पठेत् स्तोत्रं त्रिपुराहृदयं शुभम् ।
जपेद् यः सर्वदा साक्षाद् भवेद् देवीस्वरूपकः ॥ १७

साङ्गं त्रिपुरसुन्दर्या नित्यपूजाफलं लभेत् ।
विमुक्तो रोगसङ्घातैरारोग्यं महदश्नुते ॥ १८

प्राप्नोति महदैश्वर्यं सर्वविद्यानिधिर्भवेत् ।
तत्करस्पर्शमात्रेण नरो ब्राह्मणतां लभेत् ॥ १९

मुच्यते सकलैर्विघ्नैः स नित्यं मानवोत्तमः ।
स भुङ्क्ते सकलान् भोगान् दुर्लभांश्च दिने दिने ॥ २०

लभते पुत्रपौत्रांश्चमिहालक्ष्मीसमन्वितान् ।
परमायुष्यसंयुक्तान् साक्षच्छिवसमान् गुणैः ॥ २१

सृष्टिपालनसंहारकर्तेवायं सदा भवेत् ।
यस्ते कृपावान् भवति स त्रिमूर्तिर्न संशयः ॥ २२

तत्समीपस्थितः शीघ्रं सदा जातिस्मरोभवेत्।
तस्य गेहे सदा कामधेनुः कल्पतरुस्तथा॥ २३

चिन्तामणिश्च सततं तिष्ठत्येव न संशयः।
महाजयमवाप्नोति सदा सर्वत्र मानवः॥ २४

वज्रकायसमो भूत्वा चरत्येव जगत्ययम्।
महासुखी भवेन्नित्यं परमात्मा भवेत् सदा॥ २५

मुच्यते सकलेभ्योऽपि बन्धनैः शृङ्खलादिभिः।
तं पूजयन्तिसततं हरिरुद्रादयोऽपि च॥ २६

शुभमेव भवेन्नित्यं सदापद्भिर्विमुच्यते।
देवगन्धर्वरक्षाद्यैर्ब्रह्माद्यैरपि दुर्लभान्॥ २७

प्राप्नोति सकलान् कामान् शीघ्रमेव न संशयः।
दिव्यभोगयुतो दिव्यकन्याभिः सह संयुतः॥ २८

विमानं स समास्थाय दिव्याभरणभूषितः।
दिव्यचन्दनलिप्ताङ्गः सदा विंशतिवार्षिकः॥ २९

स भुङ्क्ते सकलान् भोगान् देवलोके नरः सदा।
तस्मादेतत् पठेत् स्तोत्रं त्रिपुराहृदयं शुभम्
जपेद्यः सततं भक्त्या भवेत् साक्षात् सदा शिवः॥ ३०

॥ इति श्री रुद्रयामले ईश्वरपार्वतीसंवादे श्री त्रिपुर सुन्दरी हृदय स्तोत्रम्॥

Śrī Tripura-Sundarī Kavacam

Kavacam is the armour or shield what warriors wear to protect their bodies during battles. This is a mantra shield, to protect our body, soul and mind.

|| *Pūrva Pīṭhikā* ||

Oṃ Namaḥ Śivāya Gurave, Nāda-Bindu-Kalātmane |

Śrī Gaṇeśāya Namaḥ | Śrī Manmahā-Tripura-Sundaryai Namaḥ |

|| *Śrī Bhairava Uvāca* ||

Krama-Dīkṣā-Vidhānāni, Mayoktāni Maheśvari! |
Tvayātmanaḥ Kulāgāre, Kavacaṃ Yat Su-Gopitam || 1

Adhunā Kṛpayā Tvaṃ Ca, Tat-Sarvaṃ Vaktumarhasi |

|| *Śrī Bhairavyuvāca* ||

Śṛṇu ! Nātha Pravakṣyāmi, Tantra-Sāramidaṃ Mahat || 2

Etacchrī-Kavacasyāsya, Para-Brahma Ṛṣiḥ Śivaḥ |
Mahatī Jagatīcchandaścicchaktirdevatocyate || 3

Aiṃ Bījaṃ Hrīṃ Tathā Śaktiḥ, Sakalahrīṃ Kīlakaṃ Tathā |
Para-Brahma-Prāpti-Hetau, Viniyogaḥ Prakīrtitaḥ || 4

Atha Viniyoga ||

Oṃ Asya Śrī Parā-Mahā-Yoni-Kavacasya Śrī Para-Brahma-Śivaḥ Ṛṣiḥ |
Mahatī Jagatīḥ Chandaḥ | Śrī Cicchaktiḥ Devatā | Aiṃ Bījam |
Hrīṃ Śaktiḥ | Sakalahrīṃ Kīlakam |
Para-Brahma-Prāpti-Hetau Pāṭhe Viniyogaḥ |

|| *Ṛṣyādi-Nyāsa* ||

Śrī Para-Brahma-Śivaḥ-Ṛṣaye Namaḥ Śirasi |
Mahatī Jagatīḥ - Chandase Namaḥ Mukhe |

Śrī Cicchaktiḥ - Devatāyai Namaḥ Hṛdaye |

Aiṃ-Vījāya Namaḥ Guhye |

Hrīṃ-Śaktye Namaḥ Nābhau |

Sakalahrīṃ-Kīlakāya Namaḥ Pādayoḥ |
Para-Brahma-Prāpti-Hetau Pāṭhe Viniyogāya Namaḥ Sarvāṅge

(Sarvāṅge) |

|| Dhyāna ||

Oṃ Ādhāre Taruṇārka-Bimba-Ruciraṃ Hema-Prabhaṃ Vāgbhavam |
Bījaṃ Manmathamindra-Gopa-Sadṛśaṃ Hṛt-Paṅkaje Saṃsthitam ||

Viṣṇu-Brahma-Padastha-Śakti-Kalitaṃ Soma-Prabhā-Bhāsuram |
Ye Dhyāyanti Pada-Trayaṃ Tava Śive ! Te Yānti Saukhyaṃ Padam ||

Atha Kavaca Pāṭha |
Oṃ Hrī Strīṃ Hūṃ Phaṭ Ugra-Tārā, Mūlādhāraṃ Mamāvatu |
Hrīṃ Bhuvaneśvarī Pātu, Svādhiṣṭhānaṃ Ca Me Sadā || 1

Krīṃ Hūṃ Hrīṃ Dakṣiṇā Pātu, Maṇipuraṃ Tathā Mama |
Namo Bhagavatyai Haskhphreṃ, Kubjikāyai Śrāṃ Śrīṃ Śrūṃ Śrāṃ Śrīṃ

Śrūm |

Ṅañaṇaname-Aghorā-Mukhi Chāṃ Chīṃ Kiṇi-Kiṇi Vicce || 2

Anāhataṃ Sadā Pātu, Kubjikā Parameśvarī |
Phreṃ Khphreṃ Guhya-Kālī Sā, Viśuddhaṃ Me Ca Rakṣatu || 3

Ka-E-Ī-La-Hrīṃ Ha-Sa-Ka-Ha-La-Hrīṃ Sa-Ka-La-Hrīṃ Śrīm |
Ājñā-Cakraṃ Mahā-Devī, Ṣoḍaśī Pātu Me Sadā || 4

Haskṣmlavarayūṃ̐ Śakṣmlavarayīm |
Nāda-Cakraṃ Ca Me Pātu, Śrīmadānanda-Bhairavaḥ || 5

Hsauṃḥ Śauṃḥ Ardha-Nārīśvarī Binduśca Me'vatu |
Haṃsaḥ So'haṃ Sadā Pātu, Sahasrāraṃ Sadā Mama || 6

Kaeīlahrīṃ Hasakahalahrīṃ Sakalahrīṃ Śrīm |
Śiro Me Pātu Sā Devī, Mahā-Tripura-Sundarī || 7

``Kaeīlahrīṃ'' Kāmeśī, Bhrū-Madhyaṃ Me Sadā'vatu |

``Hasakahalahrīṃ'' Vajreśī, Dakṣa-Netraṃ Sadā'vatu || 8

``Sakalahrīṃ'' Vāma-Netraṃ, Rakṣatu Bhaga-Mālinī |

``Hasreṃ Haskalahrīṃ Hsauṃḥ'', Tri-Netraṃ Pātu Bhairavī || 9

``Hrīṃ Śrīṃ Sauḥ'' Tripurā-Siddhā, Karṇau Me Pari-Rakṣatu |

``Hrīṃ Klīṃ Kṣuṃ'' Māṃ Sadā Pātu, Mukhaṃ Tripura-Mālinī || 10

``Hasaiṃ Hasklīṃ Hasauṃ'' Kaṇṭhaṃ, Pātu Śrītripurā-Śrīrme |

``Haiṃ Haklīṃ Hasauṃ'' Pātu, Vakṣastripura-Vāsinī || 11

Dauvārijau Sadā Pātu, Hyāṇimādyaṣṭa-Siddhayaḥ |

``Hrīṃ Klīṃ Sauḥ'' Pātu Me Nābhiṃ, Parā Tripura-Sundarī || 12

Daśa-Mudrā-Yutā Devī, Mamoru Pātu Sarvadā |

``Aiṃ Klīṃ Sauḥ'' Pātu Me Jānū, Śrīmahā-Tripureśvarī || 13

Ṣaḍ-Darśanaṃ Sadā Pātu, Jaṅghā-Yugmaṃ Ca Sarvadā |

``Aṃ Āṃ Sauḥ'' Tripurā Pātu, Pādau Ca Satata Namaḥ || 14

``Oṃ Hrīṃ Śrīṃ'' Pātu Māṃ Pūrve, Śrīmahā-Bhuvaneśvarī |

``Kaeīlahrīṃ'' Dakṣiṇe Māṃ, Parā''dyā Pari-Rakṣatu || 15

``Sauḥ Aiṃ Klīṃ Hrīṃ Śrīṃ'' Śrīkujā, Paścime Māṃ Sadā'vatu |

``Śrīṃ Hrīṃ Klīṃ Aiṃ Sauḥ'' Cottare Māṃ, Pātu Yogeśvarī Parā || 16

``Hasakahalahrīṃ'' Pātu, Māmadho Vajra-Yoginī |

``Sakalahrīṃ'' Sā Lalitā, Hyūrdhve Māṃ Pari-Rakṣatu || 17

Śrīṃ-5 Oṃ-3 Ka-5 Ha-6 Sa-4 Sauḥ-5 Sadā'vatu |

Sarvāṅgaṃ Me Ca Cidrūpā, Mahā-Tripura-Sundarī || 18

(Śrīṃ-5 -- Śrīṃ Hrī Klīṃ Aiṃ Sauḥ, Oṃ-3 -- Oṃ Hrīṃ Śrīṃ,
Ka-5 -- Ka E Ī La Hrīṃ,   Ha-6 -- Ha Sa Ka Ha La Hrīṃ,
Sa-4 -- Sa Ka La Hrīṃ, Sauḥ-5 -- Sauḥ Aiṃ Klīṃ Hrīṃ Śrīṃ)

|| *Phala-Śruti* ||

Iti Te Kathitaṃ Deva!, Brahmānanda-Mayaṃ Param |
Śrī Mahā-Yonirākhyātaṃ, Kavacaṃ Deva-Durlabham || 1

Mama Tejasā Racitaṃ, Śrīvidyā-Krama-Saṃyutam |
Tava Snehānmahā-Deva!, Tavāgre Tu Mayoditam || 2

Rājyaṃ Deyaṃ Śiro Deyaṃ, Na Deyaṃ Kavacaṃ Param |
Deyaṃ Pūrṇābhiṣiktāya, Sva-Śiṣyāya Maheśvara ! || 3

Anyathā Nārakī Bhūyāt, Kalpa-Koṭi-Śatairapi |
Dik-Sahasreṇa Pāṭhena, Hyāsādhyaṃ Sādhyate Kṣaṇāt || 4

Lakṣaṃ Japatvā Mahā-Deva!, Taddaśāṃśaṃ Huned Yadi |
Brahma-Jñānamavāpnoti, Para-Brahmaṇi Līyate || 5

Bhūrje Vilikhya Guṭikāṃ, Svarṇasthāṃ Dhārayed Yadi |
Kaṇṭhe Vā Dakṣiṇe Bāhau, Sākṣāt Kāmeśvaro Bhavet |
Nārī Vāma-Bhuje Dhṛtvā, Bhavet Tripura-Sundarī || 6

Oṃ Tatsat ||

Śrīmahā-Nirvāṇa-Tantre Śrīmahā-Yoni-Nāma Śrīmahā-Tripura-Sundarī-
Kavacaṃ Sampūrṇam ||

श्री त्रिपुर-सुन्दरी कवचम्

|| पूर्व पीठिका ||

ॐ नमः शिवाय गुरवे, नाद-विन्दु-कलात्मने ।

श्री गणेशाय नमः । श्री मन्महा-त्रिपुर-सुन्दर्यै नमः ।

|| श्री भैरव उवाच ||

क्रम-दीक्षा-विधानानि, मयोक्तानि महेश्वरि! ।
त्वयात्मनः कुलागारे, कवचं यत् सु-गोपितम् || १
अधुना कृपया त्वं च तत्-सर्वं वक्तुमर्हसि ।

॥ श्री भैरव्युवाच ॥

श्रृणु ! नाथ प्रवक्ष्यामि, तन्त्र-सारमिदं महत् ॥ २

एतच्छ्री-कवचस्यास्य, पर-ब्रह्म ऋषिः शिवः ।
महती जगतीच्छन्दश्रिच्छक्तिर्देवतोच्यते ॥ ३

ऐं वीजं ह्रीं तथा शक्तिः, सकलह्रीं कीलकं तथा ।
पर-ब्रह्म-प्राप्ति-हेतौ, विनियोगः प्रकीर्तितः ॥ ४

अथ ॥ विनियोग ॥

ॐ अस्य श्री परा-महा-योनि-कवचस्य श्री पर-ब्रह्म-शिवः ऋषिः ।
महती जगतीः छन्दः । श्री चिच्छक्तिः देवता । ऐं वीजम् । ह्रीं शक्तिः ।
सकलह्रीं कीलकम् । पर-ब्रह्म-प्राप्ति-हेतौ पाठे विनियोगः ।

॥ ऋष्यादि-न्यास ॥

श्री पर-ब्रह्म-शिवः-ऋषये नमः शिरसि ।
महती जगतीः - छन्दसे नमः मुखे ।　श्री चिच्छक्तिः - देवतायै नमः हृदये ।
ऐं-वीजाय नमः गुह्ये ।　　　　ह्रीं-शक्त्ये नमः नाभौ ।
सकलह्रीं-कीलकाय नमः पादयोः ।
पर-ब्रह्म-प्राप्ति-हेतौ पाठे विनियोगाय नमः सर्वाङ्गे (सर्वाङ्गे) ।

॥ ध्यान ॥

ॐ आधारे तरुणार्क-बिम्ब-रुचिरं हेम-प्रभं वाग्भवम् ।
बीजं मन्मथमिन्द्र-गोप-सदृशं हृत्-पङ्कजे संस्थितम् ॥

विष्णु-ब्रह्म-पदस्थ-शक्ति-कलितं सोम-प्रभा-भासुरम् ।
ये ध्यायन्ति पद-त्रयं तव शिवे ! ते यान्ति सौख्यं पदम् ॥

अथ कवच पाठ ।

ॐ ह्रीं स्त्रीं हूं फट् उग्र-तारा, मूलाधारं ममावतु ।
ह्रीं भुवनेश्वरी पातु, स्वाधिष्ठानं च मे सदा ॥ १

क्रीं हूं ह्रीं दक्षिणा पातु मणिपुरं तथा मम।

नमो भगवत्यै हस्ख्फ्रें, कुब्जिकायै श्रां श्रीं श्रूं श्रां श्रीं श्रूम्

ङऽणनमे-अघोरा-मुखि छां छ्रीं किणिक्रिणि विच्चे॥ २

अनाहतं सदा पातु कुब्जिका परमेश्वरी।

फ्रें ख्फ्रें गुह्य-काली सा, विशुद्धं मे च रक्षतु॥ ३

क-ए-ई-ल-ह्रीं ह-स-क-ह-ल-ह्रीं स-क-ल-ह्रीं श्रीम्।

आज्ञा-चक्रं महा-देवी, षोडशी पातु मे सदा॥ ४

हस्क्म्लवरयूँ शक्स्म्लवरयीम्।

नाद-चक्रं च मे पातु, श्रीमदानन्द-भैरवः ॥ ५

ह्सौंः शौंः अर्ध-नारीश्वरी बिन्दुश्च मेऽवतु।

हंसः सोऽहं सदा पातु, सहस्रारं सदा मम॥ ६

कएईलह्रीं हसकहलह्रीं सकलह्रीं श्रीम्।

शिरो मे पातु सा देवी, महा-त्रिपुर-सुन्दरी॥ ७

``कएईलह्रीं" कामेशी, भ्रू-मध्यं मे सदाऽवतु।

``हसकहलह्रीं" वज्रेशी, दक्ष-नेत्रं सदाऽवतु॥ ८

``सकलह्रीं" वाम-नेत्रं, रक्षतु भग-मालिनी।

``हस्रें हस्कलह्रीं ह्सौंः", त्रि-नेत्रं पातु भैरवी॥ ९

``ह्रीं श्रीं सौंः" त्रिपुरा-सिद्धा, कर्णौं मे परि-रक्षतु।

``ह्रीं क्लीं क्षुं" मां सदा पातु मुखं त्रिपुरमालिनी॥ १०

``हसैं हस्क्लीं हसौं" कण्ठं, पातु श्रीत्रिपुरा-श्रीर्मे।

``हैं हक्लीं हसौं" पातु, वक्षस्त्रिपुर-वासिनी॥ ११

दौवारिजौ सदा पातु, ह्याणिमाद्यष्ट-सिद्धयः।

``ह्रीं क्लीं सौंः" पातु मे नाभिं, परा त्रिपुर-सुन्दरी॥ १२

दश-मुद्रा-युता देवी, ममोरु पातु सर्वदा।

``ऐं क्लीं सौंः" पातु मे जानू, श्रीमहा-त्रिपुरेश्वरी॥ १३

षड्-दर्शनं सदा पातु, जङ्घा-युग्मं च सर्वदा।

``अं आं सौंः" त्रिपुरा पातु, पादौ च सतत नमः ॥ १४

''ॐ ह्रीं श्रीं'' पातु मां पूर्वे, श्रीमहा-भुवनेश्वरी।
''कएईलह्रीं'' दक्षिणे मां, पराऽऽद्या परि-रक्षतु॥ १५

''सौः ऐं क्लीं ह्रीं श्रीं'' श्रीकुजा, पश्चिमे मां सदाऽवतु।
''श्रीं ह्रीं क्लीं ऐं सौः'' चोत्तरे मां, पातु योगेश्वरी परा॥ १६

''हसकहलह्रीं'' पातु, मामधो वज्र-योगिनी।
''सकलह्रीं'' सा ललिता, ह्यूर्ध्वे मां परिरक्षतु॥ १७

श्रीं-५ ॐ-३ क-५ ह-६ स-४ सौः-५ सदाऽवतु।
सर्वाङ्गं मे च चिद्रूपा महा-त्रिपुर-सुन्दरी॥ १८

(श्रीं-५ -- श्रीं ही क्लीं ऐं सौः,   ॐ-३ -- ॐ ह्रीं श्रीं,
क-५ -- क ए ई ल ह्रीं,   ह-६ -- ह स क ह ल ह्रीं,
स-४ -- स क ल ह्रीं,   सौः-५ -- सौः ऐं क्लीं ह्रीं श्रीं)

॥ फल-श्रुति॥

इति ते कथितं देव!, ब्रह्मानन्द-मयं परम्।
श्री महा-योनिराख्यातं, कवचं देव-दुर्लभम्॥ १

मम तेजसा रचितं, श्रीविद्या-क्रम-संयुतम्।
तव स्नेहान्महा-देव!, तवाग्रे तु मयोदितम्॥ २

राज्यं देयं शिरो देयं न देयं कवचं परम्।
देयं पूर्णाभिषिक्ताय, स्व-शिष्याय महेश्वर !॥ ३

अन्यथा नारकी भूयात्, कल्प-कोटि-शतैरपि।
दिक्-सहस्रेण पाठेन, ह्यासाध्यं साध्यते क्षणात्॥ ४

लक्षं जपत्वा महा-देव!, तद्दशांशं हुनेद् यदि।
ब्रह्म-ज्ञानमवाप्नोति, पर-ब्रह्मणि लीयते॥ ५

भूर्जे विलिख्य गुटिकां, स्वर्णस्थां धारयेद् यदि।
कण्ठे वा दक्षिणे बाहौ, साक्षात् कामेश्वरो भवेत्।
नारी वाम-भुजे धृत्वा, भवेत् त्रिपुरसुन्दरी॥ ६

ॐ तत्सत् ॥

श्रीमहा-निर्वाण-तन्त्रे श्रीमहा-योनि-नाम श्रीमन्महा-त्रिपुर-सुन्दरी-कवचं सम्पूर्णम्॥

*****

Śrī Tripura Sundaryaṣṭottara Śatanāmā Stotram

One hundred divine names of the holy mother in verses form.

Asya Śrī Tripura Sundaryaṣṭottara Śatanāma Stotramahāmantrasya

Dakṣiṇāmūrtiḥ Ṛṣiḥ | Anuṣṭup Chandaḥ | ŚrīTripurasundarī Devatā |

Aiṃ Bījam | Sauḥ Śaktiḥ | Klīṃ Kīlakam |

Śrī Tripurasundarī Prasādasiddhyarthe Nāmapārāyaṇe Viniyogaḥ |

Oṃ Aiṃ Aṅguṣṭhābhyāṃ Namaḥ | Klīṃ Tarjanībhyāṃ Namaḥ |

Sauḥ Madhyamābhyāṃ Namaḥ | Aiṃ Anāmikābhyāṃ Namaḥ |

Klīṃ Kaniṣṭhikābhyāṃ Namaḥ | Sauḥ Karatalakaraprṣṭhābhyāṃ Namaḥ |

Oṃ Aiṃ Hṛdayāya Namaḥ | Klīṃ Śirase Svāhā | Sauḥ Śikhāyai Vaṣaṭ |

Aiṃ Kavacāya Hum | Klīṃ Netratrayāya Vauṣaṭ | Sauḥ Astrāya Phaṭ |

Bhūrbhuvassuvaroṃ Iti Digbandhaḥ |

Dhyānam

Pāśāṅkuśe Pustakākṣasūtre Ca Dadhatī Karaiḥ |

Raktā Tryakṣā Candraphālā Pātu Bālā Surārcitā ||

Lamityādi Pañcapūjā

Laṃ Pṛthivyātmikāyai Gandhaṃ Samarpayāmi |

Haṃ Ākāśātmikāyai Puṣpāṇi Samarpayāmi |

Yaṃ Vāyvātmikāyai Dhūpamāghrāpayāmi |

Raṃ Agnyātmikāyai Dīpaṃ Darśayāmi |

Vaṃ Amṛtātmikāyai Amṛtopahāraṃ Nivedayāmi |

Saṃ Sarvātmikāyai Sarvopacārapūjāḥ Samarpayāmi ||

Atha Śrī Aṣṭottaraśatanāmastotram |

Oṃ Kalyāṇī Tripurā Bālā Māyā Tripurasundarī |

Sundarī Saubhāgyavatī Klīṅkārī Sarvamaṅgalā || 1

Hrīṅkārī Skandajananī Parā Pañcadaśākṣarī |
Trilokī Mohanādhīśā Sarveśī Sarvarūpiṇī || 2

Sarvasaṃkṣobhiṇī Pūrṇā Navamudreśvarī Śivā |
Anaṅgakusumā Khyātā Anaṅgā Bhuvaneśvarī || 3

Japyā Stavyā Śrutirnitā Nityaklinnā'mṛtodbhavā |
Mohinī Paramā''nandā Kāmeśataruṇā Kalā || 4

Kalāvatī Bhagavatī Padmarāgakirīṭinī |
Saugandhinī Saridveṇī Mantriṇi Mantrarūpiṇi || 5

Tattvatrayī Tattvamayī Siddhā Tripuravāsinī |
Śrīrmatiśca Mahādevī Kaulinī Paradevatā || 6

Kaivalyarekhā Vaśinī Sarveśī Sarvamātṛkā |
Viṣṇusvasā Devamātā Sarvasampatpradāyinī || 7

Kiṅkarī Mātā Gīrvāṇī Surāpānānumodinī |
Ādhārāhitapatnīkā Svādhiṣṭhānasamāśrayā || 8

Anāhatābjanilayā Maṇipūrāsamāśrayā |
Ājñā Padmāsanāsīnā Viśuddhasthalasaṃsthitā || 9

Aṣṭātriṃśatkalāmūrti Ssuṣumnā Cārumadhyamā |
Yogeśvarī Munidhyeyā Parabrahmasvarūpiṇī || 10

Caturbhujā Candracūḍā Purāṇāgamarūpinī |
Aiṃkārādirmahāvidyā Pañcapraṇavarūpiṇī || 11

Bhūteśvarī Bhūtamayī Pañcāśadvarṇarūpiṇī |
Ṣoḍhānyāsa Mahābhūṣā Kāmākṣī Daśamātṛkā || 12

Ādhāraśaktiḥ Taruṇī Lakṣmīḥ Tripurabhairavī |
Śāmbhavī Saccidānandā Saccidānandarūpiṇī || 13

Māṅgalya Dāyinī Mānyā Sarvamaṅgalakāriṇī |
Yogalakṣmīḥ Bhogalakṣmīḥ Rājyalakṣmīḥ Trikoṇagā || 14

Sarvasaubhāgyasampannā Sarvasampattidāyinī |

Navakoṇapurāvāsā Bindutrayasamanvitā || 15

Nāmnāmaṣṭottaraśataṃ Paṭhennyāsasamanvitaṃ |

Sarvasiddhimavāpnotī Sādhakobhīṣṭamāpnuyāt || 16

Iti Śrī Rudrayāmalatantre Umāmaheśvarasaṃvāde Śrī

Aṣṭottaraśatanāmastotram Sampūrṇam |

श्रीत्रिपुरसुन्दर्यष्टोत्तरशतनाम स्तोत्रम्

अस्य श्रीत्रिपुरसुन्दर्यष्टोत्तरशतनामस्तोत्रमहामन्त्रस्य

दक्षिणामूर्तिः ऋषिः। अनुष्टुप् छन्दः। श्री त्रिपुरसुन्दरी देवता।

ऐं बीजम्। सौः शक्तिः। क्लीं कीलकम्।

श्रीत्रिपुरसुन्दरीप्रसादसिद्ध्यर्थे नामपारायणे विनियोगः।

ओं ऐं अङ्गुष्ठाभ्यां नमः। क्लीं तर्जनीभ्यां नमः।

सौः मध्यमाभ्यां नमः। ऐं अनामिकाभ्यां नमः।

क्लीं कनिष्ठिकाभ्यां नमः। सौः करतलकरपृष्ठाभ्यां नमः।

ओं ऐं हृदयाय नमः। क्लीं शिरसे स्वाहा। सौः शिखायै वषट्।

ऐं कवचाय हुम्। क्लीं नेत्रत्रयाय वौषट्। सौः अस्त्राय फट्।

भूर्भुवस्सुवरों इति दिग्बन्धः।

ध्यानम्

पाशाङ्कुशे पुस्तकाक्षसूत्रे च दधती करैः।

रक्ता त्र्यक्षा चन्द्रफाला पातु बाला सुरार्चिता॥

लमित्यादि पञ्चपूजा

लं पृथिव्यात्मिकायै गन्धं समर्पयामि।

हं आकाशात्मिकायै पुष्पाणि समर्पयामि।

यं वाय्वात्मिकायै धूपमाघ्रापयामि।

रं अग्न्यात्मिकायै दीपं दर्शयामि।

वं अमृतात्मिकायै अमृतोपहारं निवेदयामि।

सं सर्वात्मिकायै सर्वोपचारपूजाः समर्पयामि॥

अथ स्तोत्रम् ।

ॐ कल्याणी त्रिपुरा बाला माया त्रिपुरसुन्दरी।
सुन्दरी सौभाग्यवती क्लीङ्कारी सर्वमङ्गला॥ १

हीङ्कारी स्कन्दजननी परा पञ्चदशाक्षरी ।
त्रिलोकी मोहनाधीशा सर्वेशी सर्वरूपिणी ॥ २

सर्वसंक्षोभिणी पूर्णा नवमुद्रेश्वरी शिवा।
अनङ्गकुसुमा ख्याता अनङ्गा भुवनेश्वरी॥ ३

जप्या स्तव्या श्रुतिर्निता नित्यक्लिन्नाऽमृतोद्भवा।
मोहिनी परमाऽऽनन्दा कामेशतरुणा कला ॥ ४

कलावती भगवती पद्मरागकिरीटिनी ।
सौगन्धिनी सरिद्वेणी मन्त्रिणि मन्त्ररूपिणि ॥ ५

तत्त्वत्रयी तत्त्वमयी सिद्धा त्रिपुरवासिनी ।
श्रीर्मतिश्च महादेवी कौलिनी परदेवता ॥ ६

कैवल्यरेखा वशिनी सर्वेशी सर्वमातृका ।
विष्णुस्वसा देवमाता सर्वसम्पत्प्रदायिनी॥ ७

किङ्करी माता गीर्वाणी सुरापानानुमोदिनी।
आधाराहितपत्नीका स्वाधिष्ठानसमाश्रया ॥ ८

अनाहताब्जनिलया मणिपूरासमाश्रया ।
आज्ञा पद्मासनासीना विशुद्धस्थलसंस्थिता ॥ ९

अष्टात्रिंशत्कलामूर्ति स्सुषुम्ना चारुमध्यमा।
योगेश्वरी मुनिध्येया परब्रह्मस्वरूपिणी ॥ १०

चतुर्भुजा चन्द्रचूडा पुराणागमरूपिणी।
ऐंकारादिर्महाविद्या पञ्चप्रणवरूपिणी ॥ ११

भूतेश्वरी भूतमयी पञ्चाशद्वर्णरूपिणी।
षोढान्यास महाभूषा कामाक्षी दशमातृका॥ १२

आधारशक्तिः तरुणी लक्ष्मीः त्रिपुरभैरवी।
शाम्भवी सच्चिदानन्दा सच्चिदानन्दरूपिणी॥ १३

माङ्गल्य दायिनी मान्या सर्वमङ्गलकारिणी।
योगलक्ष्मीः भोगलक्ष्मीः राज्यलक्ष्मीः त्रिकोणगा॥ १४
सर्वसौभाग्यसम्पन्ना सर्वसम्पत्तिदायिनी।
नवकोणपुरावासा बिन्दुत्रयसमन्विता॥ १५

नाम्नामष्टोत्तरशतं पठेन्यासससमन्वितं।
सर्वसिद्धिमवाप्नोती साधकोभीष्टमाप्नुयात्॥ १६

इति श्री रुद्रयामलतन्त्रे उमामहेश्वरसंवादे श्री श्रीत्रिपुरसुन्दर्यष्टोत्तरशतनामस्तोत्रम्
सम्पूर्णम्।

*****

Śrī Tripura Sundaryaṣṭottara Śatanāmāvalī

One hundred divine names of the holy mother.

Oṃ Kalyāṇyai Namaḥ |

Oṃ Tripurāyai Namaḥ |

Oṃ Bālāyai Namaḥ |

Oṃ Māyāyai Namaḥ |

Oṃ Tripurasundaryai Namaḥ |

Oṃ Sundaryai Namaḥ |

Oṃ Saubhāgyavatyai Namaḥ |

Oṃ Klīṃkāryai Namaḥ |

Oṃ Sarvamaṅgalāyai Namaḥ |

Oṃ Hrīṃkāryai Namaḥ | 10

Oṃ Skandajananyai Namaḥ |

Oṃ Parāyai Namaḥ |

Oṃ Pañcadaśākṣaryai Namaḥ |

Oṃ Trilokyai Namaḥ |

Oṃ Mohanādhīśāyai Namaḥ |

Oṃ Sarveśvaryai Namaḥ |

Oṃ Sarvarūpiṇyai Namaḥ |

Oṃ Sarvasaṅkṣobhiṇyai

Namaḥ |

Oṃ Pūrṇāyai Namaḥ |

Oṃ Navamudreśvaryai

Namaḥ | 20

Oṃ Śivāyai Namaḥ |

Oṃ Anaṅgakusumāyai Namaḥ |

Oṃ Khyātāyai Namaḥ |

Oṃ Anaṅgāyai Namaḥ |

Oṃ Bhuvaneśvaryai Namaḥ |

Oṃ Japyāyai Namaḥ |

Oṃ Stavyāyai Namaḥ |

Oṃ Śrutyai Namaḥ |

Oṃ Nityāyai Namaḥ |

Oṃ Nityaklinnāyai Namaḥ | 30

Oṃ Amṛtodbhavāyai Namaḥ |

Oṃ Mohinyai Namaḥ |

Oṃ Paramāyai Namaḥ |

Oṃ Ānandāyai Namaḥ |

Oṃ Kāmeśyai Namaḥ |

Oṃ Tāruṇāyai Namaḥ |

Var Kāmeśataruṇāyai Namaḥ

Oṃ Kalāyai Namaḥ |

Oṃ Kalāvatyai Namaḥ |

Oṃ Bhagavatyai Namaḥ |

Oṃ Padmarāgakirīṭinyai

Namaḥ |

Oṃ Saugandhinyai Namaḥ | 40

Oṃ Saridveṇyai Namaḥ |

Oṃ Mantriṇyai Namaḥ |

Oṃ Mantrarūpiṇyai Namaḥ |

Oṃ Tattvatrayyai Namaḥ |

Oṃ Tattvamayyai Namaḥ |

Oṃ Siddhāyai Namaḥ |

Oṃ Tripuravāsinyai Namaḥ |

Oṃ Śriyai Namaḥ |

Oṃ Matyai Namaḥ |

Oṃ Mahādevyai Namaḥ | 50

Oṃ Kālinyai Namaḥ |
Oṃ Paradevatāyai Namaḥ |
Oṃ Kaivalyarekhāyai Namaḥ |
Oṃ Vaśinyai Namaḥ |
Oṃ Sarveśyai Namaḥ |
Oṃ Sarvamātṛkāyai Namaḥ |
Oṃ Viṣṇusvasre Namaḥ |
Oṃ Devamātre Namaḥ |
Oṃ Sarvasampatpradāyinyai
                    Namaḥ | 60

Oṃ Kiṃkaryai Namaḥ |
Oṃ Mātre Namaḥ |
Oṃ Gīrvāṇyai Namaḥ |
Oṃ Surāpānānumodinyai
                    Namaḥ |
Oṃ Ādhārāyai Namaḥ |
Oṃ Hitapatnikāyai Namaḥ |
Oṃ Svādhiṣṭhānasamāśrayāyai
                    Namaḥ |
Oṃ Anāhatābjanilayāyai
                    Namaḥ |
Oṃ Maṇipūrasamāśrayāyai
                    Namaḥ | 70

Oṃ Ājñāyai Namaḥ |
Oṃ Padmāsanāsīnāyai Namaḥ |
Oṃ Viśuddhasthalasaṃsthitāyai
                    Namaḥ |
Oṃ Aṣṭātriṃśatkalāmūrtyai
                    Namaḥ |
Oṃ Suṣumnāyai Namaḥ |

Oṃ Cārumadhyamāyai Namaḥ |
Oṃ Yogeśvaryai Namaḥ |
Oṃ Munidhyeyāyai Namaḥ |
Oṃ Parabrahmasvarūpiṇyai
                    Namaḥ |
Oṃ Caturbhujāyai Namaḥ |
Oṃ Candracūḍāyai Namaḥ | 80

Oṃ Purāṇāgamarūpiṇyai
                    Namaḥ |
Oṃ Aiṃkāravidyāyai Namaḥ |
Oṃ Mahāvidyāyai Namaḥ |
Oṃ Pañcapraṇavarūpiṇyai
                    Namaḥ |
Oṃ Bhūteśvaryai Namaḥ |
Oṃ Bhūtamayyai Namaḥ |
Oṃ Pañcāśadvarṇarūpiṇyai
                    Namaḥ |
Oṃ Ṣoḍhānyāsamahābhūṣāyai
                    Namaḥ |
Oṃ Kāmākṣyai Namaḥ |
Oṃ Daśamātṛkāyai Namaḥ |
Oṃ Ādhāraśaktyai Namaḥ | 90

Oṃ Taruṇyai Namaḥ |
Oṃ Lakṣmyai Namaḥ |
Oṃ Tripurabhairavyai Namaḥ |
Oṃ Śāmbhavyai Namaḥ |
Oṃ Saccidānandāyai Namaḥ |
Oṃ Saccidānandarūpiṇyai
                    Namaḥ |
Oṃ Māṅgalyadāyinyai Namaḥ |
Oṃ Mānyāyai Namaḥ |

Oṃ Sarvamaṅgalakāriṇyai
                    Namaḥ |
Oṃ Yogalakṣmyai Namaḥ | 100

Oṃ Bhogalakṣmyai Namaḥ |
Oṃ Rājyalakṣmyai Namaḥ |
Oṃ Trikoṇagāyai Namaḥ |

Oṃ Sarvasaubhāgya
              Sampannāyai Namaḥ |
Oṃ Sarvasampattidāyinyai
                    Namaḥ |
Oṃ Navakoṇapurāvāsāyai
                    Namaḥ |
Oṃ Bindutrayasamanvitāyai
                    Namaḥ |

Iti Śrī Rudrayāmalatantre Umāmaheśvarasaṃvāde Niṣpannā
Śrītripurasundaryaṣṭottaraśatanāmāvalī Samāptā |

श्री त्रिपुरसुन्दर्यष्टोत्तरशतनामावली

ॐ कल्याण्यै नमः |

ॐ त्रिपुरायै नमः |

ॐ बालायै नमः |

ॐ मायायै नमः |

ॐ त्रिपुरसुन्दर्यै नमः |

ॐ सुन्दर्यै नमः |

ॐ सौभाग्यवत्यै नमः |

ॐ क्लींकायै नमः |

ॐ सर्वमङ्गलायै नमः |

ॐ ह्रींकायै नमः | १०

ॐ स्कन्दजनन्यै नमः |

ॐ परायै नमः |

ॐ पञ्चदशाक्षर्यै नमः |

ॐ त्रिलोक्यै नमः |

ॐ मोहनाधीशायै नमः |

ॐ सर्वेश्वर्यै नमः |

ॐ सर्वरूपिण्यै नमः |

ॐ सर्वसङ्क्षोभिण्यै नमः |

ॐ पूर्णायै नमः |

ॐ नवमुद्रेश्वर्यै नमः | २०

ॐ शिवायै नमः |

ॐ अनङ्गकुसुमायै नमः |

ॐ ख्यातायै नमः |

ॐ अनङ्गायै नमः |

ॐ भुवनेश्वर्यै नमः |

ॐ जप्यायै नमः |

ॐ स्तव्यायै नमः |

ॐ श्रुत्यै नमः |

ॐ नित्यायै नमः |

ॐ नित्यक्लिन्नायै नमः | ३०

ॐ अमृतोद्भवायै नमः |

ॐ मोहिन्यै नमः |

ॐ परमायै नमः |

ॐ आनन्दायै नमः |

ॐ कामेश्यै नमः |

ॐ तारुणायै नमः |

ॐ कलायै नमः |

ॐ कलावत्यै नमः |

ॐ भगवत्यै नमः ।

ॐ पद्मरागकिरीटिन्यै नमः ।

ॐ सौगन्धिन्यै नमः । ४०

ॐ सरिद्वेण्यै नमः ।

ॐ मन्त्रिण्यै नमः ।

ॐ मन्त्ररूपिण्यै नमः ।

ॐ तत्त्वत्रय्यै नमः ।

ॐ तत्त्वमय्यै नमः ।

ॐ सिद्धायै नमः ।

ॐ त्रिपुरवासिन्यै नमः ।

ॐ श्रियै नमः ।

ॐ मत्यै नमः ।

ॐ महादेव्यै नमः । ५०

ॐ कालिन्यै नमः ।

ॐ परदेवतायै नमः ।

ॐ कैवल्यरेखायै नमः ।

ॐ वशिन्यै नमः ।

ॐ सर्वेश्यै नमः ।

ॐ सर्वमातृकायै नमः ।

ॐ विष्णुस्वस्रे नमः ।

ॐ देवमात्रे नमः ।

ॐ सर्वसम्पत्प्रदायिन्यै नमः । ६०

ॐ किंकर्यै नमः ।

ॐ मात्रे नमः ।

ॐ गीर्वाण्यै नमः ।

ॐ सुरापानानुमोदिन्यै नमः ।

ॐ आधारायै नमः ।

ॐ हितपत्निकायै नमः ।

ॐ स्वाधिष्ठानसमाश्रयायै नमः ।

ॐ अनाहताब्जनिलयायै नमः ।

ॐ मणिपूरसमाश्रयायै नमः ।

ॐ आज्ञायै नमः । ७०

ॐ पद्मासनासीनायै नमः ।

ॐ विशुद्धस्थलसंस्थितायै नमः ।

ॐ अष्टात्रिंशत्कलामूर्त्यै नमः ।

ॐ सुषुम्नायै नमः ।

ॐ चारुमध्यमायै नमः ।

ॐ योगेश्वर्यै नमः ।

ॐ मुनिध्येयायै नमः ।

ॐ परब्रह्मस्वरूपिण्यै नमः ।

ॐ चतुर्भुजायै नमः ।

ॐ चन्द्रचूडायै नमः । ८०

ॐ पुराणागमरूपिण्यै नमः ।

ॐ ओंकारविद्यायै नमः ।

ॐ महाविद्यायै नमः ।

ॐ पञ्चप्रणवरूपिण्यै नमः ।

ॐ भूतेश्वर्यै नमः ।

ॐ भूतमय्यै नमः ।

ॐ पञ्चाशद्वर्णरूपिण्यै नमः ।

ॐ षोढान्यासमहाभूषायै नमः ।

ॐ कामाक्ष्यै नमः ।

ॐ दशमातृकायै नमः ।

ॐ आधारशक्त्यै नमः । ९०

ॐ तरुण्यै नमः ।

ॐ लक्ष्म्यै नमः ।

ॐ त्रिपुरभैरव्यै नमः ।

ॐ शाम्भव्यै नमः ।

ॐ सच्चिदानन्दायै नमः ।

ॐ सच्चिदानन्दरूपिण्यै नमः ।

ॐ माङ्गल्यदायिन्यै नमः ।

ॐ मान्यायै नमः ।　　　ॐ त्रिकोणगायै नमः ।

ॐ सर्वमङ्गलकारिण्यै नमः ।　　　ॐ सर्वसौभाग्यसम्पन्नायै नमः ।

ॐ योगलक्ष्म्यै नमः । १००　　　ॐ सर्वसम्पत्तिदायिन्यै नमः ।

ॐ भोगलक्ष्म्यै नमः ।　　　ॐ नवकोणपुरावासायै नमः ।

ॐ राज्यलक्ष्म्यै नमः ।　　　ॐ बिन्दुत्रयसमन्वितायै नमः ।

इति श्री रुद्रयामलतन्त्रे उमामहेश्वरसंवादे निष्पन्ना श्रीत्रिपुरसुन्दर्यष्टोत्तरशतनामावली समाप्ता ।

*****

Śrī Tripura Sundarī Cakrarāja Stotram

Stotras pertaining to the 15 syllables of the *Moola Mantra* and for the *Beejakshara* viz. *Śrīm*.

|| *Ka* ||

Kartuṃ Devi ! Jagad-Vilāsa-Vidhinā Sṛṣṭena Te Māyayā
Sarvānanda-Mayena Madhya-Vilasacchrī-Vinadunā' laṅkṛtam |
Śrīmad-Sad-Guru-Pūjya-Pāda-Karuṇā-Saṃvedya-Tattvātmakaṃ
Śrī-Cakraṃ Śaraṇaṃ Vrajāmi Satataṃ Sarveṣṭa-Siddhi-Pradam || 1

|| *E* ||

Ekasminnaṇimādibhirvilasitaṃ Bhūmī-Gṛhe Siddhibhiḥ
Vāhyādyābhirupāśritaṃ Ca Daśabhirmudrābhirudbhāsitam |
Cakreśyā Prakateḍyayā Tripurayā Trailokya-Sammohanaṃ
Śrī-Cakraṃ Śaraṇaṃ Vrajāmi Satataṃ Sarveṣṭa-Siddhi-Pradam || 2

|| *Ī* ||

Īḍyābhirnava-Vidruma-Cchavi-Samābhikhyābhiraṅgī-Kṛtaṃ
Kāmākarṣiṇī Kādibhiḥ Svara-Dale Guptābhidhābhiḥ Sadā |
Sarvāśā-Pari-Pūrake Pari-Lasad-Devyā Pureśyā Yutaṃ
Śrī-Cakraṃ Śaraṇaṃ Vrajāmi Satataṃ Sarveṣṭa-Siddhi-Pradam || 3

|| *La* ||

Labdha-Projjvala-Yauvanābhirabhito' naṅga-Prasūnādibhiḥ
Sevyaṃ Gupta-Tarābhiraṣṭa-Kamale Saṅkṣobhakākhye Sadā |
Cakreśyā Pura-Sundarīti Jagati Prakhyātayāsaṅgatam
Śrī-Cakraṃ Śaraṇaṃ Vrajāmi Satataṃ Sarveṣṭa-Siddhi-Pradam || 4

|| *Hrīṃ* ||

Hrīṅkārāṅkita-Mantra-Rāja-Nilayaṃ Śrīsarva-Saṅkṣobhiṇī
Mukhyābhiścala-Kuntalābhiruṣitaṃ Manvasra-Cakre Śubhe |
Yatra Śrī-Pura-Vāsinī Vijayate Śrī-Sarva-Saubhāgyade
Śrī-Cakraṃ Śaraṇaṃ Vrajāmi Satataṃ Sarveṣṭa-Siddhi-Pradam || 5

|| *Ha* ||

Haste Pāśa-Gadādi-Śastra-Nicayaṃ Dīptaṃ Vahantībhiḥ
Uttīrṇākhyābhirupāsya Pāti Śubhade Sarvārtha-Siddhi-Prade |
Cakre Bāhya-Daśārake Vilasitaṃ Devyā Pūra-Śryākhyayā
Śrī-Cakraṃ Śaraṇaṃ Vrajāmi Satataṃ Sarveṣṭa-Siddhi-Pradam || 6

|| *Sa* ||

Sarvajñādibhirinadu-Kānti-Dhavalā Kālābhirārakṣite
Cakre'ntardaśa-Koṇake'ti-Vimale Nāmnā Ca Rakṣā-Kare |
Yatra Śrītripura-Mālinī Vijayate Nityaṃ Nigarbhā Stutā
Śrī-Cakraṃ Śaraṇaṃ Vrajāmi Satataṃ Sarveṣṭa-Siddhi-Pradam || 7

|| *Ka* ||

Kartuṃ Mūkamanargala-Sravadita-Drākṣādi-Vāg-Vaibhavaṃ
Dakṣābhirvaśinī-Mukhābhirabhito Vāg-Devatābhiryutām |
Aṣṭāre Pura-Siddhayā Vilasitaṃ Roga-Praṇāśe Śubhe
Śrī-Cakraṃ Śaraṇaṃ Vrajāmi Satataṃ Sarveṣṭa-Siddhi-Pradam || 8

|| *Ha* ||

Hantuṃ Dānava-Saṅghamāhava Bhuvi Svecchā Samākalpitaiḥ
Śastrairastra-Cayaiśca Cāpa-Nivahairatyugra-Tejo-Bharaiḥ |
Ārta-Trāṇa-Parāyaṇairari-Kula-Pradhvaṃsibhiḥ Saṃvṛtaṃ
Śrī-Cakraṃ Śaraṇaṃ Vrajāmi Satataṃ Sarveṣṭa-Siddhi-Pradam || 9

|| *La* ||

Lakṣmī-Vāga-Gajādibhiḥ Kara-Lasat-Pāśāsi-Ghaṇṭādibhiḥ
Kāmeśyādibhirāvṛtaṃ Śubha~Ṅkaraṃ Śrī-Sarva-Siddhi-Pradam |
Cakreśī Ca Purāmbikā Vijayate Yatra Trikoṇe Mudā
Śrī-Cakraṃ Śaraṇaṃ Vrajāmi Satataṃ Sarveṣṭa-Siddhi-Pradam || 10

|| *Hrīṃ* ||

Hrīṅkāraṃ Paramaṃ Japadbhiraniśaṃ Mitreśa-Nāthādibhiḥ
Divyaughairmanujaugha-Siddha-Nivahaiḥ Sārūpya-Muktiṃ Gataiḥ |
Nānā-Mantra-Rahasya-Vidbhirakhilairanvāsitaṃ Yogibhiḥ
Śrī-Cakraṃ Śaraṇaṃ Vrajāmi Satataṃ Sarveṣṭa-Siddhi-Pradam || 11

|| *Sa* ||

Sarvotkṛṣṭa-Vapurdharābhirabhito Devī Samābhirjagat
Saṃrakṣārthamupāgatā'bhirasakṛnnityābhidhābhirmudā |
Kāmeśyādibhirājñayaiva Lalitā-Devyāḥ Samudbhāsitaṃ
Śrī-Cakraṃ Śaraṇaṃ Vrajāmi Satataṃ Sarveṣṭa-Siddhi-Pradam || 12

|| *Ka* ||

Kartuṃ Śrīlalitāṅga-Rakṣaṇa-Vidhiṃ Lāvaṇya-Pūrṇāṃ Tanūṃ
Āsthāyāstra-Varollasat-Kara-Payojātābhiradhyāsitam |
Devībhirhṛdayādibhiśca Parito Vinduṃ Sadā''nandadaṃ
Śrī-Cakraṃ Śaraṇaṃ Vrajāmi Satataṃ Sarveṣṭa-Siddhi-Pradam || 13

|| *La* ||

Lakṣmīśādi-Padairyutena Mahatā Mañcena Saṃśobhitaṃ
Ṣaṭ-Trimśadbhiranargha-Ratna-Khacitaiḥ Sopānakairbhūṣitam |
Cintā-Ratna-Vinirmitena Mahatā Siṃhāsanenojjvalaṃ
Śrī-Cakraṃ Śaraṇaṃ Vrajāmi Satataṃ Sarveṣṭa-Siddhi-Pradam || 14

|| *Hrīṃ* ||

Hrīṅkāraika-Mahā-Manuṃ Prajapatā Kāmeśvareṇoṣitaṃ
Tasyāṅke Ca Niṣaṇṇayā Tri-Jagatāṃ Mātrā Cidākirayā |
Kāmeśyā Karuṇā-Rasaika-Nidhinā Kalyāṇa-Dātryā Yutaṃ
Śrī-Cakraṃ Śaraṇaṃ Vrajāmi Satataṃ Sarveṣṭa-Siddhi-Pradam || 15

|| *Śrīṃ* ||

Śrīmat-Pañca-Daśākṣaraika-Nilayaṃ Śrīṣoḍaśī-Mandiraṃ
Śrīnāthādibhirarcitaṃ Ca Bahudhā Devaiḥ Samārādhitam |
Śrīkāmeśa-Rahassakhī-Nilayanaṃ Śrīmad-Guhārādhitaṃ
Śrī-Cakraṃ Śaraṇaṃ Vrajāmi Satataṃ Sarveṣṭa-Siddhi-Pradam || 16

*****

श्री त्रिपुर सुन्दरी चक्रराज स्तोत्रम्

॥ क॥

कर्तुं देवि ! जगद्-विलास-विधिना सृष्टेन ते मायया
सर्वानन्द-मयेन मध्य-विलसच्छ्री-विन्दुनाऽलङ्कृतम् ।
श्रीमद्-सद्-गुरु-पूज्य-पाद-करुणा-संवेद्य-तत्त्वात्मकं
श्री-चक्रं शरणं व्रजामि सततं सर्वेष्ट-सिद्धि-प्रदम्॥ १

॥ ए॥

एकस्मिन्ननिमादिभिर्विलसितं भूमी-गृहे सिद्धिभिः
वाह्याद्याभिरुपाश्रितं च दशभिर्मुद्राभिरुद्भासितम्।
चक्रेश्या प्रकटेड्यया त्रिपुरया त्रैलोक्य-सम्मोहनं
श्री-चक्रं शरणं व्रजामि सततं सर्वेष्ट-सिद्धि-प्रदम्॥ २

॥ ई॥

ईड्याभिर्नव-विद्रुम-च्छवि-समाभिख्याभिरङ्गी-कृतं
कामाकर्षिणी कादिभिः स्वर-दले गुप्ताभिधाभिः सदा।
सर्वाशा-परि-पूरके परि-लसद्-देव्या पुरेश्या युतं
श्री-चक्रं शरणं व्रजामि सततं सर्वेष्ट-सिद्धि-प्रदम् ॥ ३

॥ ल॥

लब्ध-प्रोज्ज्वल-यौवनाभिरभितोऽनङ्ग-प्रसूनादिभिः
सेव्यं गुप्ततराभिरष्ट-कमले सङ्क्षोभकाख्ये सदा ।
चक्रेश्या पुर-सुन्दरीति जगति प्रख्यातयासङ्गतं
श्री-चक्रं शरणं व्रजामि सततं सर्वेष्ट-सिद्धि-प्रदम्॥ ४

॥ ह्रीं॥

ह्रीङ्काराङ्कित-मन्त्र-राज-निलयं श्रीसर्व-सङ्क्षोभिणी
मुख्याभिश्चल-कुन्तलाभिरुषितं मन्वस्र-चक्रे शुभे।
यत्र श्री-पुर-वासिनी विजयते श्री-सर्व-सौभाग्यदे
श्री-चक्रं शरणं व्रजामि सततं सर्वेष्ट-सिद्धि-प्रदम् ॥ ५

॥ ह॥

हस्ते पाश-गदादि-शस्त्र-निचयं दीप्तं वहन्तीभिः
उत्तीर्णाख्याभिरुपास्य पाति शुभदे सर्वार्थ-सिद्धि-प्रदे ।
चक्रे बाह्य-दशारके विलसितं देव्या पूरःश्रयाख्यया
श्री-चक्रं शरणं व्रजामि सततं सर्वेष्ट-सिद्धि-प्रदम् ॥ ६

॥ सा॥

सर्वज्ञादिभिरिन्दु-कान्ति-धवला कालाभिरारक्षिते
चक्रेऽन्तर्दश-कोणकेऽति-विमले नाम्ना च रक्षा-करे ।
यत्र श्रीत्रिपुर-मालिनी विजयते नित्यं निगर्भा स्तुता
श्री-चक्रं शरणं व्रजामि सततं सर्वेष्ट-सिद्धि-प्रदम् ॥ ७

॥ क॥

कर्तुं मूकमनर्गल-स्रवदित-द्राक्षादि-वाग्-वैभवं
दक्षाभिर्वशिनी-मुखाभिरभितो वाग्-देवताभिर्युताम् ।
अष्टारे पुर-सिद्धया विलसितं रोग-प्रणाशे शुभे
श्री-चक्रं शरणं व्रजामि सततं सर्वेष्ट-सिद्धि-प्रदम् ॥ ८

॥ ह॥

हन्तुं दानव-सङ्घमाहव भुवि स्वेच्छा समाकल्पितैः
शस्त्रैरस्त्र-चयैश्च चाप-निवहैरत्युग्र-तेजो-भरैः ।
आर्त-त्राण-परायणैररि-कुल-प्रध्वंसिभिः संवृतं
श्री-चक्रं शरणं व्रजामि सततं सर्वेष्ट-सिद्धि-प्रदम् ॥ ९

॥ ल॥

लक्ष्मी-वाग-गजादिभिः कर-लसत्-पाशासि-घण्टादिभिः
कामेश्यादिभिरावृतं शुभ-ङ्करं श्री-सर्व-सिद्धि-प्रदम् ।
चक्रेशी च पुराम्बिका विजयते यत्र त्रिकोणे मुदा
श्री-चक्रं शरणं व्रजामि सततं सर्वेष्ट-सिद्धि-प्रदम् ॥ १०

॥ ह्रीं॥

ह्रीङ्कारं परमं जपद्भिरनिशं मित्रेशभनाथादिभिः
दिव्यौघैर्मनुजौघ-सिद्ध-निवहैः सारूप्य-मुक्तिं गतैः ।
नाना-मन्त्र-रहस्य-विद्भिरखिलैरन्वासितं योगिभिः
श्री-चक्रं शरणं व्रजामि सततं सर्वेष्ट-सिद्धि-प्रदम् ॥ ११

॥ सा॥

सर्वोत्कृष्ट-वपुर्धराभिरभितो देवी समाभिर्जगत्
संरक्षार्थमुपागताऽभिरसकृन्नित्याभिधाभिर्मुदा ।
कामेश्यादिभिराज्ञयैव ललिता-देव्याः समुद्भासितं
श्री-चक्रं शरणं व्रजामि सततं सर्वेष्ट-सिद्धि-प्रदम् ॥ १२

॥ का॥

कर्तुं श्रीललिताङ्ग-रक्षण-विधिं लावण्य-पूर्णा तनूं
आस्थायास्त्र-वरोल्लसत्-कर-पयोजाताभिरध्यासितम् ।
देवीभिर्हृदयादिभिश्च परितो विन्दुं सदाऽऽनन्ददं
श्री-चक्रं शरणं व्रजामि सततं सर्वेष्ट-सिद्धि-प्रदम् ॥ १३

॥ ल॥

लक्ष्मीशादि-पदैर्युतेन महता मञ्चेन संशोभितं
षट्-त्रिंशद्भिरनर्घ-रत्न-खचितैः सोपानकैर्भूषितम् ।
चिन्ता-रत्न-विनिर्मितेन महता सिंहासनेनोज्ज्वलं
श्री-चक्रं शरणं व्रजामि सततं सर्वेष्ट-सिद्धि-प्रदम् ॥ १४

॥ ह्रीं॥

ह्रीङ्कारैक-महा-मनुं प्रजपता कामेश्वरेणोषितं
तस्याङ्के च निषण्णया त्रि-जगतां मात्रा चिदाकिरया ।
कामेश्या करुणा-रसैक-निधिना कल्याण-दात्र्या युतं
श्री-चक्रं शरणं व्रजामि सततं सर्वेष्ट-सिद्धि-प्रदम् ॥ १५

॥ श्रीं॥

श्रीमत्-पञ्च-दशाक्षरैक-निलयं श्रीषोडशी-मन्दिरं
श्रीनाथादिभिरर्चितं च बहुधा देवैः समाराधितम्।
श्रीकामेश-रहस्सखी-निलयनं श्रीमद्-गुहाराधितं
श्री-चक्रं शरणं व्रजामि सततं सर्वेष्टसिद्धि-प्रदम्॥ १६

*****

Śrī Tripura Sundarī Sahasranāma Stotram

One thousand divine names of the holy mother in verses form.

Samādhyuparataṃ Kāle Kadācidvijane Mudā |

Paramānandasandohamuditaṃ Prāha Pārvatī || 1

Śrīdevyuvāca -
Śrīmannātha Tavānandakāraṇaṃ Brūhi Śaṅkara |

Yogīndropāsya Deveśa Premapūrṇa Sudhānidhe |

Kṛpāsti Yadi Me Śambho Sugopyamapi Kathyatām || 2

Śrībhairavaḥ
Nirbharānandasandohaḥ Śaktibhāvena Jāyate |

Lāvaṇyasindhustatrāsti Bālāyā Rasakandaraḥ || 3

Tāmevānukṣaṇaṃ Devīṃ Cintayāmi Tataḥ Śivām |

Tasyā Nāmasahasrāṇi Kathayāmi Tava Priye || 4

Sugopyānyapi Rambhoru Gambhīrasnehavibhramāt |

Tāmeva Stuvato Devi Dhyāyato'nukṣaṇaṃ Mama |

Sukhasandohasambhāvo Jñānānandasya Kāraṇam || 5

Nyāsaḥ ||

Asya Śrītripurasundarī Sahasranāmastotrasya Śaṅkara Ṛṣiḥ,
Anuṣṭup Chandaḥ | Śrītripurasundarī Devatā |

Aiṃ Bījam | Sauḥ Śaktiḥ | Klīṃ Kīlakam |
Śrītripurasundarī Prītyarthe Samastapuruṣārthasiddhyarthe
Pārāyaṇe Viniyogaḥ |

Aiṃ Aṅguṣṭhābhyāṃ Namaḥ | Klīṃ Tarjanībhyāṃ Namaḥ |
Sauḥ Madhyamābhyāṃ Namaḥ | Aiṃ Anāmikābhyāṃ Namaḥ |
Klīṃ Kaniṣṭhikābhyāṃ Namaḥ | Sauḥ Karatalakarapṛṣṭhābhyāṃ Namaḥ |
Evaṃ Hṛdayādinyāsaḥ |

Aiṃ Hrudayāya Namaḥ | Klīṃ Śirase Namaḥ |
Sauḥ Shikāyai Vaśat | Aiṃ Kavacāya Hum |

Klīṃ Netratrayāya Vouśat | Sauḥ Astrāya Vaśat |

Bhūḥ Bhuvasvarom Iti Dik Bandhaḥ |

Dhyānam |

*Bālārkāyutatejasam Trinayanām Raktāmbarollāsinīm
Nānālankruti Rājamānavapuśam Bālodurātśekharam |
Hastairikṣudhanuḥ Sruṇim Sumaśaram Pāśam Mudaa Bibhratīm
Śrīcakrasthitasundarīm Trijagatāmādhārabhūtām Smaret ||*

Pañca Pūja ||

*Lam Prutviyātmikāyai Gandam Samarpayāmi |
Ham Ākāśātmikāyai Puṣpaiḥ Pūjayāmi |
Yam Vāyvātmikāyai Dhūpamākrāpayāmi |
Ram Vahṇiyātmikāyai Dīpam Darśayāmi |
Vam Amrutātmikāyai Amrutam Mahānaivēdyam Nivēdayāmi |
Sam Sarvātmikāyai Sarvōpacāra Pūjām Samarpayāmi ||*

Ata Stōtraḥ |

*Ānandasindhurānandā''nandamūrtirvinodinī |
Tripurā Sundarī Premapāthonidhiranuttamā || 1*

*Vāmārdhagahvarā Bhūtirvibhūtiḥ Śaṅkarī Śivā |
Śṛṅgāramūrtirvaradā Rasā Ca Śubhagocarā || 2*

*Paramānandalaharī Ratī Raṅgavatī Gatiḥ |
Raṅgamālānaṅgakalā Kelī Kaivalyadā Kalā || 3*

*Rasakalpā Kalpalatā Kutūhalavatī Gatiḥ |
Vinodadigdhā Susnigdhā Mugdhamūrtirmanoramā || 4*

*Bālārkakoṭikiraṇā Candrakoṭisuśītalā |
Sravatpīyūṣadigdhāṅgī Svargārthaparikalpitā || 5*

*Kuraṅganayanā Kāntā Sugatiḥ Sukhasantatiḥ |
Rājarājeśvarī Rājñī Mahendraparivanditā || 6*

Prapañcagatirīśānī Prapañcagatiruttamā |

Durvāsā Duḥsahā Śaktiḥ Śiñjatkanakanūpurā || 7

Merumandaravakṣojā Sṛṇipāśavarāyudhā |
Śarakodaṇḍasaṃsaktapāṇidvayavirājitā || 8

Candrabimbānanā Cārumukuṭottaṃsacandrikā |
Sindūratilakā Cārudhammillāmalamālikā || 9

Mandāradāmamuditā Ratnamālāvibhūṣitā |
Suvarṇābharaṇaprītā Muktādāmamanoramā || 10

Tāmbūlapūrṇavadanā Madanānandamānasā |
Sukhārādhyā Tapaḥ Sārā Kṛpāpārā Vidhīśvarī || 11

Vakṣaḥsthalalasadratnaprabhā Madhurasonmadā |
Bindunādātmakoccārarahitā Turyarūpiṇī || 12

Kamanīyākṛtirdhanyā Śāṅkarī Prītimañjarī |
Prapañcā Pañcamī Pūrṇā Pūrṇapīṭhanivāsinī || 13

Rājyalakṣmīśca Śrīlakṣmīrmahālakṣmīḥ Surājikā |
Santoṣasīmā Sampattiḥ Śātakaumbhī Tathā Dyutiḥ || 14

Paripūrṇā Jagaddhātrī Vidhātrī Balavardhinī |
Sārvabhaumanṛpaśrīśca Sāmrājyagatirambikā || 15

Sarojākṣī Dīrghadṛṣṭiḥ Sācīkṣaṇavicakṣaṇā |
Raṅgasravantī Rasikā (100) *Pradhānā Rasarūpiṇī* || 16

Rasasindhuḥ Sugātrī Ca Dhūsarī Maithunonmukhā |
Nirantaraguṇāsaktā Śaktirnidhuvanātmikā || 17

Kāmākṣī Kamanīyā Ca Kāmeśī Bhagamaṅgalā |
Subhagā Bhoginī Bhogyā Bhagyadā Subhagā Bhagā || 18

Bhagaliṅgānandakalā Bhagamadhyanivāsinī |
Bhagarūpā Bhagamayī Bhagayantrā Bhagottamā || 19

Yonimudrā Kāmakalā Kulāmṛtaparāyaṇā |

Kulakuṇḍālayā Sūkṣmā Jīvātmā Liṅgarūpiṇī ‖ 20

Mūlakriyā Mūlarūpā Mūlākṛtisvarūpiṇī ǀ
Sotsukā Kamalānandā Cidbhāvā''tmagatiḥ Śivā ‖ 21

Śvetāruṇā Bindurūpā Vedayonirdhvanikṣaṇā ǀ
Ghaṇṭākoṭi Ravārāvā Ravibimbotthitā'dbhutā ‖ 22

Nādāntalīnā Sampūrṇā Pūrṇasthā Bahurūpikā ǀ
Bhṛṅgārāvā Vaṃśagatirvāditrā Murajadhvaniḥ ‖ 23

Varṇamālā Siddhikalā Ṣaṭ Cakrakramavāsinī ǀ
Mūlakelīratā Svādhiṣṭhānā Turyanivāsinī ‖ 24

Maṇipūrasthitiḥ Snigdhā Kūrmacakraparāyaṇā ǀ
Anāhatagatirdīpaśikhā Maṇimayākṛtiḥ ‖ 25

Viśuddhā Śabdasaṃśuddhā Jīvabodhasthalī Ravā ǀ
Ājñācakrābjasaṃsthā Ca Sphurantī Nipuṇā Trivṛt ‖ 26

Candrikā Candrakoṭi Śrīḥ Sūryakoṭiprabhāmayī ǀ
Padmarāgāruṇacchāyā Niścalā'mṛtanandinī ǀ
Kāntāṅgasaṅgamuditā Sudhāmādhuryasambhṛtā ‖ 28

Mahāmañcasthitā'liptā Tṛptā Dṛptā Susambhṛtiḥ ǀ
Sravatpīyūṣasaṃsiktā Raktārṇavavivardhinī ‖ 29

Suraktā Priyasaṃsiktā Śaśvatkuṇḍālayā'bhayā ǀ (200) ǀ
Śreyaḥ Śrutiśca Pratyekānavakeśiphalāvalī ‖ 30

Prītā Śivā Śivapriyā Śāṅkarī Śāmbhavī Vibhā ǀ
Svayambhūḥ Svapriyā Svīyā Svakīyā Janamātṛkā ‖ 31

Svārāmā Svāśrayā Sādhvī Sudhādhārā'dhikādhikā ǀ
Maṅgalojjayinī Mānyā Sarvamaṅgalasaṅginī ‖ 32

Bhadrā Bhadrāvalī Kanyā Kalitārdhendubimbabhāk ǀ
Kalyāṇalatikā Kāmyā Kukarmā Kumatirmanuḥ ‖ 33

Kuraṅgākṣī Kṣībanetrā Kṣārā Rasamadonmadā |
Vāruṇīpānamuditā Madirāracitāśrayā ‖ 34

Kādambarīpānarucirvipāśā Pāśabhītinut |
Muditā Muditāpāṅgā Daradolitadīrghadṛk ‖ 35

Daityakulānalaśikhā Manorathasudhādyutiḥ |
Suvāsinī Pīnagātrī Pīnaśroṇipayodharā ‖ 36

Sucārukabarī Dantadīdhitidīpramauktikā |
Bimbādharā Dyutimukhā Pravālottamadīdhitiḥ ‖ 37

Tilaprasūnanāsāgrā Hemakakkolabhālakā |
Niṣkalaṅkenduvadanā Bālendumukuṭojjvalā ‖ 38

Nṛtyatkhañjananetraśrīrvisphuratkarṇaśaṣkulī |
Bālacandrātapatrārdhā Maṇisūryakirīṭinī ‖ 39

Hemamāṇikyatāṭaṅkā Maṇikāñcanakuṇḍalā |
Sucārucibukā Kambukaṇṭhī Maṇimanoramā ‖ 40

Gaṅgātaraṅgahārormirmattakokilaniḥsvanā |
Mṛṇālavilasadbāhuḥ Pāśāṅkuśadhanurdharā ‖ 41

Keyūrakaṭakācchannā Nānāratnamanoramā |
Tāmrapaṅkajapāṇiśrīrnakharatnaprabhāvatī ‖ 42

Aṅgulīyamaṇiśreṇicañcadaṅgulisantatiḥ |
Mandaradvandvasukucā Romarājībhujaṅgakā ‖ 43

Gambhīranābhistrivalīvalayā Ca Sumadhyamā |
Raṇatkāñcīguṇonnaddhā Paṭṭāṃśukasunīvikā ‖ 44

Meruguṇḍīnitambāḍhyā Gajagaṇḍoruyugmayuk |
Sujānumandarāsaktalasajjaṅghādvayānvitā ‖ 45

Gūḍhagulphā Mañjuśiñjanmaṇinūpuramaṇḍitā |
Yogidhyeyapadadvandvā Sudhāmā'mṛtasāriṇī ‖ 46

Lāvaṇyasindhuḥ Sindūratilakā Kuṭilālakā |

Sādhusiddhā Subuddhā Ca Budhā Vṛndārakodayā || 47

Bālārkakiraṇaśreṇīśoṇā Śrīpremakāmadhuk |

Rasagambhīrasarasī Padminī (300) Rasasārasā || 48

Prasannā''sannavaradā Śāradā Ca Subhāgyadā |

Naṭarājapriyā Viśvanāṭyā Nartakanartakī || 49

Vicitrayantrā Cittantrā Vidyāvallī Gatiḥ Śubhā |

Kūṭārakūṭā Kūṭasthā Pañcakūṭā Ca Pañcamī || 50

Catuṣkūṭā Trikūṭādyā Ṣaṭkūṭā Vedapūjitā |

Kūṭaṣoḍaśasampannā Turīyā Paramā Kalā || 51

Ṣoḍaśī Mantrayantrāṇāmīśvarī Merumaṇḍalā |

Ṣoḍaśārṇā Trivarṇā Ca Bindunādasvarūpiṇī || 52

Varṇātītā Varṇamātā Śabdabrahmamahāsukhā |

Caitanyavallī Kūṭātmā Kāmeśī Svapradṛśyagā || 53

Svapnāvatī Bodhakarī Jāgṛtirjāgarāśrayā |

Svapnāśrayā Suṣuptiśca Tandrāmuktā Ca Mādhavī || 54

Lopāmudrā Kāmarājñī Mānavī Vittapārcitā |

Śākambharī Nandividyā Bhāsvadvidyotamālinī || 55

Māhendrī Svargasampattirdurvāsaḥsevitā Śrutiḥ |

Sādhakendragatiḥ Sādhvī Sulabhā Siddhikandarā || 56

Puratrayeśī Purajidarcitā Puradevatā |

Puṣṭirvighnaharī Bhūtirviguṇā Pūjyakāmadhuk || 57

Hiraṇyamātā Gaṇapā Guhamātā Nitambinī |

Sarvasīmantinī Mokṣā Dīkṣā Dīkṣitamātṛkā || 58

Sādhakāmbā Siddhamātā Sādhakendrā Manoramā |

Yauvanonmādinī Tuṅgā Suśroṇirmadamantharā || 59

Padmaraktotpalavatī Raktamālyānulepanā |

Raktamālāruciḥ Śikhāśikhaṇḍinyatisundarī ‖ 60

Śikhaṇḍinṛttasantuṣṭā Saurabheyī Vasundharā |

Surabhiḥ Kāmadā Kāmyā Kamanīyārthakāmadā ‖ 61

Nandinī Lakṣaṇavatī Vasiṣṭhālayadevatā |

Golokadevī (400) Lokaśrīrgolokaparipālikā ‖ 62

Havirdhānī Devamātā Vṛndārakavarānuyuk |

Rudrapatnī Bhadramātā Sudhādhārā'mbuvikṣatiḥ ‖ 63

Dakṣiṇā Yajñasammūrtiḥ Subālā Dhīranandinī |

Kṣīrapūrṇārṇavagatiḥ Sudhāyoniḥ Sulocanā ‖ 64

Rāmānugā Susevyā Ca Sugandhālayavāsagā |

Sucāritrā Sutripurā Sustanī Stanavatsalā ‖ 65

Rajasvalā Rajoyuktā Rañjikā Raṅgamālikā |

Raktapriyā Suraktā Ca Ratiraṅgasvarūpiṇī ‖ 66

Rajaḥ Śukrāmbikā Niṣṭhā Rataniṣṭhā Ratispṛhā |

Hāvabhāvā Kāmakelisarvasvā Surajīvikā ‖ 67

Svayambhūkusumānandā Svayambhūkusumapriyā |

Svayambhūprītisantuṣṭā Svayambhūnindakāntakṛt ‖ 68

Svayambhūsthā Śaktipuṭī Ratisarvasvapīṭhikā |

Atyantasabhikā Dūtī Vidagdhā Prītipūjitā ‖ 69

Kullikā Yantranilayā Yogapīṭhādhivāsinī |

Sulakṣaṇā Rasarūpā Sarvalakṣaṇalakṣitā ‖ 70

Nānālaṅkārasubhagā Pañcabāṇasamarcitā |

Ūrdhvatrikoṇanilayā Bālā Kāmeśvarī Tathā ‖ 71

Gaṇādhyakṣā Kulādhyakṣā Lakṣmīścaiva Sarasvatī |

Vasantasamayaprītā Prītiḥ Kucabharānatā ‖ 72

Kalādharamukhā' mūrdhā Pādavṛddhiḥ Kalāvatī |

Puṣpapriyā Dhṛtiścaiva Ratikaṇṭhī Manoramā || 73

Madanonmādinī Caiva Mohinī Pārvaṇīkalā |

Śoṣiṇī Vaśinī Rājinyatyantasubhagā Bhagā || 74

Pūṣā Vaśā Ca Sumanā Ratiḥ Prītirdhṛtistathā |

Ṛddhiḥ Saumyā Marīcyaṃśumālā Pratyaṅgirā Tathā || 75

Śaśinī Caiva Succhāyā Sampūrṇamaṇḍalodayā |

Tuṣṭā Cāmṛtapūrṇā Ca Bhagayantranivāsinī || 76

Liṅgayantrālayā (500) Śambhurūpā Saṃyogayoginī |

Drāviṇī Bījarūpā Ca Akṣubdhā Sādhakapriyā || 77

Rājabījamayī Rājyasukhadā Vāñchitapradā |

Rajaḥ Saṃvīryaśaktiśca Śukravicchivarūpiṇī || 78

Sarvasārā Sāramayā Śivaśaktimayī Prabhā |

Saṃyogānandanilayā Saṃyogaprītimātṛkā || 79

Saṃyogakusumānandā Saṃyogā Yogavardhinī |

Saṃyogasukhadārasthā Cidānandaikasevitā || 80

Ardhyapūjakasampattirarghyadravyasvarūpiṇī |

Sāmarasyā Parā Prītā Priyasaṅgamarūpiṇī || 81

Jñānadūtī Jñānagamyā Jñānayoniḥ Śivālayā |

Citkalā Jñānasakalā Sakulā Sakulātmikā || 82

Kalācatuṣṭayī Padminyatisūkṣmā Parātmikā |

Haṃsakelisthalī Cchāyā Haṃsadvayavikāsinī || 83

Virāgatā Mokṣakalā Paramātmakalāvatī |

Vidyākalāntarātmasthā Catuṣṭayakalāvatī || 84

Vidyāsantoṣiṇī Tṛptiḥ Parabrahmaprakāśikā |

Paramātmaparā Vastulīnaśakticatuṣṭayī || 85

Śāntirbodhakalāvāptiḥ Parajñānātmikā Kalā |

Paśyantī Paramātmasthā Cāntarātmakalākulā ‖ 86

Madhyamā Vaikharī Cātmakalānandā Kalāvatī |

Tāriṇī Taraṇī Tārā Śivaliṅgālayā''tmavit ‖ 87

Parasparaśubhācārā Brahmānandavinodinī |

Rasālasā Dūtarāsā Sārthā Sārthapriyā Hyumā ‖ 88

Jātyādirahitā Yogiyoginyānandavardhinī |

Vīrabhāvapradā Divyā Vīrasūrvīrabhāvadā ‖ 89

Paśutvābhivīragatirvīrasaṅgamahodayā |

Mūrdhābhiṣikta Rājaśrīḥ Kṣatriyottamamātṛkā ‖ 90

Śastrāstrakuśalā Śobhā Rasasthā Yuddhajīvikā |

Vijayā Yoginī Yātrā Parasainyavimardinī ‖ 91

Pūrṇā (600) Vittaiṣiṇī Vittā Vittasañcayaśālinī |

Bhāṇḍāgārasthitā Ratnā Ratnaśreṇyadhivāsinī ‖ 92

Mahiṣī Rājabhogyā Ca Gaṇikā Gaṇabhogabhṛt |

Kariṇī Vaḍavā Yogyā Mallasenā Padātikā ‖ 93

Sainyaśreṇī Śauryaratā Patākādhvajavāsinī |

Succhatrā Cāmbikā Cāmbā Prajāpālanasadgatiḥ ‖ 94

Surabhiḥ Pūjakācārā Rājakāryaparāyaṇā |

Brahmakṣatramayī Somasūryāntaryāminī Sthitiḥ ‖ 95

Paurohityapriyā Sādhvī Brahmāṇī Yajñasantatiḥ |

Somapānaparā Prītā Janāḍhyā Tapanā Kṣamā ‖ 96

Pratigrahaparā Dātrī Sṛṣṭājātiḥ Satāṅgatiḥ |

Gāyatrī Vedalabhyā Ca Dīkṣā Sandhyāparāyaṇā ‖ 97

Ratnasaddīdhitirviśvavāsanā Viśvajīvikā |

Kṛṣivāṇijyabhūtiśca Vṛddhirdhīśca Kusīdikā ‖ 98

Kulādhārā Suprasārā Manonmanī Parāyaṇā |

Śūdrā Vipragatiḥ Karmakarī Kautukapūjitā ǁ 99

Nānāvicāracaturā Bālā Prauḍhā Kalāmayī |

Sukarṇadhārā Nauḥ Pārā Sarvāśā Durgamocanī ǁ 100

Durgā Vindhyavanasthā Ca Kandarpanayapūraṇī |

Bhūbhāraśamanī Kṛṣṇā Rakṣārādhyā Rasollasā ǁ 101

Trividhotpātaśamanī Samagrasukhaśevadhiḥ |

Pañcāvayavavākyaśrīḥ Prapañcodyānacandrikā ǁ 102

Siddhasandohasukhitā Yoginīvṛndavanditā |

Nityāṣoḍaśārūpā Ca Kāmeśī Bhagamālinī ǁ 103

Nityaklinnā Ca Bhī(Bhe) Ruṇḍā Vahnimaṇḍalavāsinī |

Mahāvidyeśvarī Nityā Śivadūtīti Viśrutā ǁ 104

Tvaritā Prathitā Khyātā Vikhyātā Kulasundarī |

Nityā Nīlapatākā Ca Vijayā Sarvamaṅgalā ǁ 105

Jvālāmālā(700) Vicitrā Ca Mahātripurasindarī |

Guruvṛndā Paraguruḥ Prakāśānandanāthinī ǁ 106

Śivānandanātharūpā Śaktyānandasvarūpiṇī |

Devyānandanāthamayī Kauleśānandanāthinī ǁ 107

Divyaughagururūpā Ca Samayānandanāthinī |

Śukladevyānandanāthā Kuleśānandanāthinī 1 ǁ 108

Klinnāṅgānandarūpā Ca Samayānandanāthinī |

Vedānandanāthamayī Sahajānandanāthinī ǁ 109

Siddhaughagururūpā Ca Aparāgururūpiṇī |

Gaganānandanāthā Ca Viśvānandasvanāthinī ǁ 110

Vimalānandanāthā Ca Madanānandanāthinī |

Bhuvanādyā Ca Līlādyā Nandanānandanāthinī ǁ 111

Svātmānandānandarūpā Priyādyānandanāthinī |
Mānavaughaguruśreṣṭhā Parameṣṭhi Guruprabhā || 112

Paraguhyā Guruśaktiḥ Svagurukīrtanapriyā |
Trailokyamohanakhyātā Sarvāśāparipūrakā || 113

Sarvasaṅkṣobhiṇī Pūrvāmnāyaprathitavaibhavā |
Śivāśaktiḥ Śivaśaktiḥ Śivacakratrayālayā || 114

Sarvasaubhāgyadākhyā Ca Sarvārthasādhikāhvayā |
Sarvarakṣākarākhyā Ca Dakṣiṇāmnāyadevatā || 115

Madhyārkacakranilayā Paścimāmnāyadevatā |
Navacakrakṛtāvāsā Kauberāmnāyadevatā || 116

Kuberapūjyā Kulajā Kulāmnāyapravartinī |
Binducakrakṛtāvāsā Madhyasiṃhāsaneśvarī || 117

Śrīvidyā Ca Mahālakṣmīḥ Lakṣmīḥ Śaktitrayātmikā |
Sarvasāmrājyalakṣmīśca Pañcalakṣmītiviśrutā || 118

Śrīvidyā Ca Parañjyotiḥ Paraniṣkalaśāmbhavī |
Mātṛkā Pañcakośī Ca Śrīvidyā Tvaritā Tathā || 119

Pārijāteśvarī Caiva Trikūṭā Pañcabāṇagā |
Pañcakalpalatā Pañcavidyā Cāmṛtapīṭhikā || 120

Sudhāsū Ramaṇeśānā Cānnapūrṇā Ca Kāmadhuk |
Śrīvidyā Siddhalakṣmīśca Mātaṅgī Bhuvaneśvarī || 121

Vārāhī Pañcaratnānāmīśvarī Mātṛvarṇagā |
Parāñjyotiḥ Kośarūpā Aindavī Kalayā Yutā || 122

Paritaḥ Svāminī Śaktidarśanā Ravibinduyuk |
Brahmadarśanarūpā Ca Śivadarśanarūpiṇī || 123

Viṣṇudarśanarūpā Ca Sṛṣṭicakranivāsinī |
Sauradarśanarūpā Ca Sthiticakrakṛtālayā || 124

Bauddhadarśanarūpā Ca Mahātripurasundarī |
Tattvamudrāsvarūpā Ca Prasannā(800) Jñānamudrikā || 125

Sarvopacārasantuṣṭā Hṛnmayī Śīrṣadevatā |
Śikhāsthitā Brahmamayī Netratrayavilāsinī || 126

Astrasthā Caturasrā Ca Dvārakādvāravāsinī |
Aṇimā Paścimasthā Ca Laghimottaradevatā || 127

Pūrvasthā Mahimeśitvā Dakṣiṇadvāradevatā |
Vaśitvā Vāyukoṇasthā Prākāmyeśānadevatā || 128

Agnikoṇasthitā Bhuktiricchā Nairṛtavāsinī |
Prāptisiddhiravasthā Ca Prākāmyārdhavilāsinī || 129

Brāhmī Māheśvarī Caiva Kaumārī Vaiṣṇavī Tathā |
Vārāhyaundrī Ca Cāmuṇḍā Mahālakṣmīrdiśāṅgatiḥ || 130

Kṣobhiṇī Drāviṇī Mudrā''karṣonmādanakāriṇī |
Mahāṅkuśā Khecarī Ca Bījākhyā Yonimudrikā || 131

Sarvāśāpūracakrasthā Kāryasiddhikarī Tathā |
Kāmākarṣiṇikāśaktirbuddhyākarṣaṇarūpiṇī || 132

Ahaṅkārākarṣiṇī Ca Śabdākarṣaṇarūpiṇī |
Sparśākarṣaṇarūpā Ca Rūpākarṣaṇarūpiṇī || 133

Rasākarṣaṇarūpā Ca Gandhākarṣaṇarūpiṇī |
Cittākarṣaṇarūpā Ca Dhairyākarṣaṇarūpiṇī || 134

Smṛtyākarṣaṇarūpā Ca Bījākarṣaṇarūpiṇī |
Amṛtākarṣiṇī Caiva Nāmākarṣaṇarūpiṇī || 135

Śarīrākarṣiṇīdevī Ātmākarṣaṇarūpiṇī |
Ṣoḍaśasvararūpā Ca Sravatpīyūṣamandirā || 136

Tripureśī Siddharūpā Kalādalanivāsinī |
Sarvasaṅkṣobhacakreśī Śaktirguptatarābhidhā || 137

Anaṅgakusumāśaktiranaṅgakaṭimekhalā |

Anaṅgamadanā'naṅgamadanāturarūpiṇī || 138

Anaṅgarekhā Cānaṅgavegānaṅgāṅkuśābhidhā |

Anaṅgamālinī Śaktiraṣṭavargadiganvitā || 139

Vasupatrakṛtāvāsā Śrīmattripurasundarī |

Sarvasāmrājyasukhadā Sarvasaubhāgyadeśvarī || 140

Sampradāyeśvarī Sarvasaṅkṣobhaṇakarī Tathā |

Sarvavidrāviṇī Sarvākarṣaṇāṭopakāriṇī || 141

Sarvāhlādanaśaktiśca Sarvajṛmbhaṇakāriṇī |

Sarvastambhana Śaktiśca Sarvasammohinī Tathā || 142

Sarvavaśyakarīśaktiḥ Sarvasarvānurañjinī |

Sarvonmādanaśaktiśca Sarvārthasiddhikāriṇī || 143

Sarvasampattidā Śaktiḥ Sarvamantramayī Tathā |

Sarvadvandvakṣayakarī(900) Siddhistripuravāsinī || 144

Sarvārthasādhakeśī Ca Sarvakāryārthasiddhidā |

Caturdaśāracakreśī Kalāyogasamanvitā || 145

Sarvasiddhipradā Devī Sarvasampatpradā Tathā |

Sarvapriyaṅkarī Śaktiḥ Sarvamaṅgalakāriṇī || 146

Sarvakāmaprapūrṇā Ca Sarvaduḥkhapramocinī |

Sarvamṛtyupraśamanī Sarvavighnavināśinī || 147

Sarvāṅgasundarī Devī Sarvasaubhāgyadāyinī |

Tripureśī Sarvasiddhipradā Ca Daśakoṇagā || 148

Sarvarakṣākareśī Ca Nigarbhā Yoginī Tathā |

Sarvajñā Sarvaśaktiśca Sarvaiśvaryapradā Tathā || 149

Sarvajñānamayīdevī Sarvavyādhivināśinī |

Sarvādhārasvarūpā Ca Sarvapāpaharā Tathā || 150

Sarvānandamayīdevī Sarvarakṣāsvarūpiṇī |

Mahimāśaktidevī Ca Devī Sarvasamṛddhidā ‖ 151

Antardaśāracakreśī Devī Tripuramālinī |

Sarvarogahareśī Ca Rahasyā Yoginī Tathā ‖ 152

Vāgdevī Vaśinī Caiva Devīkāmeśvarī Tathā |

Modinī Vimalā Caiva Aruṇā Jayinī Tathā ‖ 153

Sarveśvarī Kaulinī Ca Hyaṣṭārasarvasiddhidā |

Sarvakāmapradeśī Ca Parāpararahasyavit ‖ 154

Trikoṇacaturaśrasthā Sarvaiśvaryā''yudhātmikā |

Kāmeśvarībāṇarūpā Kāmeśīcāparūpiṇī ‖ 155

Kāmeśīpāśarūpā Ca Kāmeśyaṅkuśarūpiṇī |

Kāmeśvarīndraśaktiśca Agnicakrakṛtālayā ‖ 156

Kāmagiryadhidevī Ca Trikoṇasthā'grakoṇagā |

Dakṣakoṇeśvarī Viṣṇuśaktirjālandharāśrayā ‖ 157

Sūryacakrālayā Rudraśaktirvāmāṅgakoṇagā |

Somacakrā Brahmaśaktiḥ Pūrṇagiryanurāgiṇī ‖ 158

Śrīmattrikoṇabhuvanā Tripurātmā Maheśvarī |

Sarvānandamayeśī Ca Bindugātirahasyabhṛt ‖ 159

Parabrahmasvarūpā Ca Mahātripurasundarī |

Sarvacakrāntarasthā Ca Samastacakranāyikā ‖ 160

Sarvacakreśvarī Sarvamantrāṇāmīśvarī Tathā |

Sarvavidyeśvarī Caiva Sarvavāgīśvarī Tathā ‖ 161

Sarvayogīśvarī Caiva Pīṭheśvaryakhileśvarī |

Sarvakāmeśvarī Sarvatattveśvaryāgameśvarī ‖ 162

Śaktiḥ Śaktidhṛgullāsā Nirdvandvā Dvaitagarbhiṇī |

Niṣprapañcā Mahāmāyā Saprapañcā Suvāsinī ‖ 163

Sarvaviśvotpattidhātrī Paramānandasundarī (1000) |

Phala Śruti ||

Ityetatkathitaṃ Divyaṃ Paramānandakāraṇam || 164

Lāvaṇyasindhulaharībālāyāstoṣamandiram |
Sahasranāma Tantrāṇāṃ Sāramākṛṣya Pārvati || 165

Anena Stuvato Nityamardharātre Niśāmukhe |
Prātaḥ Kāle Ca Pūjāyāṃ Sarvakālamataḥ Priye || 166

Sarvasāmrājyasukhadā Bālā Ca Parituṣyati |
Ratnāni Vividhānyasya Vittāni Pracurāṇi Ca || 167

Manorathapathasthāni Dadāti Parameśvarī |
Putrāḥ Pautrāśca Vardhante Santatiḥ Sārvakālikī || 168

Śatravastasya Naśyanti Vardhante'sya Balāni Ca |
Vyādhayastasya Dūrasthāḥ Sakalānyauṣadhāni Ca || 169

Mandirāṇi Vicitrāṇi Rājante Tasya Sarvadā |
Kṛṣiḥ Phalavatī Tasya Bhūmiḥ Kāmadughā'vyayā || 170

Sphīto Janapadastasya Rājyaṃ Tasya Nirītikam |
Mātaṅgāḥ Pakṣiṇastuṅgāḥ Siñcanto Madavāribhiḥ || 171

Dvāre Tasya Virājante Hṛṣṭā Nāgaturaṅgamāḥ |
Prajāstasya Virājante Nirvivādāśca Mantriṇaḥ || 172

Jñātayastasya Tuṣyanti Śīlaṃ Tasyātisundaram |
Lakṣmīstasya Vaśe Nityaṃ Svāsanā Ca Manoramā || 173

Gadyapadyamayī Vāṇī Tasya Gaṅgātaraṅgavat |
Nānāpadapadārthānāṃ Vādacāturyasambhṛtā || 174

Samagrarasasampattiśālinī Lāsyamālinī |
Adṛṣṭānyapi Śāstrāṇī Prakāśyante Nirantaram || 175

Nigrahaḥ Paravākyānāṃ Sabhāyāṃ Tasya Jāyate |

Stuvanti Vandinastaṃ Vai Rājāno Dāsavattathā || 176

Śastrāṇyastrāṇi Tadaṅge Janayanti Rujāṃ Na Hi |

Mahilāstasya Vaśagāḥ Sarvāvasthā Bhavanti Vai || 177

Viṣaṃ Nirviṣatāṃ Yāti Pānīyamamṛtaṃ Bhavet |

Parapakṣastambhanaṃ Ca Pratipakṣasya Jṛmbhaṇam || 178

Navarātreṇa Jāyeta Sa Tadabhyāsayogavit |

Ahorātraṃ Paṭhedyastu Nistandraḥ Śāntamānasaḥ || 179

Vaśe Tasya Prajā Yāti Sarve Lokāḥ Suniścitam |

Ṣaṇmāsābhyāsayogena Yogamāyāti Niścitam || 180

Nityaṃ Kāmakalāṃ Dhyāyan Yaḥ Paṭhet Stotramuttamam |

Madanonmādakalitāḥ Puraṅghryāstadvaśānugāḥ || 181

Lāvaṇyamadanāḥ Sākṣādvaidagdhyamuditekṣaṇāḥ |

Premapūrṇāmapi Vaśe Hyurvaśīṃ Sa Hi Vindati || 182

Bhūrjapatre Rocanayā Kuṅkumena Śubhe Dine |

Lākṣārasadraveṇāpi Yāvakairvā Viśeṣataḥ || 183

Dhāturāgeṇa Vā Devi Likhitaṃ Yantramañcitam |

Suvarṇaraupyagarbhasthaṃ Susampūtaṃ Susādhitam || 184

Bālābuddhyā Pūjitaṃ Ca Pratiṣṭhitasamīraṇam |

Dhārayenmastake Kaṇṭhe Bāhumūle Tathā Hṛdi || 185

Nābhau Vāpi Dhṛtaṃ Dhanyaṃ Jayadaṃ Sarvakāmadam |

Rakṣaṇaṃ Nāparaṃ Kiñcidvidyate Bhuvanatraye || 186

Graharogādibhayahṛt Sukhakṛtyavivardhanam |

Balavīryakaraṃ Krūrabhūtaśatruvināśanam || 187

Putrapautrān Guṇagaṇairvardhanaṃ Dhanadhānyakṛt |

Dharaṇyāṃ Sā Purī Dhanyā Yatrāyaṃ Sādhakottamaḥ || 188

Yadgṛhe Likhitaṃ Tiṣṭhet Stotrametadvarānane |
Tatra Cāhaṃ Śive Nityaṃ Hariśca Kamalā Tathā || 189

Vasāmaḥ Sarvatīrthānāmutpattistatra Jāyate |
Yo Vāpi Pāṭhayedbhaktyā Paṭhedvai Sādhakottamaḥ || 190

Jñānānandakalāyogādaikyavṛttiṃ Sa Vindati |
Stotreṇānena Deveśi Tava Pūjāphalaṃ Labhet || 191

Śoḍhānyāsatanurbhūtvā Paṭhitavyaṃ Prayatnataḥ |
Uttamā Sarvatantrāṇāṃ Bālāyāḥ Pūjanasrutiḥ || 192

Tatrottamā Ṣoḍaśārṇā Tatredaṃ Stotramuttamam |
Nāśiṣyāya Pradātavyamaśuddhāya Śaṭhāya Ca || 193

Alasāyāprayatnāyāśivābhaktāya Sundari |
Bhaktihīnāya Maline Gurunindāparāya Ca || 194

Viṣṇubhaktivihīnāya Vikalpāvṛtabuddhaye |
Deyaṃ Bhaktavare Mukteḥ Kāraṇaṃ Bhaktivardhanam || 195

Latāyoge Paṭhedyastu Stotrametadvarānane |
Saiva Kalpalatā Tasya Vāñchāphalakarī Tathā || 196

Puṣpitāyā Latāyoge Kuraṅgamukhi Sādhakaḥ |
Akṣubdhaḥ San Paṭhedyastu Śatayajñasya Puṇyabhāk || 197

Brahmādayo'pi Deveśi Prārthayanti Padadvayam |
Svayaṃ Śivaḥ Sa Vijñeyo Yo Bālābhāvalampaṭaḥ || 198

Brahmānandamayī Jyotsnā Sadāśivavidhūditā |
Ānando Yo'pi Yaṃ Vedā Vadantyasyā Vaśe Sthitāḥ || 199

Āhlādanaṃ Bālādhyānādbālāyā Nāmakīrtanāt |
Sadānandābhyāsayogāt Sadānandaḥ Prajāyate || 200

Iti Śrīrudrayāmale Tantre Bhairavabhairavīsaṃvāde Śrī Tripura Sundarī
Sahasranāma Stotraṃ Sampūrṇam ||

श्री त्रिपुरसुन्दरीसहस्रनाम स्तोत्रम्

समाध्युपरतं काले कदाचिद्द्विजने मुदा।
परमानन्दसन्दोहमुदितं प्राह पार्वती॥ १

श्रीदेव्युवाच -
श्रीमन्नाथ तवानन्दकारणं ब्रूहि शङ्कर।
योगीन्द्रोपास्य देवेश प्रेमपूर्ण सुधानिधे।
कृपास्ति यदि मे शम्भो सुगोप्यमपि कथ्यताम्॥ २

श्रीभैरवः
निर्भरानन्दसन्दोहः शक्तिभावेन जायते।
लावण्यसिन्धुस्तत्रास्ति बालाया रसकन्दरः॥ ३

तामेवानुक्षणं देवीं चिन्तयामि ततः शिवाम्।
तस्या नामसहस्राणि कथयामि तव प्रिये॥ ४

सुगोप्यान्यपि रम्भोरु गम्भीरस्नेहविभ्रमात्।
तामेव स्तुवतो देवि ध्यायतोऽनुक्षणं मम।
सुखसन्दोहसम्भावो ज्ञानानन्दस्य कारणम्॥ ५

अस्य श्रीत्रिपुरसुन्दरी सहस्रनामस्तोत्रस्य शङ्कर ऋषिः;
अनुष्टुप् छन्दः। श्रीत्रिपुरसुन्दरी देवता। ऐं बीजम्। सौः शक्तिः।
क्लीं कीलकम्।
श्रीत्रिपुरसुन्दरी प्रीत्यर्थे समस्तपुरुषार्थसिद्ध्यर्थे पारायणे विनियोगः।

ॐ ऐं अङ्गुष्ठाभ्यां नमः। ॐ क्लीं तर्जनीभ्यां नमः।
ॐ सौः मध्यमाभ्यां नमः। ॐ ऐं अनामिकाभ्यां नमः।
ॐ क्लीं कनिष्ठिकाभ्यां नमः। ॐ सौः करतलकरपृष्ठाभ्यां नमः।

ॐ ऐं हृदयाय नमः।   ॐ क्लीं शिरसे स्वाहा।
ॐ सौः शिखायै वषट्।   ॐ ऐं कवचाय हुं।
ॐ क्लीं नेत्रत्रयाय वौषट्।   ॐ सौः अस्त्राय फट्।
भूर्भुवस्सुवरोमितिदिग्बन्धः॥

॥ ध्यानम्॥

बालार्कायुततेजसं त्रिनयनं रक्ताम्बरोल्लासिनीं
नानालंकृति राजमानवपुषं बालोडुराट्शेखरम्।
हस्तैरिक्षु धनुः सृणिं सुमशरं पाशं मुदा
बिभ्रतीं श्रीचक्रस्थितसुन्दरीं त्रिजगतामाधारभूतां स्मरेत्॥

॥ लं इत्यादि पञ्चपूजा॥

लं पृथिव्यात्मिकायै गन्धं समर्पयामि।
हं आकाशात्मिकायै पुष्पैः पूजयामि।
यं वाय्वात्मिकायै कुङ्कुमं आवाहयामि।
रं वह्यात्मिकायै दीपं दर्शयामि।
वं अमृतात्मिकायै अमृतं महानैवेद्यं निवेदयामि।
सं सर्वात्मिकायै सर्वोपचारपूजां समर्पयामि॥

अथ सहस्रनाम स्तोत्र: ॥

आनन्दसिन्धुरानन्दाऽऽनन्दमूर्तिर्विनोदिनी।
त्रिपुरा सुन्दरी प्रेमपाथोनिधिरनुत्तमा॥ १

वामार्धगह्वरा भूतिर्विभूतिः शङ्करी शिवा।
शृङ्गारमूर्तिर्वरदा रसा च शुभगोचरा॥ २

परमानन्दलहरी रती रङ्गवती गतिः।
रङ्गमालानङ्गकला केली कैवल्यदा कला॥ ३

रसकल्पा कल्पलता कुतूहलवती गतिः।
विनोददिग्धा सुस्निग्धा मुग्धमूर्तिर्मनोरमा॥ ४

बालार्ककोटिकिरणा चन्द्रकोटिसुशीतला।
स्रवत्पीयूषदिग्धाङ्गी स्वर्गार्थपरिकल्पिता॥ ५

कुरङ्गनयना कान्ता सुगतिः सुखसन्ततिः।
राजराजेश्वरी राज्ञी महेन्द्रपरिवन्दिता॥ ६

प्रपञ्चगतिरीशानी प्रपञ्चगतिरुत्तमा।
दुर्वासा दुःसहा शक्तिः शिञ्जत्कनकनूपुरा॥ ७

मेरुमन्दरवक्षोजा सृणिपाशवरायुधा ।
शरकोदण्डसंसक्तपाणिद्वयविराजिता ॥ ८

चन्द्रबिम्बानना चारुमुकुटोत्तंसचन्द्रिका ।
सिन्दूतिलका चारुधम्मिल्लामलमालिका ॥ ९

मन्दारदाममुदिता रत्नमालाविभूषिता ।
सुवर्णाभरणप्रीता मुक्तादाममनोरमा ॥ १०

ताम्बूलपूर्णवदना मदनानन्दमानसा ।
सुखाराध्या तपः सारा कृपापारा विधीश्वरी ॥ ११

वक्षःस्थललसद्रत्नप्रभा मधुरसोन्मदा ।
बिन्दुनादात्मकोच्चाररहिता तुर्यरूपिणी ॥ १२

कमनीयाकृतिर्धन्या शाङ्करी प्रीतिमञ्जरी ।
प्रपञ्चा पञ्चमी पूर्णा पूर्णपीठनिवासिनी ॥ १३

राज्यलक्ष्मीश्च श्रीलक्ष्मीर्महालक्ष्मीः सुराजिका ।
सन्तोषसीमा सम्पत्तिः शातकौम्भी तथा द्युतिः ॥ १४

परिपूर्णा जगद्धात्री विधात्री बलवर्धिनी ।
सार्वभौमनृपश्रीश्च साम्राज्यगतिरम्बिका ॥ १५

सरोजाक्षी दीर्घदृष्टिः साचीक्षणविचक्षणा ।
रङ्गस्त्रवन्ती रसिका (१००) प्रधाना रसरूपिणी ॥ १६

रससिन्धुः सुगात्री च धूसरी मैथुनोन्मुखा ।
निरन्तरगुणासक्ता शक्तिर्निधुवनात्मिका ॥ १७

कामाक्षी कमनीया च कामेशी भगमङ्गला ।
सुभगा भोगिनी भोग्या भग्यदा सुभगा भगा ॥ १८

भगलिङ्गानन्दकला भगमध्यनिवासिनी ।
भगरूपा भगमयी भगयन्त्रा भगोत्तमा ॥ १९

योनिमुद्रा कामकला कुलामृतपरायणा ।
कुलकुण्डालया सूक्ष्मा जीवात्मा लिङ्गरूपिणी ॥ २०

मूलक्रिया मूलरूपा मूलाकृतिस्वरूपिणी।
सोत्सुका कमलानन्दा चिद्द्रावाऽऽत्मगतिः शिवा ॥ २१

श्वेतारुणा बिन्दुरूपा वेदयोनिर्ध्वनिक्षणा ।
घण्टाकोटि खारावा रविबिम्बोत्थिताऽद्भुता॥ २२

नादान्तलीना सम्पूर्णा पूर्णस्था बहुरूपिका।
भृङ्गारावा वंशगतिर्वादित्रा मुरजध्वनिः॥ २३

वर्णमाला सिद्धिकला षट् चक्रक्रमवासिनी ।
मूलकेलीरता स्वाधिष्ठाना तुर्यनिवासिनी॥ २४

मणिपूरस्थितिः स्निग्धा कूर्मचक्रपरायणा ।
अनाहतगतिर्दीपशिखा मणिमयाकृतिः ॥ २५

विशुद्धा शब्दसंशुद्धा जीवबोधस्थली रवा।
आज्ञाचक्राब्जसंस्था च स्फुरन्ती निपुणा त्रिवृत्॥ २६

चन्द्रिका चन्द्रकोटि श्रीः सूर्यकोटिप्रभामयी।
पद्मरागारुणच्छाया निश्चलाऽमृतनन्दिनी ।
कान्ताङ्गसङ्गमुदिता सुधामाधुर्यसम्भृता॥ २८

महामञ्चस्थिताऽलिप्ता तृप्ता दृप्ता सुसम्भृतिः ।
स्रवत्पीयूषसंसिक्ता रक्तार्णवविवर्धिनी ॥ २९

सुरक्ता प्रियसंसिक्ता शश्वत्कुण्डालयाऽभया। (२००)।
श्रेयः श्रुतिश्च प्रत्येकानवकेशिफलावली॥ ३०

प्रीता शिवा शिवप्रिया शाङ्करी शाम्भवी विभा।
स्वयम्भूः स्वप्रिया स्वीया स्वकीया जनमातृका॥ ३१

स्वारामा स्वाश्रया साध्वी सुधाधाराऽधिकाधिका ।
मङ्गलोज्जयिनी मान्या सर्वमङ्गलसङ्गिनी॥ ३२

भद्रा भद्रावली कन्या कलितार्धेन्दुबिम्बभाक् ।
कल्याणलतिका काम्या कुकर्मा कुमतिर्मनुः॥ ३३

कुरङ्गाक्षी क्षीबनेत्रा क्षारा रसमदोन्मदा ।
वारुणीपानमुदिता मदिरारचिताश्रया ॥ ३४

कादम्बरीपानरुचिर्विपाशा पाशभीतिनुत् ।
मुदिता मुदितापाङ्गा दरदोल्लितदीर्घदृक् ॥ ३५

दैत्यकुलानलशिखा मनोरथसुधाद्युतिः ।
सुवासिनी पीनगात्री पीनश्रोणिपयोधरा ॥ ३६

सुचारुकबरी दन्तदीधितिदीप्रमौक्तिका ।
बिम्बाधरा द्युतिमुखा प्रवालोत्तमदीधितिः ॥ ३७

तिलप्रसूननासाग्रा हेमकक्कोलभालका ।
निष्कलङ्केन्दुवदना बालेन्दुमुकुटोज्ज्वला ॥ ३८

नृत्यत्खञ्जननेत्रश्रीर्विस्फुरत्कर्णशष्कुली ।
बालचन्द्रातपत्रार्धा मणिसूर्यकिरीटिनी १ ॥ ३९

हेममाणिक्यताटङ्का मणिकाञ्चनकुण्डला ।
सुचारुचिबुका कम्बुकण्ठी मणिमनोरमा ॥ ४०

गङ्गातरङ्गहारोर्मिर्मत्तकोकिलनिःस्वना ।
मृणालविलसद्बाहुः पाशाङ्कुशधनुर्धरा ॥ ४१

केयूरकटकाच्छन्ना नानारत्नमनोरमा ।
ताम्रपङ्कजपाणिश्रीर्नखरत्नप्रभावती ॥ ४२

अङ्गुलीयमणिश्रेणिचञ्चदङ्गुलिसन्ततिः ।
मन्दरद्वन्द्वसुकुचा रोमराजीभुजङ्गका ॥ ४३

गम्भीरनाभिस्त्रिवलीवलया च सुमध्यमा ।
रणत्काञ्चीगुणोन्नद्धा पट्टांशुकसुनीविका ॥ ४४

मेरुगुण्डीनितम्बाढ्या गजगण्डोरुयुग्मयुक् ।
सुजानुमन्दरासक्तलसज्जङ्घाद्वयान्विता ॥ ४५

गूढगुल्फा मञ्जुशिञ्जन्मणिनूपुरमण्डिता ।
योगिध्येयपदद्वन्द्वा सुधामोऽमृतसारिणी ॥ ४६

लावण्यसिन्धुः सिन्दूतिलका कुटिलालका ।
साधुसिद्धा सुबुद्धा च बुधा वृन्दारकोदया ॥ ४७

बालार्ककिरणश्रेणीशोणा श्रीप्रेमकामधुक् ।
रसगम्भीरसरसी पद्मिनी (३००) रससारसा ॥ ४८

प्रसन्नाऽऽसन्नवरदा शारदा च सुभाग्यदा ।
नटराजप्रिया विश्वनाट्या नर्तकनर्तकी ॥ ४९

विचित्रयन्त्रा चित्तन्त्रा विद्यावल्ली गतिः शुभा ।
कूटारकूटा कूटस्था पञ्चकूटा च पञ्चमी ॥ ५०

चतुष्कूटा त्रिकूटाढ्या षट्कूटा वेदपूजिता ।
कूटषोडशसम्पन्ना तुरीया परमा कला ॥ ५१

षोडशी मन्त्रयन्त्राणामीश्वरी मेरुमण्डला ।
षोडशार्णा त्रिवर्णा च बिन्दुनादस्वरूपिणी ॥ ५२

वर्णातीता वर्णमाता शब्दब्रह्ममहासुखा ।
चैतन्यवल्ली कूटात्मा कामेशी स्वप्रदृश्यगा ॥ ५३

स्वप्नावती बोधकरी जागृतिर्जागराश्रया ।
स्वप्नाश्रया सुषुप्तिश्च तन्द्रामुक्ता च माधवी ॥ ५४

लोपामुद्रा कामराज्ञी मानवी वित्तपार्चिता ।
शाकम्भरी नन्दिविद्या भास्वद्विद्योतमालिनी ॥ ५५

माहेन्द्री स्वर्गसम्पत्तिर्दुर्वासःसेविता श्रुतिः ।
साधकेन्द्रगतिः साध्वी सुलभा सिद्धिकन्दरा ॥ ५६

पुरत्रयेशी पुरजिदर्चिता पुरदेवता ।
पुष्टिर्विघ्नहरी भूतिर्विगुणा पूज्यकामधुक् ॥ ५७

हिरण्यमाता गणपा गुहमाता नितम्बिनी ।
सर्वसीमन्तिनी मोक्षा दीक्षा दीक्षितमातृका ॥ ५८

साधकाम्बा सिद्धमाता साधकेन्द्रा मनोरमा ।
यौवनोन्मादिनी तुङ्गा सुश्रोणिर्मदमन्थरा ॥ ५९

पद्मरक्तोत्पलवती रक्तमाल्यानुलेपना ।
रक्तमालारुचिः शिखाशिखण्डिन्यतिसुन्दरी ॥ ६०

शिखण्डिनृत्तसन्तुष्टा सौरभेयी वसुन्धरा।
सुरभिः कामदा काम्या कमनीयार्थकामदा॥ ६१

नन्दिनी लक्षणवती वसिष्ठालयदेवता।
गोलोकदेवी (४००) लोकश्रीर्गोलोकपरिपालिका॥ ६२

हविर्धानी देवमाता वृन्दारकवरानुयुक्।
रुद्रपत्नी भद्रमाता सुधाधाराम्बुविक्षतिः॥ ६३

दक्षिणा यज्ञसम्मूर्तिः सुबाला धीरनन्दिनी।
क्षीरपूर्णार्णवगतिः सुधायोनिः सुलोचना॥ ६४

रामानुगा सुसेव्या च सुगन्धालयवासगा।
सुचारित्रा सुत्रिपुरा सुस्तनी स्तनवत्सला॥ ६५

रजस्वला रजोयुक्ता रञ्जिका रङ्गमालिका।
रक्तप्रिया सुरक्ता च रतिरङ्गस्वरूपिणी॥ ६६

रजः शुक्राम्बिका निष्ठा रतनिष्ठा रतिस्पृहा।
हावभावा कामकेलिसर्वस्वा सुरजीविका॥ ६७

स्वयम्भूकुसुमानन्दा स्वयम्भूकुसुमप्रिया।
स्वयम्भूप्रीतिसन्तुष्टा स्वयम्भूनिन्दकान्तकृत्॥ ६८

स्वयम्भूस्था शक्तिपुटी रतिसर्वस्वपीठिका।
अत्यन्तसभिका दूती विदग्धा प्रीतिपूजिता॥ ६९

कुल्लिका यन्त्रनिलया योगपीठाधिवासिनी।
सुलक्षणा रसरूपा सर्वलक्षणलक्षिता॥ ७०

नानालङ्कारसुभगा पञ्चबाणसमर्चिता।
ऊर्ध्वत्रिकोणनिलया बाला कामेश्वरी तथा॥ ७१

गणाध्यक्षा कुलाध्यक्षा लक्ष्मीश्चैव सरस्वती।
वसन्तसमयप्रीता प्रीतिः कुचभरानता॥ ७२

कलाधरमुखाऽमूर्धा पादवृद्धिः कलावती।
पुष्पप्रिया धृतिश्चैव रतिकण्ठी मनोरमा॥ ७३

मदनोन्मादिनी चैव मोहिनी पार्वणीकला ।
शोषिणी वशिनी राजिन्यत्यन्तसुभगा भगा॥ ७४

पूषा वशा च सुमना रतिः प्रीतिर्धृतिस्तथा ।
ऋद्धिः सौम्या मरीच्यंशुमाला प्रत्यङ्गिरा तथा॥ ७५

शशिनी चैव सुच्छाया सम्पूर्णमण्डलोदया ।
तुष्टा चामृतपूर्णा च भगयन्त्रनिवासिनी ॥ ७६

लिङ्गयन्त्रालया (५००) शम्भुरूपा संयोगयोगिनी ।
द्राविणी बीजरूपा च अक्षुब्धा साधकप्रिया॥ ७७

राजबीजमयी राज्यसुखदा वाञ्छितप्रदा ।
रजः संवीर्यशक्तिश्च शुक्रविच्छिवरूपिणी॥ ७८

सर्वसारा सारमया शिवशक्तिमयी प्रभा ।
संयोगानन्दनिलया संयोगप्रीतिमातृका॥ ७९

संयोगकुसुमानन्दा संयोगा योगवर्धिनी।
संयोगसुखदारस्थाचिदानन्दैकसेविता ॥ ८०

अर्ध्यपूजकसम्पत्तिरर्घ्यद्रव्यस्वरूपिणी ।
सामरस्या परा प्रीता प्रियसङ्गमरूपिणी॥ ८१

ज्ञानदूती ज्ञानगम्या ज्ञानयोनिः शिवालया ।
चित्कला ज्ञानसकला सकुला सकुलात्मिका ॥ ८२

कलाचतुष्ट्यी पद्मिन्यतिसूक्ष्मा परात्मिका ।
हंसकेलिस्थली च्छाया हंसद्वयविकासिनी ॥ ८३

विरागता मोक्षकला परमात्मकलावती ।
विद्याकलान्तरात्मस्था चतुष्ट्यकलावती ॥ ८४

विद्यासन्तोषिणी तृप्तिः परब्रह्मप्रकाशिका ।
परमात्मपरा वस्तुलीनशक्तिचतुष्ट्यी॥ ८५

शान्तिर्बोधकलावाप्तिः परज्ञानात्मिका कला ।
पश्यन्ती परमात्मस्था चान्तरात्मकलाकुला॥ ८६

मध्यमा वैखरी चात्मकलानन्दा कलावती ।
तारिणी तरणी तारा शिवलिङ्गालयाऽऽत्मवित् ॥ ८७

परस्परशुभाचारा ब्रह्मानन्दविनोदिनी ।
रसालसा दूतरासा सार्थरा सार्थप्रिया ह्युमा ॥ ८८

जात्यादिरहिता योगियोगिन्यानन्दवर्धिनी ।
वीरभावप्रदा दिव्या वीरसूर्वीरभावदा ॥ ८९

पशुत्वाभिवीरगतिर्वीरसङ्गमहोदया ।
मूर्धाभिषिक्त राजश्रीः क्षत्रियोत्तममातृका ॥ ९०

शस्त्रास्त्रकुशला शोभा रसस्था युद्धजीविका ।
विजया योगिनी यात्रा परसैन्यविमर्दिनी ॥ ९१

पूर्णा (६००) वित्तैषिणी वित्ता वित्तसञ्चयशालिनी ।
भाण्डागारस्थिता रत्ना रत्नश्रेण्यधिवासिनी ॥ ९२

महिषी राजभोग्या च गणिका गणभोगभृत् ।
करिणी वडवा योग्या मल्लसेना पदातिका ॥ ९३

सैन्यश्रेणी शौर्यरता पताकाध्वजवासिनी ।
सुच्छत्रा चाम्बिका चाम्बा प्रजापालनसद्व्रतिः ॥ ९४

सुरभिः पूजकाचारा राजकार्यपरायणा ।
ब्रह्मक्षत्रमयी सोमसूर्यान्तर्यामिनी स्थितिः ॥ ९५

पौरोहित्यप्रिया साध्वी ब्रह्माणी यज्ञसन्ततिः ।
सोमपानपरा प्रीता जनाढ्या तपना क्षमा ॥ ९६

प्रतिग्रहपरा दात्री सृष्टाजातिः सताङ्गतिः ।
गायत्री वेदलभ्या च दीक्षा सन्ध्यापरायणा ॥ ९७

रत्नसद्दीधितिर्विश्ववासना विश्वजीविका ।
कृषिवाणिज्यभूतिश्च वृद्धिर्धीश्च कुसीदिका ॥ ९८

कुलाधारा सुप्रसारा मनोन्मनी परायणा ।
शूद्रा विप्रगतिः कर्मकरी कौतुकपूजिता ॥ ९९

नानाविचारचतुरा बाला प्रौढा कलामयी ।
सुकर्णधारा नौः पारा सर्वाशा दुर्गमोचनी ॥ १००

दुर्गा विन्ध्यवनस्था च कन्दर्पनयपूरणी ।
भूभारशमनी कृष्णा रक्षाराध्या रसोल्लसा ॥ १०१

त्रिविधोत्पातशमनी समग्रसुखशेवधिः ।
पञ्चावयववाक्यश्रीः प्रपञ्चोद्यानचन्द्रिका ॥ १०२

सिद्धसन्दोहसुखिता योगिनीवृन्दवन्दिता ।
नित्याषोडशारूपा च कामेशी भगमालिनी ॥ १०३

नित्यक्लिन्ना च भी(भे) रुण्डा वह्निमण्डलवासिनी ।
महाविद्येश्वरी नित्या शिवदूतीति विश्रुता ॥ १०४

त्वरिता प्रथिता ख्याता विख्याता कुलसुन्दरी ।
नित्या नीलपताका च विजया सर्वमङ्गला ॥ १०५

ज्वालामाला(७००) विचित्रा च महात्रिपुरसिन्दरी ।
गुरुवृन्दा परगुरुः प्रकाशानन्दनाथिनी ॥ १०६

शिवानन्दनाथरूपा शक्त्यानन्दस्वरूपिणी ।
देव्यानन्दनाथमयी कौलेशानन्दनाथिनी ॥ १०७

दिव्यौघगुरुरूपा च समयानन्दनाथिनी ।
शुक्लदेव्यानन्दनाथा कुलेशानन्दनाथिनी १ ॥ १०८

क्लिन्नाङ्गानन्दरूपा च समयानन्दनाथिनी ।
वेदानन्दनाथमयी सहजानन्दनाथिनी ॥ १०९

सिद्धौघगुरुरूपा च अपरागुरुरूपिणी ।
गगनानन्दनाथा च विश्वानन्दस्वनाथिनी ॥ ११०

विमलानन्दनाथा च मदनानन्दनाथिनी ।
भुवनाद्या च लीलाद्या नन्दनानन्दनाथिनी ॥ १११

स्वात्मिनन्दानन्दरूपा प्रियाद्यानन्दनाथिनी ।
मानवौघगुरुश्रेष्ठा परमेष्ठि गुरुप्रभा ॥ ११२

परगुह्या गुरुशक्तिः स्वगुरुकीर्तनप्रिया।
त्रैलोक्यमोहनख्याता सर्वाशापरिपूरका॥ ११३

सर्वसङ्क्षोभिणी पूर्वाम्नायप्रथितवैभवा।
शिवाशक्तिः शिवशक्तिः शिवचक्रत्रयालया॥ ११४

सर्वसौभाग्यदाख्या च सर्वार्थसाधिकाह्वया।
सर्वरक्षाकराख्या च दक्षिणाम्नायदेवता॥ ११५

मध्यार्कचक्रनिलया पश्चिमाम्नायदेवता।
नवचक्रकृतावासा कौबेराम्नायदेवता॥ ११६

कुबेरपूज्या कुलजा कुलाम्नायप्रवर्तिनी।
बिन्दुचक्रकृतावासा मध्यसिंहासनेश्वरी॥ ११७

श्रीविद्या च महालक्ष्मीः लक्ष्मीः शक्तित्रयात्मिका।
सर्वसाम्राज्यलक्ष्मीश्च पञ्चलक्ष्मीतिविश्रुता॥ ११८

श्रीविद्या च परञ्ज्योतिः परनिष्कलशाम्भवी।
मातृका पञ्चकोशी च श्रीविद्या त्वरिता तथा॥ ११९

पारिजातेश्वरी चैव त्रिकूटा पञ्चबाणगा।
पञ्चकल्पलता पञ्चविद्या चामृतपीठिका॥ १२०

सुधासू रमणेशाना चान्नपूर्णा च कामधुक्।
श्रीविद्या सिद्धलक्ष्मीश्च मातङ्गी भुवनेश्वरी॥ १२१

वाराही पञ्चरत्नानामीश्वरी मातृवर्णगा।
पराञ्ज्योतिः कोशरूपा ऐन्दवी कलया युता॥ १२२

परितः स्वामिनी शक्तिदर्शना रविबिन्दुयुक्।
ब्रह्मदर्शनरूपा च शिवदर्शनरूपिणी॥ १२३

विष्णुदर्शनरूपा च सृष्टिचक्रनिवासिनी।
सौरदर्शनरूपा च स्थितिचक्रकृतालया॥ १२४

बौद्धदर्शनरूपा च महात्रिपुरसुन्दरी।
तत्त्वमुद्रास्वरूपा च प्रसन्ना(८००) ज्ञानमुद्रिका॥ १२५

सर्वोपचारसन्तुष्टा हृन्मयी शीर्षदेवता ।
शिखास्थिता ब्रह्ममयी नेत्रत्रयविलासिनी ॥ १२६

अस्त्रस्था चतुरस्ना च द्वारकाद्द्वारवासिनी ।
अणिमा पश्चिमस्था च लघिमोत्तरदेवता ॥ १२७

पूर्वस्था महिमेशित्वा दक्षिणद्वारदेवता ।
वशित्वा वायुकोणस्था प्राकाम्येशानदेवता ॥ १२८

अग्निकोणस्थिता भुक्तिरिच्छा नैरृतवासिनी ।
प्राप्तिसिद्धिरवस्था च प्राकाम्यार्धविलासिनी ॥ १२९

ब्राह्मी माहेश्वरी चैव कौमारी वैष्णवी तथा ।
वाराह्यैन्द्री च चामुण्डा महालक्ष्मीर्दिशाङ्गतिः ॥ १३०

क्षोभिणी द्राविणी मुद्राऽऽकर्षोन्मादनकारिणी ।
महाङ्कुशा खेचरी च बीजाख्या योनिमुद्रिका ॥ १३१

सर्वाशापूरचक्रस्था कार्यसिद्धिकरी तथा ।
कामाकर्षिणिकाशक्तिर्बुद्ध्याकर्षणरूपिणी ॥ १३२

अहङ्काराकर्षिणी च शब्दाकर्षणरूपिणी ।
स्पर्शाकर्षणरूपा च रूपाकर्षणरूपिणी ॥ १३३

रसाकर्षणरूपा च गन्धाकर्षणरूपिणी ।
चित्ताकर्षणरूपा च धैर्याकर्षणरूपिणी ॥ १३४

स्मृत्याकर्षणरूपा च बीजाकर्षणरूपिणी ।
अमृताकर्षिणी चैव नामाकर्षणरूपिणी ॥ १३५

शरीराकर्षिणीदेवी आत्माकर्षणरूपिणी ।
षोडशस्वररूपा च स्रवत्पीयूषमन्दिरा ॥ १३६

त्रिपुरेशी सिद्धरूपा कलादलनिवासिनी ।
सर्वसङ्क्षोभचक्रेशी शक्तिर्गुप्ततराभिधा ॥ १३७

अनङ्गकुसुमाशक्तिरनङ्गकटिमेखिला ।
अनङ्गमदनाऽनङ्गमदनातुररूपिणी ॥ १३८

अनङ्गरेखा चानङ्गवेगानङ्गाङ्कुशाभिधा ।
अनङ्गमालिनी शक्तिरष्टवर्गदिगन्विता ॥ १३९

वसुपत्रकृतावासा श्रीमत्त्रिपुरसुन्दरी ।
सर्वसाम्राज्यसुखदा सर्वसौभाग्यदेश्वरी ॥ १४०

सम्प्रदायेश्वरी सर्वसङ्क्षोभणकरी तथा ।
सर्वविद्राविणी सर्वाकर्षणाटोपकारिणी ॥ १४१

सर्वाह्लादनशक्तिश्च सर्वजृम्भणकारिणी ।
सर्वस्तम्भन शक्तिश्च सर्वसम्मोहिनी तथा ॥ १४२

सर्ववश्यकरीशक्तिः सर्वसर्वानुरञ्जिनी ।
सर्वोन्मादनशक्तिश्च सर्वार्थसिद्धिकारिणी ॥ १४३

सर्वसम्पत्तिदा शक्तिः सर्वमन्त्रमयी तथा ।
सर्वद्वन्द्वक्षयकरी(९००) सिद्धिस्त्रिपुरवासिनी ॥ १४४

सर्वार्थसाधकेशी च सर्वकार्यार्थसिद्धिदा ।
चतुर्दशारचक्रेशी कलायोगसमन्विता ॥ १४५

सर्वसिद्धिप्रदा देवी सर्वसम्पत्प्रदा तथा ।
सर्वप्रियङ्करी शक्तिः सर्वमङ्गलकारिणी ॥ १४६

सर्वकामप्रपूर्णा च सर्वदुःखप्रमोचिनी ।
सर्वमृत्युप्रशमनी सर्वविघ्नविनाशिनी ॥ १४७

सर्वाङ्गसुन्दरी देवी सर्वसौभाग्यदायिनी ।
त्रिपुरेशी सर्वसिद्धिप्रदा च दशकोणगा ॥ १४८

सर्वरक्षाकरेशी च निगर्भा योगिनी तथा ।
सर्वज्ञा सर्वशक्तिश्च सर्वैश्वर्यप्रदा तथा ॥ १४९

सर्वज्ञानमयीदेवी सर्वव्याधिविनाशिनी ।
सर्वाधारस्वरूपा च सर्वपापहरा तथा ॥ १५०

सर्वानन्दमयीदेवी सर्वरक्षास्वरूपिणी ।
महिमाशक्तिदेवी च देवी सर्वसमृद्धिदा ॥ १५१

अन्तर्दशारचक्रेशी देवी त्रिपुरमालिनी।
सर्वरोगहरेशी च रहस्या योगिनी तथा॥ १५२

वाग्देवी वशिनी चैव देवीकामेश्वरी तथा।
मोदिनी विमला चैव अरुणा जयिनी तथा॥ १५३

सर्वेश्वरी कौलिनी च ह्यष्टारसर्वसिद्धिदा।
सर्वकामप्रदेशी च परापररहस्यवित्॥ १५४

त्रिकोणचतुरश्रस्था सर्वैश्वर्याऽऽयुधात्मिका।
कामेश्वरीबाणरूपा कामेशीचापरूपिणी॥ १५५

कामेशीपाशरूपा च कामेश्यङ्कुशरूपिणी।
कामेश्वरीन्द्रशक्तिश्च अग्निचक्रकृतालया॥ १५६

कामगिर्यधिदेवी च त्रिकोणस्थाऽग्रकोणगा।
दक्षकोणेश्वरी विष्णुशक्तिर्जालन्धराश्रया॥ १५७

सूर्यचक्रालया रुद्रशक्तिर्वामाङ्गकोणगा।
सोमचक्रा ब्रह्मशक्तिः पूर्णगिर्यनुरागिणी॥ १५८

श्रीमत्त्रिकोणभुवना त्रिपुरात्मा महेश्वरी।
सर्वानन्दमयेशी च बिन्दुगातिरहस्यभृत्॥ १५९

परब्रह्मस्वरूपा च महात्रिपुरसुन्दरी।
सर्वचक्रान्तरस्था च समस्तचक्रनायिका॥ १६०

सर्वचक्रेश्वरी सर्वमन्त्राणामीश्वरी तथा।
सर्वविद्येश्वरी चैव सर्ववागीश्वरी तथा॥ १६१

सर्वयोगीश्वरी चैव पीठेश्वर्यखिलेश्वरी।
सर्वकामेश्वरी सर्वतत्त्वेश्वर्यागमेश्वरी॥ १६२

शक्तिः शक्तिधृगुल्लासा निर्द्वन्द्वा द्वैतगर्भिणी।
निष्प्रपञ्चा महामाया सप्रपञ्चा सुवासिनी॥ १६३

सर्वविश्वोत्पत्तिधात्री परमानन्दसुन्दरी (१०००)।

फलश्रुतिः ॥

इत्येतत्कथितं दिव्यं परमानन्दकारणम्॥ १६४

लावण्यसिन्धुलहरीबालायास्तोषमन्दिरम् ।
सहस्रनाम तन्त्राणां सारमाकृष्य पार्वति ॥ १६५

अनेन स्तुवतो नित्यमर्धरात्रे निशामुखे ।
प्रातः काले च पूजायां सर्वकालमतः प्रिये॥ १६६

सर्वसाम्राज्यसुखदा बाला च परितुष्यति ।
रत्नानि विविधान्यस्य वित्तानि प्रचुराणि च॥ १६७

मनोरथपथस्थानि ददाति परमेश्वरी ।
पुत्राः पौत्राश्च वर्धन्ते सन्ततिः सार्वकालिकी॥ १६८

शत्रवस्तस्य नश्यन्ति वर्धन्तेऽस्य बलानि च ।
व्याधयस्तस्य दूरस्थाः सकलान्यौषधानि च ॥ १६९

मन्दिराणि विचित्राणि राजन्ते तस्य सर्वदा ।
कृषिः फलवती तस्य भूमिः कामदुघाऽव्यया ॥ १७०

स्फीतो जनपदस्तस्य राज्यं तस्य निरीतिकम् ।
मातङ्गाः पक्षिणस्तुङ्गाः सिञ्चन्तो मदवारिभिः॥ १७१

द्वारे तस्य विराजन्ते हृष्टा नागतुरङ्गमाः ।
प्रजास्तस्य विराजन्ते निर्विवादाश्च मन्त्रिणः ॥ १७२

ज्ञातयस्तस्य तुष्यन्ति शीलं तस्यातिसुन्दरम् ।
लक्ष्मीस्तस्य वशे नित्यं स्वासना च मनोरमा॥ १७३

गद्यपद्यमयी वाणी तस्य गङ्गातरङ्गवत् ।
नानापदपदार्थानां वादचातुर्यसम्भृता ॥ १७४

समग्ररससम्पत्तिशालिनी लास्यमालिनी ।
अदृष्टान्यपि शास्त्राणि प्रकाश्यन्ते निरन्तरम् ॥ १७५

निग्रहः परवाक्यानां सभायां तस्य जायते ।
स्तुवन्ति वन्दिनस्तं वै राजानो दासवत्तथा॥ १७६

शस्त्राण्यस्त्राणि तदङ्गे जनयन्ति रुजां न हि।
महिलास्तस्य वशगाः सर्वावस्था भवन्ति वै ॥ १७७

विषं निर्विषितां याति पानीयममृतं भवेत्।
परपक्षस्तम्भनं च प्रतिपक्षस्य जृम्भणम् ॥ १७८

नवरात्रेण जायेत स तदभ्यासयोगवित्।
अहोरात्रं पठेद्यस्तु निस्तन्द्रः शान्तमानसः॥ १७९

वशे तस्य प्रजा याति सर्वे लोकाः सुनिश्चितम्।
षण्मासाभ्यासयोगेन योगमायाति निश्चितम् ॥ १८०

नित्यं कामकलां ध्यायन् यः पठेत् स्तोत्रमुत्तमम्।
मदनोन्मादकलिताः पुरन्ध्र्यास्तद्द्रशानुगाः ॥ १८१

लावण्यमदनाः साक्षाद्वैदग्ध्यमुदितेक्षणाः।
प्रेमपूर्णामपि वशे ह्यु र्वशीं स हि विन्दति॥ १८२

भूर्जपत्रे रोचनया कुङ्कुमेन शुभे दिने।
लाक्षारसद्रवेणापि यावकैर्वा विशेषतः ॥ १८३

धातुरागेण वा देवि लिखितं यन्त्रमञ्चितम्।
सुवर्णरौप्यगर्भस्थं सुसम्पूतं सुसाधितम्॥ १८४

बालाबुद्ध्या पूजितं च प्रतिष्ठितसमीरणम्।
धारयेन्मस्तके कण्ठे बाहुमूले तथा हृदि॥ १८५

नाभौ वापि धृतं धन्यं जयदं सर्वकामदम्।
रक्षणं नापरं किञ्चिद्विद्यते भुवनत्रये॥ १८६

ग्रहरोगादिभयहृत् सुखकृत्यविवर्धनम्।
बलवीर्यकरं क्रूरभूतशत्रुविनाशनम्॥ १८७

पुत्रपौत्रान् गुणगणैर्वर्धनं धनधान्यकृत्।
धरण्यां सा पुरी धन्या यत्रायं साधकोत्तमः॥ १८८

यद्गृहे लिखितं तिष्ठेत् स्तोत्रमेतद्वरानने।
तत्र चाहं शिवे नित्यं हरिश्च कमला तथा॥ १८९

वसामः सर्वतीर्थानामुत्पत्तिस्तत्र जायते।
यो वापि पाठयेद्भक्त्या पठेद्वै साधकोत्तमः ॥ १९०

ज्ञानानन्दकलायोगादैक्यवृत्तिं स विन्दति।
स्तोत्रेणानेन देवेशि तव पूजाफलं लभेत् ॥ १९१

षोढान्यासतनुर्भूत्वा पठितव्यं प्रयत्नतः।
उत्तमा सर्वतन्त्राणां बालायाः पूजनस्तुतिः ॥ १९२

तत्रोत्तमा षोडशार्णा तत्रेदं स्तोत्रमुत्तमम्।
नाशिष्याय प्रदातव्यमशुद्धाय शठाय च ॥ १९३

अलसायाप्रयत्नायाशिवाभक्ताय सुन्दरि।
भक्तिहीनाय मलिने गुरुनिन्दापराय च ॥ १९४

विष्णुभक्तिविहीनाय विकल्पावृतबुद्धये।
देयं भक्तवरे मुक्तेः कारणं भक्तिवर्धनम् ॥ १९५

लतायोगे पठेद्यस्तु स्तोत्रमेतद्वरानने।
सैव कल्पलता तस्य वाञ्छाफलकरी तथा ॥ १९६

पुष्पिताया लतायोगे कुरङ्गमुखि साधकः।
अक्षुब्धः सन् पठेद्यस्तु शतयज्ञस्य पुण्यभाक् ॥ १९७

ब्रह्मादयोऽपि देवेशि प्रार्थयन्ति पदद्वयम्।
स्वयं शिवः स विज्ञेयो यो बालाभावलम्पटः ॥ १९८

ब्रह्मानन्दमयी ज्योत्स्ना सदाशिवविधूदिता।
आनन्दो योऽपि यं वेदा वदन्त्यस्या वशे स्थिताः ॥ १९९

आह्लादनं बालाध्यानाद्वालाया नामकीर्तनात्।
सदानन्दाभ्यासयोगात् सदानन्दः प्रजायते ॥ २००

इति श्रीरुद्रयामले तन्त्रे भैरवभैरवीसंवादे श्री त्रिपुर सुन्दरी
सहस्रनाम स्तोत्रं सम्पूर्णम् ॥

*****

Śrī Tripura Sundarī Sahasranāmāvaliḥ

One hundred divine names of the holy mother.

Oṃ Aiṃ Hrīṃ Śrīṃ-
Ānandasindhave Namaḥ.
Oṃ Ānandāyai Namaḥ.
Oṃ Ānandamūrtaye Namaḥ
Vinodinyai Namaḥ.
Oṃ Tripurāyai Sundaryai
Namaḥ.
Oṃ Premapāthonidhaye Namaḥ
Anuttamāyai Namaḥ.
Oṃ Vāmārdhagahvarāyai
Namaḥ.
Oṃ Bhūtyai Namaḥ Vibhūtyai
Namaḥ.
Oṃ Śaṅkaryai Namaḥ.
Oṃ Śivāyai Namaḥ.
Oṃ Śṛṅgāramūrtaye Namaḥ
Oṃ Varadāyai Namaḥ.
Oṃ Rasāyai Namaḥ.
Oṃ Śubhagocarāyai Namaḥ
Oṃ Paramānandalaharyai
Namaḥ.
Oṃ Raṅgavatyai Gataye Namaḥ.
Oṃ Raṅgamālāyai Namaḥ. 20

Oṃ Anaṅgakalāyai Namaḥ.
Oṃ Kelyai Namaḥ.
Oṃ Kaivalyadāyai Namaḥ.
Oṃ Kalāyai Namaḥ
Oṃ Rasakalpāyai Namaḥ.
Oṃ Kalpalatāyai Namaḥ.
Oṃ Kutūhalavatyai Gataye
Namaḥ.
Oṃ Vinodadigdhāyai Namaḥ.
Oṃ Susnigdhāyai Namaḥ.
Oṃ Mugdhamūrtaye Namaḥ
Manoramāyai Namaḥ.
Oṃ Bālārkakoṭi Kiraṇāyai
Namaḥ.

Oṃ Candrakoṭisuśītalāyai
Namaḥ.
Oṃ Sravatpīyūṣadigdhāṅgyai
Namaḥ.
Oṃ Svargārthaparikalpitāyai
Namaḥ.
Oṃ Kuraṅganayanāyai Namaḥ.
Oṃ Kāntāyai Namaḥ.
Oṃ Sugataye Namaḥ.
Oṃ Sukhasantatyai Namaḥ.
Oṃ Rājarājeśvaryai Namaḥ 40.

Oṃ Rājñyai Namaḥ.
Oṃ Mahendraparivanditāyai
Namaḥ.
Oṃ Prapañcagataye Namaḥ.
Oṃ Īśānyai Namaḥ.
Oṃ Prapañcagataye Uttamāyai
Namaḥ.
Oṃ Durvāsase Namaḥ.
Oṃ Duḥsahāyai Namaḥ.
Oṃ Śaktaye Namaḥ.
Oṃ Śiñjatkanakanūpurāyai
Namaḥ
Oṃ Merumandaravakṣojāyai
Namaḥ.
Oṃ Sṛṇipāśavarāyudhāyai
Namaḥ
Oṃ Śarakodaṇḍa Saṃsakta
Pāṇidvaya Virājitāyai Namaḥ.
Oṃ Candrabimbānanāyai
Namaḥ.
Oṃ Cārumakuṭāyai Namaḥ.
Oṃ Uttaṃsacandrikāyai Namaḥ.
Oṃ Sindūratilakāyai Namaḥ.
Oṃ Cārudhammillāyai Namaḥ.
Oṃ Amalamālikāyai Namaḥ.
Oṃ Mandāradāmamuditāyai
Namaḥ

Oṃ Ratnamālāvibhūṣitāyai
                    Namaḥ. 60

Oṃ Suvarṇābharaṇaprītāyai
                    Namaḥ.
Oṃ Muktādāmamanoramāyai
                    Namaḥ.
Oṃ Tāmbūlapūrṇavadanāyai
                    Namaḥ.
Oṃ Madanānandamānasāyai
                    Namaḥ.
Oṃ Sukhārādhyāyai Namaḥ.
Oṃ Tapassārāyai Namaḥ.
Oṃ Kṛpāpārāyai Namaḥ.
Oṃ Vidhīśvaryai Namaḥ.
Oṃ Vakṣaḥ Sthalala
        Sadratnaprabhāyai Namaḥ.
Oṃ Madhurasonmadāyai
                    Namaḥ.
Oṃ Bindu Nādātmako
        Ccārarahitāyai Namaḥ.
Oṃ Turyarūpiṇyai Namaḥ.
Oṃ Kamanīyākṛtaye Namaḥ.
Oṃ Dhanyāyai Namaḥ.
Oṃ Śāṅkaryai Namaḥ.
Oṃ Prītiñjaryai Namaḥ.
Oṃ Prapañcāyai Namaḥ.
Oṃ Pañcamyai Namaḥ.
Oṃ Pūrṇāyai Namaḥ.
Oṃ Pūrṇapīṭhanivāsinyai
                    Namaḥ. 80

Oṃ Rājyalakṣmyai Namaḥ.
Oṃ Śrīlakṣmyai Namaḥ.
Oṃ Mahālakṣmyai Namaḥ.
Oṃ Surājikāyai Namaḥ.
Oṃ Santoṣasīmāyai Namaḥ.
Oṃ Sampattaye Namaḥ.
Oṃ Śātakaumbhyai Namaḥ.
Oṃ Dyutaye Namaḥ.
Oṃ Paripūrṇāyai Namaḥ.
Oṃ Jagaddhātryai Namaḥ.
Oṃ Vidhātryai Namaḥ.

Oṃ Balavardhinyai Namaḥ.
Oṃ Sārvabhaumanṛpaśriye
                    Namaḥ.
Oṃ Sāmrājyagataye Namaḥ.
Oṃ Ambikāyai Namaḥ.
Oṃ Sarojākṣyai Namaḥ.
Oṃ Dīrghadṛṣṭaye Namaḥ.
Oṃ Sācīkṣaṇavicakṣaṇāyai
                    Namaḥ.
Oṃ Raṅgasravantyai Namaḥ.
Oṃ Rasikāyai Namaḥ. 100

Oṃ Pradhānāyai Namaḥ.
Oṃ Rasarūpiṇyai Namaḥ.
Oṃ Rasasindhave Namaḥ.
Oṃ Sugātryai Namaḥ.
Oṃ Dhūsaryai Namaḥ.
Oṃ Maithunonmukhāyai
                    Namaḥ.
Oṃ Nirantaraguṇāsaktāyai
                    Namaḥ
Oṃ Nidhuvanātmikāyai Śaktaye
                    Namaḥ.
Oṃ Kāmākṣyai Namaḥ.
Oṃ Kamanīyāyai Namaḥ.
Oṃ Kāmeśyai Namaḥ.
Oṃ Bhagamaṅgalāyai Namaḥ.
Oṃ Subhagāyai Namaḥ.
Oṃ Bhoginyai Namaḥ Bhogyāyai
                    Namaḥ.
Oṃ Bhāgyadāyai Namaḥ.
Oṃ Subhagāyai Namaḥ.
Oṃ Bhagāyai Namaḥ.
Oṃ Bhagaliṅgāyai Namaḥ.
Oṃ Ānandakalāyai Namaḥ. 120

Oṃ Bhagamadhyanivāsinyai
                    Namaḥ.
Oṃ Bhagarūpāyai Namaḥ.
Oṃ Bhagamayyai Namaḥ.
Oṃ Bhagayantrāyai Namaḥ.
Oṃ Bhagottamāyai Namaḥ.
Oṃ Yonimudrāyai Namaḥ.

Oṃ Kāmakalāyai Namaḥ.
Oṃ Kulāmṛtaparāyaṇāyai Namaḥ.
Oṃ Kulakuṇḍālayāyai Namaḥ.
Oṃ Sūkṣmāyai Namaḥ.
Oṃ Jīvātmane Namaḥ.
Oṃ Liṅgarūpiṇyai Namaḥ.
Oṃ Mūlakriyāyai Namaḥ.
Oṃ Mūlarūpāyai Namaḥ.
Oṃ Mūlākṛtisvarūpiṇyai Namaḥ.
Oṃ Sotsukāyai Namaḥ.
Oṃ Kamalānandāyai Namaḥ.
Oṃ Cidbhāvāyai Namaḥ.
Oṃ Ātmagataye Namaḥ.
Oṃ Śivāyai Namaḥ. 140

Oṃ Śvetāyai Namaḥ.
Oṃ Aruṇāyai Namaḥ.
Oṃ Bindurūpāyai Namaḥ.
Oṃ Vedayonaye Namaḥ.
Oṃ Dhvanikṣaṇāyai Namaḥ.
Oṃ Ghaṇṭākoṭiravārāvāyai Namaḥ.
Oṃ Ravivimbotthitāyai Namaḥ.
Oṃ Adbhutāyai Namaḥ.
Oṃ Nādāntalīnāyai Namaḥ.
Oṃ Sampūrṇāyai Namaḥ.
Oṃ Pūrṇasthāyai Namaḥ.
Oṃ Bahurūpikāyai Namaḥ.
Oṃ Bhṛṅgārāvāyai Namaḥ.
Oṃ Vaṃśagataye Namaḥ.
Oṃ Vāditrāyai Namaḥ.
Oṃ Murajadhvanaye Namaḥ.
Oṃ Varṇamālāyai Namaḥ.
Oṃ Siddhikalāyai Namaḥ.
Oṃ Ṣaṭ Cakrakramavāsinyai Namaḥ.
Oṃ Mūlakelīratāyai Namaḥ. 160

Oṃ Svādhiṣṭhānāyai Namaḥ.
Oṃ Turyanivāsinyai Namaḥ.
Oṃ Maṇipurasthitaye Namaḥ.
Oṃ Snigdhāyai Namaḥ.

Oṃ Kūrmacakraparāyaṇāyai Namaḥ.
Oṃ Anāhatagataye Namaḥ.
Oṃ Dīpaśikhāyai Namaḥ.
Oṃ Maṇimayākṛtaye Namaḥ.
Oṃ Viśuddhāyai Namaḥ.
Oṃ Śabdasaṃśuddhāyai Namaḥ.
Oṃ Jīvabodhasthalyai Namaḥ.
Oṃ Ravāyai Namaḥ.
Oṃ Ājñācakrābjasaṃsthāyai Namaḥ.
Oṃ Sphurantyai Namaḥ.
Oṃ Nipuṇāyai Namaḥ.
Oṃ Trivṛte Namaḥ.
Oṃ Candrikāyai Namaḥ.
Oṃ Candrakoṭi Śriye Namaḥ.
Oṃ Sūryakoṭi Prabhāmayyai Namaḥ.
Oṃ Padmarāgāruṇacchāyāyai Namaḥ. 180

Oṃ Nityāyai Namaḥ.
Oṃ Āhlādamayyai Namaḥ.
Oṃ Prabhāyai Namaḥ.
Oṃ Pānaśriye Namaḥ.
Oṃ Priyāmātyāyai Namaḥ.
Oṃ Niścalāyai Namaḥ.
Oṃ Amṛtanandinyai Namaḥ.
Oṃ Kāntāṅgasaṅgamuditāyai Namaḥ.
Oṃ Sudhāmādhurya Sambhṛtāyai Namaḥ.
Oṃ Mahāmañcasthitāyai Namaḥ.
Oṃ Aliptāyai Namaḥ.
Oṃ Tṛptāyai Namaḥ.
Oṃ Dṛptāyai Namaḥ.
Oṃ Susambhṛtaye Namaḥ.
Oṃ Sravatpīyūṣasaṃsiktāyai Namaḥ.
Oṃ Raktārṇavavivardhinyai Namaḥ.

Oṃ Suraktāyai Namaḥ.

Oṃ Priyasaṃsiktāyai Namaḥ.

Oṃ Śaśvatkuṇḍālayāyai Namaḥ.

Oṃ Abhayāyai Namaḥ. 200

Oṃ Śreyaḥ Śrutaye Namaḥ.

Oṃ Pratyekānava
       Keśiphalāvalyai Namaḥ.

Oṃ Prītāyai Namaḥ Śivāyai
          Namaḥ.

Oṃ Śivapriyāyai Namaḥ.

Oṃ Śāṅkaryai Namaḥ.

Oṃ Śāmbhavyai Namaḥ.

Oṃ Vibhāyai Namaḥ.

Oṃ Svayambhuve Namaḥ.

Oṃ Svapriyāyai Namaḥ.

Oṃ Svīyāyai Namaḥ.

Oṃ Svakīyāyai Namaḥ.

Oṃ Janamātṛkāyai Namaḥ.

Oṃ Svārāmāyai Namaḥ.

Oṃ Svāśrayāyai Namaḥ.

Oṃ Sādhvyai Namaḥ.

Oṃ Sudhādhārādhikādhikāyai
          Namaḥ.

Oṃ Maṅgalāyai Namaḥ.

Oṃ Ujjayinyai Namaḥ.

Oṃ Mānyāyai Namaḥ. 220

Oṃ Sarvamaṅgalasaṅgiḥnyai
          Namaḥ.

Oṃ Bhadrāyai Namaḥ.

Oṃ Bhadrāvalyai Namaḥ.

Oṃ Kanyāyai Namaḥ.

Oṃ Kalitārdhendubimbabhāje
          Namaḥ.

Oṃ Kalyāṇalatikāyai Namaḥ.

Oṃ Kāmyāyai Namaḥ.

Oṃ Kukarmaṇe Namaḥ.

Oṃ Kumataye Namaḥ.

Oṃ Manave Namaḥ.

Oṃ Kuraṅgākṣyai Namaḥ.

Oṃ Kṣībanetrāyai Namaḥ.

Oṃ Kṣārāyai Namaḥ.

Oṃ Rasamadonmadāyai
          Namaḥ.

Oṃ Vāruṇīpānamuditāyai
          Namaḥ.

Oṃ Madirāracitāśrayāyai
          Namaḥ.

Oṃ Kādambarīpānarucaye
          Namaḥ.

Oṃ Vipāśāyai Namaḥ.

Oṃ Pāśabhītinude Namaḥ.

Oṃ Muditāyai Namaḥ. 240

Oṃ Muditāpāṅgāyai Namaḥ.

Oṃ Daradolitadīrghadṛśe
          Namaḥ.

Oṃ Daityakulānalaśikhāyai
          Namaḥ.

Oṃ Manorathasudhādyutaye
          Namaḥ.

Oṃ Suvāsinyai Namaḥ.

Oṃ Pīnagātryai Namaḥ.

Oṃ Pīnaśroṇipayodharāyai
          Namaḥ.

Oṃ Sucārukabaryai Namaḥ.

Oṃ Dantadīdhitidī
          Pramauktikāyai Namaḥ.

Oṃ Bimbādharāyai Namaḥ.

Oṃ Dyutimukhāyai Namaḥ.

Oṃ Pravālottamadīdhitaye
          Namaḥ.

Oṃ Tilaprasūnanāsāgrāyai
          Namaḥ.

Oṃ Hemakakkolabhālakāyai
          Namaḥ.

Oṃ Niṣkalaṅkenduvadanāyai
          Namaḥ.

Oṃ Bālendumukuṭojjvalāyai
          Namaḥ.

Oṃ Nṛtyatkhañjananetraśriye
          Namaḥ.

Oṃ Visphuratkarṇaśaṣkulyai
          Namaḥ.

Oṃ Bālacandrātapatrārdhāyai
                    Namaḥ.
Oṃ Maṇisūryakirīṭinyai
                    Namaḥ. 260.

Oṃ Hemamāṇikyatāṭaṅkāyai
                    Namaḥ.
Oṃ Maṇikāñcanakuṇḍalāyai
                    Namaḥ.
Oṃ Sucārucibukāyai Namaḥ.
Oṃ Kambukaṇṭhyai Namaḥ.
Oṃ Maṇimanoramāyai Namaḥ.
Oṃ Gaṅgātaraṅgahārormaye
                    Namaḥ.
Oṃ Mattakokilaniḥsvanāyai
                    Namaḥ.
Oṃ Mṛṇālavilasadbāhave
                    Namaḥ.
Oṃ Pāśāṅkuśadhanurdharāyai
                    Namaḥ.
Oṃ Keyūrakaṭakācchannāyai
                    Namaḥ.
Oṃ Nānāratnamanoramāyai
                    Namaḥ.
Oṃ Tāmrapaṅkajapāṇiśriye
                    Namaḥ.
Oṃ Nakharatnaprabhāvatyai
                    Namaḥ.
Oṃ Aṅgulīya Maṇiśreṇi
  Cañcadaṅgulisantataye Namaḥ.
Oṃ Mandaradvandvasukucāyai
                    Namaḥ.
Oṃ Romarājībhujakāyai Namaḥ.
Oṃ Gambhīranābhaye Namaḥ.
Oṃ Trivalīvalayāyai Namaḥ.
Oṃ Sumadhyamāyai Namaḥ.
Oṃ Raṇatkāñcīguṇonnaddhāyai
                    Namaḥ. 280

Oṃ Paṭṭāṃśukasunīvikāyai
                    Namaḥ.
Oṃ Meruguṇḍīnitambāḍhyāyai
                    Namaḥ.

Oṃ Gajagaṇḍoruyugmayuje
                    Namaḥ.
Oṃ Sujānumandarā Saktala
  Sajjaṅghādvayānvitāyai Namaḥ.
Oṃ Gūḍhagulphāyai Namaḥ.
Oṃ Mañjuśiñjanmaṇi
      Nūpuramaṇḍitāyai Namaḥ.
Oṃ Yogidhyeyapadadvandvāyai
                    Namaḥ.
Oṃ Sudhāmāyai Namaḥ.
Oṃ Amṛtasāriṇyai Namaḥ.
Oṃ Lāvaṇyasindhave Namaḥ.
Oṃ Sindūratilakāyai Namaḥ.
Oṃ Kuṭilālakāyai Namaḥ.
Oṃ Sādhusiddhāyai Namaḥ.
Oṃ Subuddhāyai Namaḥ.
Oṃ Budhāyai Namaḥ.
Oṃ Vṛndārakodayāyai Namaḥ.
Oṃ Bālārkakiraṇaśreṇīśoṇāyai
                    Namaḥ.
Oṃ Śrīpremakāmudughe
                    Namaḥ.
Oṃ Rasagambhīrasarasyai
                    Namaḥ.
Oṃ Padminyai Namaḥ. 300

Oṃ Rasasārasāyai Namaḥ.
Oṃ Prasannāyai Namaḥ.
Oṃ Āsannavaradāyai Namaḥ.
Oṃ Śāradāyai Namaḥ.
Oṃ Subhāgyadāyai Namaḥ.
Oṃ Naṭarājapriyāyai Namaḥ.
Oṃ Viśvanāṭyāyai Namaḥ.
Oṃ Nartakanartakyai Namaḥ.
Oṃ Vicitrayantrāyai Namaḥ.
Oṃ Cittantrāyai Namaḥ.
Oṃ Vidyāvallyai Namaḥ.
Oṃ Śubhāyai Gatyai Namaḥ.
Oṃ Kūṭārakuṭāyai Namaḥ.
Oṃ Kūṭasthāyai Namaḥ.
Oṃ Pañcakūṭāyai Namaḥ.
Oṃ Pañcamyai Namaḥ.
Oṃ Catuṣkūṭāyai Namaḥ.

Oṃ Trikūṭādyāyai Namaḥ.

Oṃ Ṣaṭkūṭāyai Namaḥ.

Oṃ Vedapūjitāyai Namaḥ. 320

Oṃ Kūṭaṣoḍaśasampannāyai
                        Namaḥ.

Oṃ Turīyāyai Namaḥ.

Oṃ Paramāyai Kalāyai Namaḥ

Oṃ Ṣoḍaśyai Namaḥ.

Oṃ Mantrayantrāṇāmīśvaryai
                        Namaḥ.

Oṃ Merumaṇḍalāyai Namaḥ

Oṃ Ṣoḍaśārṇayai Namaḥ.

Oṃ Trivarṇāyai Namaḥ.

Oṃ Bindunādasvarūpiṇyai
                        Namaḥ.

Oṃ Varṇātītāyai Namaḥ.

Oṃ Varṇamātre Namaḥ.

Oṃ Śabdabrahmaṇe Namaḥ.

Oṃ Mahāsukhāyai Namaḥ.

Oṃ Caitanyavallyai Namaḥ.

Oṃ Kūṭātmane Namaḥ.

Oṃ Kāmeśyai Namaḥ.

Oṃ Svapnadṛśyagāyai Namaḥ.

Oṃ Svapnāvatyai Namaḥ.

Oṃ Bodhakaryai Namaḥ.

Oṃ Jāgṛtaye Namaḥ. 340

Oṃ Jāgarāśrayāyai Namaḥ.

Oṃ Svapnāśrayāyai Namaḥ.

Oṃ Suṣuptyai Namaḥ.

Oṃ Tandrāmuktāyai Namaḥ.

Oṃ Mādhavyai Namaḥ.

Oṃ Lopāmudrāyai Namaḥ.

Oṃ Kāmarājñyai Namaḥ.

Oṃ Mānavyai Namaḥ.

Oṃ Vittapārcitāyai Namaḥ.

Oṃ Śākambharyai Namaḥ.

Oṃ Nandividyāyai Namaḥ.

Oṃ Bhasvadvidyotamālinyai
                        Namaḥ.

Oṃ Māhendrayai Namaḥ.

Oṃ Svargasampattaye Namaḥ.

Oṃ Durvāsaḥsevitāyai Namaḥ.

Oṃ Śrutyai Namaḥ.

Oṃ Sādhakendragataye Namaḥ.

Oṃ Sādhvyai Namaḥ.

Oṃ Sulabhāyai Namaḥ.

Oṃ Siddhikandarāyai
                        Namaḥ. 360

Oṃ Puratrayeśyai Namaḥ.

Oṃ Purajidarcitāyai Namaḥ.

Oṃ Puradevatāyai Namaḥ.

Oṃ Puṣṭyai Namaḥ.

Oṃ Vighnaharyai Namaḥ.

Oṃ Bhūtyai Namaḥ.

Oṃ Viguṇāyai Namaḥ.

Oṃ Pūjyakāmaduhe Namaḥ.

Oṃ Hiraṇyamātre Namaḥ.

Oṃ Gaṇapāyai Namaḥ.

Oṃ Guhamātre Namaḥ.

Oṃ Nitambinyai Namaḥ.

Oṃ Sarvasīmantinyai Namaḥ.

Oṃ Mokṣāyai Namaḥ.

Oṃ Dīkṣāyai Namaḥ.

Oṃ Dīkṣitamātṛkāyai Namaḥ.

Oṃ Sādhakāmbāyai Namaḥ.

Oṃ Siddhamātre Namaḥ.

Oṃ Sādhakendrāyai Namaḥ.

Oṃ Manoramāyai Namaḥ. 380

Oṃ Yauvanonmādinyai Namaḥ.

Oṃ Tuṅgāyai Namaḥ.

Oṃ Suśroṇyai Namaḥ.

Oṃ Madamantharāyai Namaḥ.

Oṃ Padmaraktotpalavatyai
                        Namaḥ.

Oṃ Raktamālyānulepanāyai
                        Namaḥ.

Oṃ Raktamālārucaye Namaḥ.

Oṃ Śikhāśikhaṇḍinyai Namaḥ.

Oṃ Atisundaryai Namaḥ.

Oṃ Śikhaṇḍinṛttasantuṣṭāyai
                        Namaḥ.

Oṃ Saurabheyyai Namaḥ.

Oṃ Vasundharāyai Namaḥ.
Oṃ Surabhyai Namaḥ.
Oṃ Kāmadāyai Namaḥ.
Oṃ Kāmyāyai Namaḥ.
Oṃ Kamanīyārthakāmadāyai
Namaḥ.
Oṃ Nandinyai Namaḥ.
Oṃ Lakṣaṇavatyai Namaḥ.
Oṃ Vasiṣṭhālayadevatāyai
Namaḥ.
Oṃ Golokadevyai Namaḥ. 400

Oṃ Lokaśriyai Namaḥ.
Oṃ Golokaparipālikāyai Namaḥ.
Oṃ Havirdhānyai Namaḥ.
Oṃ Devamātre Namaḥ.
Oṃ Vṛndārakavarānuyuje
Namaḥ.
Oṃ Rudrapatnyai Namaḥ.
Oṃ Bhadramātre Namaḥ.
Oṃ Sudhādhārāyai Namaḥ.
Oṃ Ambuvikṣataye Namaḥ.
Oṃ Dakṣiṇāyai Namaḥ.
Oṃ Yajñasammūrtaye Namaḥ.
Oṃ Subālāyai Namaḥ.
Oṃ Dhīranandinyai Namaḥ.
Oṃ Kṣīrapūrṇāyai Namaḥ.
Oṃ Arṇavagataye Namaḥ.
Oṃ Sudhāyonaye Namaḥ.
Oṃ Sulocanāyai Namaḥ.
Oṃ Rāmānugāyai Namaḥ.
Oṃ Susevyāyai Namaḥ.
Oṃ Sugandhālayavāsagāyai
Namaḥ. 420

Oṃ Sucāritrāyai Namaḥ.
Oṃ Sutripurāyai Namaḥ.
Oṃ Sustanyai Namaḥ.
Oṃ Stanavatsalāyai Namaḥ.
Oṃ Rajasvalāyai Namaḥ.
Oṃ Rajoyuktāyai Namaḥ.
Oṃ Rañjikāyai Namaḥ.
Oṃ Raṅgamālikāyai Namaḥ.

Oṃ Raktapriyāyai Namaḥ.
Oṃ Suraktāyai Namaḥ.
Oṃ Ratiraṅgasvarūpiṇyai
Namaḥ.
Oṃ Rajaḥśukrāmbikāyai Namaḥ.
Oṃ Niṣṭhāyai Namaḥ.
Oṃ Ratiniṣṭhāyai Namaḥ.
Oṃ Ratispṛhāyai Namaḥ.
Oṃ Hāvabhāvāyai Namaḥ.
Oṃ Kāmakelisarvasvāyai
Namaḥ.
Oṃ Surajīvikāyai Namaḥ.

Oṃ Svayambhūkusumānandāyai
Namaḥ.
Oṃ Svayambhūkusumapriyāyai
Namaḥ. 440

Oṃ Svayambhūprītisantuṣṭāyai
Namaḥ.
Oṃ Svayambhūnindakāntakṛte
Namaḥ.
Oṃ Svayambhūsthāyai Namaḥ.
Oṃ Śaktipuṭyai Namaḥ.
Oṃ Ratisarvasvapīṭhikāyai
Namaḥ.
Oṃ Atyantasabhikāyai Namaḥ.
Oṃ Dūtyai Namaḥ.
Oṃ Vidagdhāyai Namaḥ.
Oṃ Prītipūjitāyai Namaḥ.
Oṃ Kullikāyai Namaḥ.
Oṃ Yantranilayāyai Namaḥ.
Oṃ Yogapīṭhādhivāsinyai
Namaḥ.
Oṃ Sulakṣaṇāyai Namaḥ.
Oṃ Rasarūpāyai Namaḥ.
Oṃ Sarvalakṣaṇalalakṣitāyai
Namaḥ.
Oṃ Nānālaṅkārasubhagāyai
Namaḥ.
Oṃ Pañcabāṇasamarcitāyai
Namaḥ.

Oṃ Ūrdhvatrikoṇanilayāyai
             Namaḥ.

Oṃ Bālāyai Namaḥ.

Oṃ Kāmeśvaryai Namaḥ. 460

Oṃ Gaṇādhyakṣāyai Namaḥ.

Oṃ Kulādhyakṣāyai Namaḥ.

Oṃ Lakṣmyai Namaḥ.

Oṃ Sarasvatyai Namaḥ.

Oṃ Vasantasamayaprītāyai
             Namaḥ.

Oṃ Prītyai Namaḥ.

Oṃ Kucabharānatāyai Namaḥ.

Oṃ Kalādharamukhāyai Namaḥ.

Oṃ Amūrdhāyai Namaḥ.

Oṃ Pādavṛddhaye Namaḥ.

Oṃ Kalāvatyai Namaḥ.

Oṃ Puṣpapriyāyai Namaḥ.

Oṃ Dhṛtyai Namaḥ.

Oṃ Ratikaṇṭhyai Namaḥ.

Oṃ Manoramāyai Namaḥ.

Oṃ Madanonmādinyai Namaḥ.

Oṃ Mohinyai Namaḥ.

Oṃ Pārvaṇyai Kalāyai Namaḥ.

Oṃ Śoṣiṇyai Namaḥ.

Oṃ Vaśinyai Namaḥ. 480

Oṃ Rājinyai Namaḥ.

Oṃ Atyantasubhagāyai Namaḥ.

Oṃ Bhagāyai Namaḥ.

Oṃ Pūṣāyai(Ṣṇe) Namaḥ.

Oṃ Vaśāyai Namaḥ.

Oṃ Sumanāyai (Nase) Namaḥ.

Oṃ Ratyai Namaḥ.

Oṃ Prītyai Namaḥ.

Oṃ Dhṛtyai Namaḥ.

Oṃ Ṛddhyai Namaḥ.

Oṃ Saumyāyai Namaḥ.

Oṃ Marīcyaṃśumālāyai Namaḥ.

Oṃ Pratyaṅgirāyai Namaḥ.

Oṃ Śaśinyai Namaḥ.

Oṃ Succhāyāyai Namaḥ.

Oṃ Sampūrṇamaṇḍalodayāyai
             Namaḥ.

Oṃ Tuṣṭāyai Namaḥ.

Oṃ Amṛtapūrṇāyai Namaḥ.

Oṃ Bhagayantranivāsinyai
             Namaḥ.

Oṃ Liṅgayantrālayāyai
             Namaḥ. 500

Oṃ Śambhurūpāyai Namaḥ.

Oṃ Saṃyogayoginyai Namaḥ.

Oṃ Drāviṇyai Namaḥ.

Oṃ Bījarūpāyai Namaḥ.

Oṃ Akṣubdhāyai Namaḥ.

Oṃ Sādhakapriyāyai Namaḥ.

Oṃ Rājabījamayyai Namaḥ.

Oṃ Rājyasukhadāyai Namaḥ.

Oṃ Vāñchitapradāyai Namaḥ.

Oṃ Rajassaṃvīryaśaktaye
             Namaḥ.

Oṃ Śukravide Namaḥ.

Oṃ Śivarūpiṇyai Namaḥ.

Oṃ Sarvasārāyai Namaḥ.

Oṃ Sāramayāyai Namaḥ.

Oṃ Śivaśaktimayyai Namaḥ.

Oṃ Prabhāyai Namaḥ.

Oṃ Saṃyogānandanilayāyai
             Namaḥ.

Oṃ Saṃyogaprītimātṛkāyai
             Namaḥ.

Oṃ Saṃyogakusumānandāyai
             Namaḥ.

Oṃ Saṃyogāyai Namaḥ. 520

Oṃ Yogavardhinyai Namaḥ.

Oṃ Saṃyogasukhadāvasthāyai
             Namaḥ.

Oṃ Cidānandaikasevitāyai
             Namaḥ.

Oṃ Arghyapūjakasampattaye
             Namaḥ.

Oṃ Arghyadravyasvarūpiṇyai
             Namaḥ.

Oṃ Sāmarasyāyai Namaḥ.
Oṃ Parāyai Namaḥ Prītāyai
                    Namaḥ.
Oṃ Priyasaṅgamarūpiṇyai
                    Namaḥ.
Oṃ Jñānadūtyai Namaḥ.
Oṃ Jñānagamyāyai Namaḥ.
Oṃ Jñānayonaye Namaḥ.
Oṃ Śivālayāyai Namaḥ.
Oṃ Citkalāyai Namaḥ.
Oṃ Jñānasakalāyai Namaḥ.
Oṃ Sakulāyai Namaḥ.
Oṃ Sakulātmikāyai Namaḥ.
Oṃ Kalācatuṣṭayyai Namaḥ.
Oṃ Padminyai Namaḥ.
Oṃ Atisūkṣmāyai Namaḥ. 540

Oṃ Parātmikāyai Namaḥ.
Oṃ Haṃsakelasthalyai Namaḥ.
Oṃ Chāyāyai Namaḥ.
Oṃ Haṃsadvayavikāsinyai
                    Namaḥ.
Oṃ Virāgatāyai Namaḥ.
Oṃ Mokṣakalāyai Namaḥ.
Oṃ Paramātmakalāvatyai
                    Namaḥ.
Oṃ Vidyākalāyai Namaḥ.
Oṃ Antarātmasthāyai Namaḥ.
Oṃ Catuṣṭayakalāvatyai Namaḥ.
Oṃ Vidyāsantoṣiṇyai Namaḥ.
Oṃ Tṛptaye Namaḥ.
Oṃ Parabrahmaprakāśikāyai
                    Namaḥ.
Oṃ Paramātmaparāyai Namaḥ.
Oṃ Vastulīna Śakticatuṣṭayyai
                    Namaḥ.
Oṃ Śāntaye Namaḥ.
Oṃ Bodhakalāyai Namaḥ.
Oṃ Avāptaye Namaḥ.
Oṃ Parajñānātmikāyai Kalāyai
                    Namaḥ.
Oṃ Paśyantyai Namaḥ. 560

Oṃ Paramātmasthāyai Namaḥ.
Oṃ Antarātmakalākulāyai
                    Namaḥ.
Oṃ Madhyamāyai Namaḥ.
Oṃ Vaikharyai Namaḥ.
Oṃ Ātemakalānandāyai Namaḥ.
Oṃ Kalāvateyai Namaḥ.
Oṃ Tāriṇyai Namaḥ.
Oṃ Taraṇyai Namaḥ.
Oṃ Tārāyai Namaḥ.
Oṃ Śivaliṅgālayāyai Namaḥ.
Oṃ Ātmavide Namaḥ.
Oṃ Parasparaśubhācārāyai
                    Namaḥ.
Oṃ Brahmānandavinodinyai
                    Namaḥ.
Oṃ Rasālasāyai Namaḥ.
Oṃ Dūtarāsāyai Namaḥ.
Oṃ Sārthāyai Namaḥ.
Oṃ Sārthapriyāyai Namaḥ.
Oṃ Umāyai Namaḥ.
Oṃ Jātyādirahitāyai Namaḥ.
Oṃ Yogiyoginyai Namaḥ. 580

Oṃ Ānandavardhinyai Namaḥ.
Oṃ Vīrabhāvapradāyai Namaḥ.
Oṃ Vīrabhāvadāyai Namaḥ.
Oṃ Paśutvābhivīragataye
                    Namaḥ.
Oṃ Vīrasaṅgamahodayāyai
                    Namaḥ.
Oṃ Mūrdhābhiṣiktāyai Namaḥ.
Oṃ Rājaśriye Namaḥ.
Oṃ Kṣatriyāyai Namaḥ.
Oṃ Uttamamātṛkāyai Namaḥ.
Oṃ Śastrāstrakuśalāyai Namaḥ.
Oṃ Śobhāyai Namaḥ.
Oṃ Rasasthāyai Namaḥ.
Oṃ Yuddhajīvikāyai Namaḥ.
Oṃ Vijayāyai Namaḥ.
Oṃ Yoginyai Namaḥ.
Oṃ Yātrāyai Namaḥ.

Oṃ Parasainyavimardinyai
                              Namaḥ.
Oṃ Pūrṇāyai Namaḥ. 600

Oṃ Vittaiṣiṇyai Namaḥ.
Oṃ Vittāyai Namaḥ.
Oṃ Vittasañcayaśālinyai
                              Namaḥ.
Oṃ Bhāṇḍāgārasthitāyai
                              Namaḥ.
Oṃ Ratnāyai Namaḥ.
Oṃ Ratnaśreṇyadhivāsinyai
                              Namaḥ.
Oṃ Mahiṣyai Namaḥ.
Oṃ Rājabhogyāyai Namaḥ.
Oṃ Gaṇikāyai Namaḥ.
Oṃ Gaṇabhogabhṛte Namaḥ.
Oṃ Kariṇyai Namaḥ.
Oṃ Baḍavāyai Namaḥ.
Oṃ Yogayāyai Namaḥ.
Oṃ Mallasenāyai Namaḥ.
Oṃ Padātigāyai Namaḥ.
Oṃ Sainyaśreṇyai Namaḥ.
Oṃ Śauryaratāyai Namaḥ.
Oṃ Patākāyai Namaḥ.
Oṃ Dhvajavāsinyai Namaḥ.
Oṃ Succhatrāyai Namaḥ. 620

Oṃ Ambikāyai Namaḥ.
Oṃ Ambāyai Namaḥ.
Oṃ Prajāpālanasadgataye
                              Namaḥ.
Oṃ Surabhyai Namaḥ.
Oṃ Pūjakācārāyai Namaḥ.
Oṃ Rājakāryaparāyaṇāyai
                              Namaḥ.
Oṃ Brahmakṣatramayyai
                              Namaḥ.
Oṃ Somasūryāntaryāminyai
                              Namaḥ.
Oṃ Sthityai Namaḥ.
Oṃ Paurohityapriyāyai Namaḥ.
Oṃ Sādhvyai Namaḥ.

Oṃ Brahmāṇyai Namaḥ.
Oṃ Yajñasantatyai Namaḥ.
Oṃ Somapānaratāyai Namaḥ.
Oṃ Prītāyai Namaḥ.
Oṃ Janādhyāyai Namaḥ.
Oṃ Tapanāyai Namaḥ.
Oṃ Kṣamāyai Namaḥ.
Oṃ Pratigrahaparāyai Namaḥ.
Oṃ Dātryai Namaḥ. 640

Oṃ Sṛṣṭāyai Namaḥ.
Oṃ Jātyai Namaḥ.
Oṃ Satāṅgataye Namaḥ.
Oṃ Gāyatryai Namaḥ.
Oṃ Vedalabhyāyai Namaḥ.
Oṃ Dīkṣāyai Namaḥ.
Oṃ Sandhyāparāyaṇāyai
                              Namaḥ.
Oṃ Ratnasaddīdhitaye Namaḥ.
Oṃ Viśvavāsanāyai Namaḥ.
Oṃ Viśvajīvikāyai Namaḥ.
Oṃ Kṛṣivāṇījyabhūtyai Namaḥ.
Oṃ Vṛddhaye Namaḥ.
Oṃ Dhiye Namaḥ.
Oṃ Kusīdikāyai Namaḥ.
Oṃ Kulādhārāyai Namaḥ.
Oṃ Suprasārāyai Namaḥ.
Oṃ Manonmanyai Namaḥ.
Oṃ Parāyaṇāyai Namaḥ.
Oṃ Śūdrāyai Namaḥ. 660

Oṃ Vipragataye Karmakaryai
                              Namaḥ.
Oṃ Kautukapūjitāyai Namaḥ.
Oṃ Nānāvicāracaturāyai
                              Namaḥ.
Oṃ Bālāyai Namaḥ.
Oṃ Proḍhāyai Namaḥ.
Oṃ Kalāmayyai Namaḥ.
Oṃ Sukarṇadhārāyai Namaḥ.
Oṃ Nāve Namaḥ.
Oṃ Pārāyai Namaḥ.
Oṃ Sarvāśāyai Namaḥ.

Oṃ Durgāmocanyai Namaḥ.
Oṃ Durgāyai Namaḥ.
Oṃ Vindhyavanasthāyai Namaḥ.
Oṃ Kandarpanayapūraṇyai
　　　　Namaḥ.
Oṃ Bhūbhāraśamanyai Namaḥ.
Oṃ Kṛṣṇāyai Namaḥ.
Oṃ Rakṣārādhyāyai Namaḥ.
Oṃ Rasollasāyai Namaḥ.
Oṃ Trividhotpātaśamanyai
　　　　Namaḥ.
Oṃ Samagrasukhaśevadhaye
　　　　Namaḥ. 680

Oṃ Pañcāvayavavākyaśriye
　　　　Namaḥ.
Oṃ Prapañcodyānacandrikāyai
　　　　Namaḥ.
Oṃ Siddhasandohasukhitāyai
　　　　Namaḥ.
Oṃ Yoginīvṛndavanditāyai
　　　　Namaḥ.
Oṃ Nityāṣoḍaśarūpāyai Namaḥ.
Oṃ Kāmeśyai Namaḥ.
Oṃ Bhagamālinyai Namaḥ.
Oṃ Nityaklinnāyai Namaḥ.
Oṃ Bhī(Bhe)Ruṇḍāyai Namaḥ.
Oṃ Vahnimaṇḍalavāsinyai
　　　　Namaḥ.
Oṃ Mahāvidyeśvarīnityāyai
　　　　Namaḥ.
Oṃ Śivadūtīti Viśrutāyai Namaḥ.
Oṃ Tvaritāprathitāyai Namaḥ.
Oṃ Khyātāyai Namaḥ.
Oṃ Vikhyātāyai Kulasundaryai
　　　　Namaḥ.
Oṃ Nityāyai Namaḥ.
Oṃ Nīlapatākāyai Namaḥ.
Oṃ Vijayāyai Namaḥ.
Oṃ Sarvamaṅgalāyai Namaḥ.
Oṃ Jvālāmālāyai Namaḥ. 700

Oṃ Vicitrāyai Namaḥ.

Oṃ Mahātripurasundaryai
　　　　Namaḥ.
Oṃ Guruvṛndāyai Namaḥ.
Oṃ Puragurave Namaḥ.
Oṃ Prakāśānandanāthinyai
　　　　Namaḥ.
Oṃ Śivānandānātharūpāyai
　　　　Namaḥ.
Oṃ Śaktyānandasvarūpiṇyai
　　　　Namaḥ.
Oṃ Devyānandānāthamayyai
　　　　Namaḥ.
Oṃ Kauleśānandanāthinyai
　　　　Namaḥ.
Oṃ Divyaughagururūpāyai
　　　　Namaḥ.
Oṃ Samayānandanāthinyai
　　　　Namaḥ.
Oṃ Śukladevyānandanāthāyai
　　　　Namaḥ.
Oṃ Kuleśānandanāthinyai
　　　　Namaḥ.
Oṃ Klinnāṅgānandarūpāyai
　　　　Namaḥ.
Oṃ Samayānandanāthinyai
　　　　Namaḥ.
Oṃ Vedānandanāthamayyai
　　　　Namaḥ.
Oṃ Sahajānandanāthinyai
　　　　Namaḥ.
Oṃ Siddhaughagururūpāyai
　　　　Namaḥ.
Oṃ Aparāgururūpiṇyai Namaḥ.
Oṃ Gaganānandanāthāyai
　　　　Namaḥ. 720

Oṃ Viśvānandasvanāthinyai
　　　　Namaḥ.
Oṃ Vimalānandanāthāyai
　　　　Namaḥ.
Oṃ Madanānandanāthinyai
　　　　Namaḥ.
Oṃ Bhuvanādyāyai Namaḥ.

Oṃ Līlādyāyai Namaḥ.

Oṃ Nandanānandanāthinyai
Namaḥ.

Oṃ Svātmānandānandarūpāyai
Namaḥ.

Oṃ Priyādyānandanāthinyai
Namaḥ.

Oṃ Mānavaughaguruśreṣṭhāyai
Namaḥ.

Oṃ Parameṣṭhiguruprabhāyai
Namaḥ.

Oṃ Paraguhyāyai Namaḥ.

Oṃ Guruśaktyai Namaḥ.

Oṃ Svagurukīrtanapriyāyai
Namaḥ.

Oṃ Trailokyamohanakhyātāyai
Namaḥ.

Oṃ Sarvāśāparipūrakāyai
Namaḥ.

Oṃ Sarvasaṅkṣobhiṇyai Namaḥ.

Oṃ Pūrvāmnāya Prathita
Vaibhavāyai Namaḥ.

Oṃ Śivāyai Śaktyai Namaḥ.

Oṃ Śivaśaktyai Namaḥ.

Oṃ Śivacakratrayālayāyai
Namaḥ. 740

Oṃ Sarvasaubhāgyadākhyāyai
Namaḥ.

Oṃ Sarvārthasādhikāhvayāyai
Namaḥ.

Oṃ Sarvarakṣākarākhyāyai
Namaḥ.

Oṃ Dakṣiṇāmnāyadevatāyai
Namaḥ.

Oṃ Madhyārkacakranilayāyai
Namaḥ.

Oṃ Kauberāmnāya Devatāyai
Namaḥ.

Oṃ Kuberapūjyāyai Namaḥ.

Oṃ Kulajāyai Namaḥ.

Oṃ Kulāmnāyapravartinyai
Namaḥ.

Oṃ Binducakrakṛtāvāsāyai
Namaḥ.

Oṃ Madhyasiṃhāsaneśvaryai
Namaḥ.

Oṃ Śrīvidyāyai Namaḥ.

Oṃ Mahālakṣmyai Namaḥ.

Oṃ Lakṣmyai Namaḥ.

Oṃ Śaktitrayātmikāyai Namaḥ.

Oṃ Sarvasāmrājyalakṣmyai
Namaḥ.

Oṃ Pañcalakṣmītiviśrutāyai
Namaḥ.

Oṃ Śrīvidyāyai Namaḥ. 760

Oṃ Parajyotiṣe Namaḥ.

Oṃ Paraniṣkalaśāmbhavyai
Namaḥ.

Oṃ Mātṛkāyai Namaḥ.

Oṃ Pañcakośyai Namaḥ.

Oṃ Śrīvidyāyai Namaḥ.

Oṃ Tvaritāyai Namaḥ.

Oṃ Pārijāteśvaryai Namaḥ.

Oṃ Trikūṭāyai Namaḥ.

Oṃ Pañcabāṇagāyai Namaḥ.

Oṃ Pañcakalpalatāyai Namaḥ.

Oṃ Pañcavidyāyai Namaḥ.

Oṃ Amṛtapīṭhikāyai Namaḥ.

Oṃ Sudhāsuve Namaḥ.

Oṃ Ramaṇāyai Namaḥ.

Oṃ Īśānāyai Namaḥ.

Oṃ Annapūrṇāyai Namaḥ.

Oṃ Kāmaduhe Namaḥ.

Oṃ Śrīvidyāyai Namaḥ.

Oṃ Siddhalakṣmyai Namaḥ.

Oṃ Mātaṅgyai Namaḥ. 780

Oṃ Bhuvaneśvaryai Namaḥ.

Oṃ Vārāhyau Namaḥ.

Oṃ Pañcaratnānāmīśvaryai
Namaḥ.

Oṃ Mātṛvarṇagāyai Namaḥ.

Oṃ Parājyotiṣe Namaḥ.
Oṃ Kośarūpāyai Namaḥ.
Oṃ Aindavīkalayā Yutāyai
                              Namaḥ.
Oṃ Paritaḥ Svāminyai Namaḥ.
Oṃ Śaktidarśanāyai Namaḥ.
Oṃ Ravibinduyuje Namaḥ.
Oṃ Brahmadarśanarūpāyai
                              Namaḥ.
Oṃ Śivadarśanarūpiṇyai Namaḥ.
Oṃ Viṣṇudarśanarūpāyai
                              Namaḥ.
Oṃ Sṛṣṭicakranivāsinyai Namaḥ.
Oṃ Sauradarśanarūpāyai
                              Namaḥ.
Oṃ Sthiticakrakṛtālayāyai
                              Namaḥ.
Oṃ Bauddhadarśanarūpāyai
                              Namaḥ.
Oṃ Mahātripurasundaryai
                              Namaḥ.
Oṃ Tattvamudrāsvarūpāyai
                              Namaḥ.
Oṃ Prasannāyai Namaḥ. 800

Oṃ Jñānamudrikāyai Namaḥ.
Oṃ Sarvopacārasantuṣṭāyai
                              Namaḥ.
Oṃ Hṛnmayyai Namaḥ.
Oṃ Śīrṣadevatāyai Namaḥ.
Oṃ Śikhāsthitāyai Namaḥ.
Oṃ Brahmamayyai Namaḥ.
Oṃ Netratrayavilāsinyai Namaḥ.
Oṃ Astrasthāyai Namaḥ.
Oṃ Caturasrāyai Namaḥ.
Oṃ Dvārakāyai Namaḥ.
Oṃ Dvāravāsinyai Namaḥ.
Oṃ Aṇimāyai Namaḥ.
Oṃ Paścimasthāyai Namaḥ.
Oṃ Laghimāyai Namaḥ.
Oṃ Uttaradevatāyai Namaḥ.
Oṃ Pūrvasthāyai Namaḥ.
Oṃ Mahimāyai Namaḥ.

Oṃ Īśitvāyai Namaḥ.
Oṃ Dakṣiṇadvāradevatāyai
                              Namaḥ.
Oṃ Vaśitvāyai Namaḥ. 820

Oṃ Vāyukoṇasthāyai Namaḥ.
Oṃ Prākāmyāyai Namaḥ.
Oṃ Īśānadevatāyai Namaḥ.
Oṃ Agnikoṇasthitāyai Namaḥ.
Oṃ Bhuktaye Namaḥ.
Oṃ Icchāyai Namaḥ.
Oṃ Nairṛtavāsinyai Namaḥ.
Oṃ Prāptisiddhaye Namaḥ.
Oṃ Avasthāyai Namaḥ.
Oṃ Prākāmyārdhavilāsinyai
                              Namaḥ.
Oṃ Brāhmyai Namaḥ.
Oṃ Māheśvaryai Namaḥ.
Oṃ Kaumāryai Namaḥ.
Oṃ Vaiṣṇavyai Namaḥ.
Oṃ Vārāhyai Namaḥ.
Oṃ Aindryai Namaḥ.
Oṃ Cāmuṇḍāyai Namaḥ.
Oṃ Mahālakṣmyai Namaḥ.
Oṃ Diśāṅgataye Namaḥ.
Oṃ Kṣobhiṇyai Namaḥ. 840

Oṃ Drāviṇīmudrāyai Namaḥ.
Oṃ Ākarṣāyai Namaḥ.
Oṃ Unmādanakāriṇyai Namaḥ.
Oṃ Mahāṅkuśāyai Namaḥ.
Oṃ Khecaryai Namaḥ.
Oṃ Bījākhyāyai Namaḥ.
Oṃ Yonimudrikāyai Namaḥ.
Oṃ Sarvāśāpūracakrasthāyai
                              Namaḥ.
Oṃ Kāryasiddhikaryai Namaḥ.
Oṃ Kāmākarṣaṇikāśaktyai
                              Namaḥ.
Oṃ Buddhyākarṣaṇarūpiṇyai
                              Namaḥ.
Oṃ Ahaṅkārākarṣiṇyai Namaḥ.

Oṃ Śabdākarṣaṇarūpiṇyai
Namaḥ.

Oṃ Sparśākarṣaṇarūpāyai
Namaḥ.

Oṃ Rūpākarṣaṇarūpiṇyai
Namaḥ.

Oṃ Rasākarṣaṇarūpāyai Namaḥ.

Oṃ Gandhākarṣaṇarūpiṇyai
Namaḥ.

Oṃ Cittākarṣaṇarūpāyai Namaḥ.

Oṃ Dhairyākarṣaṇarūpiṇyai
Namaḥ.

Oṃ Smṛtyākarṣaṇarūpāyai
Namaḥ. 860

Oṃ Bījākarṣaṇarūpiṇyai Namaḥ.

Oṃ Amṛtākarṣiṇyai Namaḥ.

Oṃ Nāmākarṣaṇarūpiṇyai
Namaḥ.

Oṃ Śarīrākarṣiṇīdevyai Namaḥ.

Oṃ Ātmākarṣaṇarūpiṇyai
Namaḥ.

Oṃ Ṣoḍaśasvararūpāyai Namaḥ.

Oṃ Sravatpīyūṣamandirāyai
Namaḥ.

Oṃ Tripureśyai Namaḥ.

Oṃ Siddharūpāyai Namaḥ.

Oṃ Kalādalanivāsinyai Namaḥ.

Oṃ Sarvasaṅkṣobhacakreśyai
Namaḥ.

Oṃ Śaktaye Guptatarābhidhāyai
Namaḥ.

Oṃ Anaṅgakusumāśaktaye
Namaḥ.

Oṃ Anaṅgakaṭimekhalāyai
Namaḥ.

Oṃ Anaṅgamadanāyai Namaḥ.

Oṃ Anaṅgamadanāturarūpiṇyai
Namaḥ.

Oṃ Anaṅgarekhāyai Namaḥ.

Oṃ Anaṅgavegāyai Namaḥ.

Oṃ Anaṅgāṅkuśābhidhāyai
Namaḥ.

Oṃ Anaṅgamālinyai Śaktaye
Namaḥ. 880

Oṃ Aṣṭa Vargadiganvitāyai
Namaḥ.

Oṃ Vasupatrakṛtāvāsāyai
Namaḥ.

Oṃ Śrīmattripurasundaryai
Namaḥ.

Oṃ Sarvasāmrājyasukhadāyai
Namaḥ.

Oṃ Sarvasaubhāgyadeśvaryai
Namaḥ.

Oṃ Sampradāyeśvaryai Namaḥ.

Oṃ Sarvasaṅkṣobhaṇakaryai
Namaḥ.

Oṃ Sarvavidrāviṇyai Namaḥ.

Oṃ Sarvākarṣaṇāṭopa Kāriṇyai
Namaḥ.

Oṃ Sarvāhlādanaśaktaye
Namaḥ.

Oṃ Sarvajṛmbhaṇakāriṇyai
Namaḥ.

Oṃ Sarvastambhanaśaktaye
Namaḥ.

Oṃ Sarvasammohinyai Namaḥ.

Oṃ Sarvavaśyakaryai Śaktyai
Namaḥ.

Oṃ Sarvasarvānurañjanyai
Namaḥ.

Oṃ Sarvonmādanaśaktaye
Namaḥ.

Oṃ Sarvārthasiddhikāriṇyai
Namaḥ.

Oṃ Sarvasampattidāyai Śaktaye
Namaḥ.

Oṃ Sarvamantramayyai Namaḥ.

Oṃ Sarvadvandvakṣayakaryai
Namaḥ. 900

Oṃ Tripuravāsinyai Siddhyai
Namaḥ.

Oṃ Sarvārthasādhakeśyai
Namaḥ.
Oṃ Sarvakāyārthasiddhidāyai
Namaḥ.
Oṃ Caturdaśāracakreśyai
Namaḥ.
Oṃ Kalāyogasamanvitāyai
Namaḥ.
Oṃ Sarvasiddhipradāyai Devyai
Namaḥ.
Oṃ Sarvasampatpradāyai
Namaḥ.
Oṃ Sarvapriyaṅkaryai Śaktaye
Namaḥ.
Oṃ Sarvamaṅgalakāriṇyai
Namaḥ.
Oṃ Sarvakāmaprapūrṇāyai
Namaḥ.
Oṃ Sarvaduḥkhapramocinyai
Namaḥ.
Oṃ Sarvamṛtyupraśamanyai
Namaḥ.
Oṃ Sarvavighnavināśinyai
Namaḥ.
Oṃ Sarvāṅgasundaryai Devyai
Namaḥ.
Oṃ Sarvasaubhāgyadāyinyai
Namaḥ.
Oṃ Tripureśyai Namaḥ.
Oṃ Sarvasiddhipradāyai Namaḥ.
Oṃ Daśakoṇagāyai Namaḥ.
Oṃ Sarvarakṣākareśyai Namaḥ.
Oṃ Nigarbhāyai Yoginyai
Namaḥ. 920

Oṃ Sarvajñāyai Namaḥ.
Oṃ Sarvaśaktaye Namaḥ.
Oṃ Sarvaiśvaryapradāyai
Namaḥ.
Oṃ Sarvajñānamayyai Devyai
Namaḥ.
Oṃ Sarvavyādhivināśinyai
Namaḥ.

Oṃ Sarvādhārasvarūpāyai
Namaḥ.
Oṃ Sarvapāpaharāyai Namaḥ.
Oṃ Sarvānandamayyai Devyai
Namaḥ.
Oṃ Sarvarakṣāsvarūpiṇyai
Namaḥ.
Oṃ Mahimāśaktidevyai Namaḥ.
Oṃ Devyai Namaḥ.
Oṃ Sarvasamṛddhidāyai
Namaḥ.
Oṃ Antardaśāracakreśyai
Namaḥ.
Oṃ Devyai Tripuramālinyai
Namaḥ.
Oṃ Sarvarogahareśyai Namaḥ.
Oṃ Rahasyāyai Yoginyai
Namaḥ.
Oṃ Vāgdevyai Namaḥ.
Oṃ Vaśinyai Namaḥ.
Oṃ Devyai Kāmeśvaryai Namaḥ.
Oṃ Modinyai Namaḥ.
Oṃ Vimalāyai Namaḥ. 940

Oṃ Aruṇāyai Namaḥ.
Oṃ Jayinyai Namaḥ.
Oṃ Sarveśvaryai Namaḥ.
Oṃ Kaulinyai Namaḥ.
Oṃ Aṣṭārasarvasiddhidāyai
Namaḥ.
Oṃ Sarvakāmapradeśyai
Namaḥ.
Oṃ Parāpararahasyavide
Namaḥ.
Oṃ Trikoṇacaturaśrasthāyai
Namaḥ.
Oṃ Sarvaiśvaryāyai Namaḥ.
Oṃ Āyudhātmikāyai Namaḥ.
Oṃ Kāmeśvarībāṇarūpāyai
Namaḥ.
Oṃ Kāmeśīcāparūpiṇyai Namaḥ.
Oṃ Kāmeśīpāśarūpāyai Namaḥ.

Oṃ Kāmeśyaṅkuśarūpiṇyai
	Namaḥ.
Oṃ Kāmeśvaryai Namaḥ.
Oṃ Indraśaktaye Namaḥ.
Oṃ Agnicakrakṛtālayāyai
	Namaḥ.
Oṃ Kāmagiryadhidevyai Namaḥ.
Oṃ Trikoṇasthāyai Namaḥ.
Oṃ Agrakoṇagāyai Namaḥ. 960

Oṃ Dakṣakoṇeśvaryai Namaḥ.
Oṃ Viṣṇuśaktaye Namaḥ.
Oṃ Jālandharāśrayāyai Namaḥ.
Oṃ Sūryacakrālayāyai Namaḥ.
Oṃ Rudraśaktaye Namaḥ.
Oṃ Vāmāṅgakoṇagāyai Namaḥ.
Oṃ Somacakrāyai Namaḥ.
Oṃ Brahmaśaktaye Namaḥ.
Oṃ Pūrṇagiryanurāgiṇyai
	Namaḥ.
Oṃ Śrīmattrikoṇabhuvanāyai
	Namaḥ.
Oṃ Tripurātmane Namaḥ.
Oṃ Maheśvaryai Namaḥ.
Oṃ Sarvānandamayeśyai
	Namaḥ.
Oṃ Bindugāyai Namaḥ.
Oṃ Atirahasyabhṛte Namaḥ.
Oṃ Parabrahmasvarūpāyai
	Namaḥ.

Oṃ Mahātripurasundaryai
	Namaḥ.
Oṃ Sarvacakrāntarasthāyai
	Namaḥ.
Oṃ Samastacakranāyikāyai
	Namaḥ.
Oṃ Sarvacakreśvaryai
	Namaḥ. 980

Oṃ Sarvamantrāṇāmīśvaryai
	Namaḥ.
Oṃ Sarvavidyeśvaryai Namaḥ.
Oṃ Sarvavāgīśvaryai Namaḥ.
Oṃ Sarvayogīśvaryai Namaḥ.
Oṃ Pīṭheśvaryai Namaḥ.
Oṃ Akhileśvaryai Namaḥ.
Oṃ Sarvakāmeśvaryai Namaḥ.
Oṃ Sarvatattveśvaryai Namaḥ.
Oṃ Āgameśvaryai Namaḥ.
Oṃ Śaktyai Namaḥ.
Oṃ Śaktidhṛṣe Namaḥ.
Oṃ Ullāsāyai Namaḥ.
Oṃ Nirdvandvāyai Namaḥ.
Oṃ Dvaitagarbhiṇyai Namaḥ.
Oṃ Niṣprapañcāyai Namaḥ.
Oṃ Mahāmāyāyai Namaḥ.
Oṃ Saprapañcāyai Namaḥ.
Oṃ Suvāsinyai Namaḥ.
Oṃ Sarvaviśvotpattidhātryai
	Namaḥ.
Oṃ Paramānandasundaryai
	Namaḥ. 1000

Oṃ Iti Śrīrudrayāmale Tantre Bhairavabhairavīsaṃvāde Śrī Tripura
Sundarī Sahasranāmāvaliḥ Samāptā.

*****

श्री त्रिपुर सुन्दरी सहस्रनामावलिः ।

ॐ ऐं ह्रीं श्रीं-आनन्दसिन्धवे नमः ।

ॐ आनन्दमूर्तये नमः ।

ॐ विनोदिन्यै नमः ।

ॐ त्रिपुरायै सुन्दर्यै नमः ।

ॐ प्रेमपाथोनिधये नमः ।

ॐ अनुत्तमायै नमः ।

ॐ वामार्धगह्वरायै नमः ।

ॐ भूत्यै नमः ।

ॐ विभूत्यै नमः ।

ॐ शङ्करयै नमः ।

ॐ शिवायै नमः ।

ॐ शृङ्गारमूर्तये नमः ।

ॐ वरदायै नमः ।

ॐ रसायै नमः ।

ॐ शुभगोचरायै नमः ।

ॐ परमानन्दलहर्यै नमः ।

ॐ रङ्गवत्यै गतये नमः ।

ॐ रङ्गमालायै नमः । 20

ॐ अनङ्गकलायै नमः ।

ॐ केल्यै नमः ।

ॐ कैवल्यदायै नमः ।

ॐ कलायै नमः ।

ॐ रसकल्पायै नमः ।

ॐ कल्पलतायै नमः ।

ॐ कुतूहलवत्यै गतये नमः ।

ॐ विनोददिग्धायै नमः ।

ॐ सुस्निग्धायै नमः ।

ॐ मुग्धमूर्तये नमः ।

ॐ मनोरमायै नमः ।

ॐ बालार्ककोटि किरणायै नमः ।

ॐ चन्द्रकोटिसुशीतलायै नमः ।

ॐ स्रवत्पीयूषदिग्धाङ्ग्यै नमः ।

ॐ स्वर्गार्थपरिकल्पितायै नमः ।

ॐ कुरङ्गनयनायै नमः ।

ॐ कान्तायै नमः ।

ॐ सुगतये नमः ।

ॐ सुखसन्तत्यै नमः ।

ॐ राजराजेश्वर्यै नमः । 40

ॐ राज्यै नमः ।

ॐ महेन्द्रपरिवन्दितायै नमः ।

ॐ प्रपञ्चगतये नमः ।

ॐ ईशान्यै नमः ।

ॐ प्रपञ्चगतये उत्तमायै नमः ।

ॐ दुर्वाससे नमः ।

ॐ दुःसहायै नमः ।

ॐ शक्तये नमः ।

ॐ शिञ्जत्कनकनूपुरायै नमः ।

ॐ मेरुमन्दरवक्षोजायै नमः ।

ॐ सृणिपाशवरायुधायै नमः ।

ॐ शरकोदण्ड संसक्तपाणिद्वय
                 विराजितायै नमः ।

ॐ चन्द्रबिम्बाननायै नमः ।

ॐ चारुमकुटायै नमः ।

ॐ उत्तंसचन्द्रिकायै नमः ।

ॐ सिन्दूतिलकायै नमः ।

ॐ चारुधम्मिल्लायै नमः ।

ॐ अमलमालिकायै नमः ।

ॐ मन्दारदाममुदितायै नमः ।

ॐ रत्नमालाविभूषितायै नमः। 60

ॐ सुवर्णाभरणप्रीतायै नमः।

ॐ मुक्तादाममनोरमायै नमः।

ॐ ताम्बूलपूर्णवदनायै नमः।

ॐ मदनानन्दमानसायै नमः।

ॐ सुखाराध्यायै नमः।

ॐ तपस्सारायै नमः।

ॐ कृपापारायै नमः।

ॐ विधीश्वर्यै नमः।

ॐ वक्षःस्थललसद्रत्नप्रभायै नमः।

ॐ मधुरसोन्मदायै नमः।

ॐ बिन्दुनादात्मकोच्चाररहितायै
नमः।

ॐ तुर्यरूपिण्यै नमः।

ॐ कमनीयाकृतये नमः।

ॐ धन्यायै नमः।

ॐ शाङ्कर्यै नमः।

ॐ प्रीतिञ्जयै नमः।

ॐ प्रपञ्चायै नमः।

ॐ पञ्चम्यै नमः।

ॐ पूर्णायै नमः।

ॐ पूर्णपीठनिवासिन्यै नमः। 80

ॐ राज्यलक्ष्म्यै नमः।

ॐ श्रीलक्ष्म्यै नमः।

ॐ महालक्ष्म्यै नमः।

ॐ सुराजिकायै नमः।

ॐ सन्तोषसीमायै नमः।

ॐ सम्पत्तये नमः।

ॐ शातकौम्भ्यै नमः।

ॐ द्युतये नमः।

ॐ परिपूर्णायै नमः।

ॐ जगद्धात्र्यै नमः।

ॐ विधात्र्यै नमः।

ॐ बलवर्धिन्यै नमः।

ॐ सार्वभौमनृपश्रिये नमः।

ॐ साम्राज्यगतये नमः।

ॐ अम्बिकायै नमः।

ॐ सरोजाक्ष्यै नमः।

ॐ दीर्घदृष्ट्ये नमः।

ॐ साचीक्षणविचक्षणायै नमः।

ॐ रङ्गस्रवन्त्यै नमः।

ॐ रसिकायै नमः। 100

ॐ प्रधानायै नमः।

ॐ रसरूपिण्यै नमः।

ॐ रससिन्धवे नमः।

ॐ सुगात्र्यै नमः।

ॐ धूसर्यै नमः।

ॐ मैथुनोन्मुखायै नमः।

ॐ निरन्तरगुणासक्तायै नमः।

ॐ निधुवनात्मिकायै शक्तये नमः।

ॐ कामाक्ष्यै नमः।

ॐ कमनीयायै नमः।

ॐ कामेश्यै नमः।

ॐ भगमङ्गलायै नमः।

ॐ सुभगायै नमः।

ॐ भोगिन्यै नमः।

ॐ भोग्यायै नमः।

ॐ भाग्यदायै नमः।

ॐ सुभगायै नमः।

ॐ भगायै नमः।

ॐ भगलिङ्गायै नमः।

ॐ आनन्दकलायै नमः । 120

ॐ भगमध्यनिवासिन्यै नमः ।

ॐ भगरूपायै नमः ।

ॐ भगमय्यै नमः ।

ॐ भगयन्त्रायै नमः ।

ॐ भगोत्तमायै नमः ।

ॐ योनिमुद्रायै नमः ।

ॐ कामकलायै नमः ।

ॐ कुलामृतपरायणायै नमः ।

ॐ कुलकुण्डालयायै नमः ।

ॐ सूक्ष्मायै नमः ।

ॐ जीवात्मने नमः ।

ॐ लिङ्गरूपिण्यै नमः ।

ॐ मूलक्रियायै नमः ।

ॐ मूलरूपायै नमः ।

ॐ मूलाकृतिस्वरूपिण्यै नमः ।

ॐ सोत्सुकायै नमः ।

ॐ कमलानन्दायै नमः ।

ॐ चिद्द्रावायै नमः ।

ॐ आत्मगतये नमः ।

ॐ शिवायै नमः । 140

ॐ श्वेतायै नमः ।

ॐ अरुणायै नमः ।

ॐ बिन्दुरूपायै नमः ।

ॐ वेदयोनये नमः ।

ॐ ध्वनिक्षणायै नमः ।

ॐ घण्टाकोटिरवारावायै नमः ।

ॐ रविविम्बोत्थितायै नमः ।

ॐ अद्भुतायै नमः ।

ॐ नादान्तलीनायै नमः ।

ॐ सम्पूर्णायै नमः ।

ॐ पूर्णस्थायै नमः ।

ॐ बहुरूपिकायै नमः ।

ॐ भृङ्गारावायै नमः ।

ॐ वंशगतये नमः ।

ॐ वादित्रायै नमः ।

ॐ मुरजध्वनये नमः ।

ॐ वर्णमालायै नमः ।

ॐ सिद्धिकलायै नमः ।

ॐ षट् चक्रक्रमवासिन्यै नमः ।

ॐ मूलकेलीरतायै नमः । 160

ॐ स्वाधिष्ठानायै नमः ।

ॐ तुर्यनिवासिन्यै नमः ।

ॐ मणिपुरस्थितये नमः ।

ॐ स्निग्धायै नमः ।

ॐ कूर्मचक्रपरायणायै नमः ।

ॐ अनाहतगतये नमः ।

ॐ दीपशिखायै नमः ।

ॐ मणिमयाकृतये नमः ।

ॐ विशुद्धायै नमः ।

ॐ शब्दसंशुद्धायै नमः ।

ॐ जीवबोधस्थल्यै नमः ।

ॐ रवायै नमः ।

ॐ आज्ञाचक्राब्जसंस्थायै नमः ।

ॐ स्फुरन्त्यै नमः ।

ॐ निपुणायै नमः ।

ॐ त्रिवृते नमः ।

ॐ चन्द्रिकायै नमः ।

ॐ चन्द्रकोटि श्रिये नमः ।

ॐ सूर्यकोटि ।

ॐ प्रभामय्यै नमः ।

ॐ पद्मरागारुणच्छायायै नमः । 180

ॐ नित्यायै नमः ।

ॐ आह्लादमय्यै नमः ।

ॐ प्रभायै नमः ।

ॐ पानश्रिये नमः ।

ॐ प्रियामात्यायै नमः ।

ॐ निश्चलायै नमः ।

ॐ अमृतनन्दिन्यै नमः ।

ॐ कान्ताङ्गसङ्गमुदितायै नमः ।

ॐ सुधामाधुर्यसम्भृतायै नमः ।

ॐ महामञ्चस्थितायै नमः ।

ॐ अलिप्तायै नमः ।

ॐ तृप्तायै नमः ।

ॐ दृप्तायै नमः ।

ॐ सुसम्भृतये नमः ।

ॐ स्रवत्पीयूषसंसिक्तायै नमः ।

ॐ रक्तार्णवविवर्धिन्यै नमः ।

ॐ सुरक्तायै नमः ।

ॐ प्रियसंसिक्तायै नमः ।

ॐ शश्वत्कुण्डालयायै नमः ।

ॐ अभयायै नमः । 200

ॐ श्रेयः श्रुतये नमः ।

ॐ प्रत्येकानवकेशिफलावल्यै नमः ।

ॐ प्रीतायै नमः ।

ॐ शिवायै नमः ।

ॐ शिवप्रियायै नमः ।

ॐ शाङ्कर्यै नमः ।

ॐ शाम्भव्यै नमः ।

ॐ विभायै नमः ।

ॐ स्वयम्भुवे नमः ।

ॐ स्वप्रियायै नमः ।

ॐ स्वीयायै नमः ।

ॐ स्वकीयायै नमः ।

ॐ जनमातृकायै नमः ।

ॐ स्वारामायै नमः ।

ॐ स्वाश्रयायै नमः ।

ॐ साध्व्यै नमः ।

ॐ सुधाधाराधिकाधिकायै नमः ।

ॐ मङ्गलायै नमः ।

ॐ उज्जयिन्यै नमः ।

ॐ मान्यायै नमः । 220

ॐ सर्वमङ्गलसङ्गिन्यै नमः ।

ॐ भद्रायै नमः ।

ॐ भद्रावल्यै नमः ।

ॐ कन्यायै नमः ।

ॐ कलितार्धेन्दुबिम्बभाजे नमः ।

ॐ कल्याणलतिकायै नमः ।

ॐ काम्यायै नमः ।

ॐ कुकर्मणे नमः ।

ॐ कुमतये नमः ।

ॐ मनवे नमः ।

ॐ कुरङ्गाक्ष्यै नमः ।

ॐ क्षीबनेत्रायै नमः ।

ॐ क्षारायै नमः ।

ॐ रसमदोन्मदायै नमः ।

ॐ वारुणीपानमुदितायै नमः ।

ॐ मदिरारचिताश्रयायै नमः ।

ॐ स्वादम्बरीपानरुचये नमः ।

ॐ विपाशायै नमः ।

ॐ पाशभीतिनुदे नमः ।

ॐ मुदितायै नमः । 240

ॐ मुदितापाङ्गायै नमः ।

ॐ दरदोलितदीर्घदृशे नमः ।

ॐ दैत्यकुलानलशिखायै नमः ।

ॐ मनोरथसुधाद्युतये नमः ।

ॐ सुवासिन्यै नमः ।

ॐ पीनगात्रयै नमः ।

ॐ पीनश्रोणिपयोधरायै नमः ।

ॐ सुचारुकबर्यै नमः ।

ॐ दन्तदीधितिदीप्रमौक्तिकायै नमः ।

ॐ बिम्बाधरायै नमः ।

ॐ द्युतिमुखायै नमः ।

ॐ प्रवालोत्तमदीधितये नमः ।

ॐ तिलप्रसूननासाग्रायै नमः ।

ॐ हेमकक्कोलभालकायै नमः ।

ॐ निष्कलङ्केन्दुवदनायै नमः ।

ॐ बालेन्दुमुकुटोज्ज्वलायै नमः ।

ॐ नृत्यत्खञ्जननेत्रश्रिये नमः ।

ॐ विस्फुरत्कर्णशष्कुल्यै नमः ।

ॐ बालचन्द्रातपत्राधर्यै नमः ।

ॐ मणिसूर्यकिरीटिन्यै नमः । 260

ॐ हेममाणिक्यताटङ्कायै नमः ।

ॐ मणिकाञ्चनकुण्डलायै नमः ।

ॐ सुचारुचिबुकायै नमः ।

ॐ कम्बुकण्ठ्यै नमः ।

ॐ मणिमनोरमायै नमः ।

ॐ गङ्गातरङ्गहारोर्मये नमः ।

ॐ मत्तकोकिलनिःस्वनायै नमः ।

ॐ मृणालविलसद्बाहवे नमः ।

ॐ पाशाङ्कुशधनुर्धरायै नमः ।

ॐ केयूरकटकाच्छन्नायै नमः ।

ॐ नानारत्नमनोरमायै नमः ।

ॐ ताम्रपङ्कजपाणिश्रिये नमः ।

ॐ नखरत्नप्रभावत्यै नमः ।

ॐ अङ्गुलीय मणिश्रेणि
चञ्चदङ्गुलि सन्ततये नमः ।

ॐ मन्दरद्वन्द्वसुकुचायै नमः ।

ॐ रोमराजीभुजकायै नमः ।

ॐ गम्भीरनाभये नमः ।

ॐ त्रिवलीवलयायै नमः ।

ॐ सुमध्यमायै नमः ।

ॐ रणत्काञ्चीगुणोन्नद्धायै
नमः । 280

ॐ पट्टांशुकसुनीविकायै नमः ।

ॐ मेरुगुण्डीनितम्बाढ्यायै नमः ।

ॐ गजगण्डोरुयुग्मयुजे नमः ।

ॐ सुजानुमन्दरासक्त
लसज्जङ्घाद्वयान्वितायै नमः ।

ॐ गूढगुल्फायै नमः ।

ॐ मञ्जुशिञ्जन्मणिनूपुरमण्डितायै
नमः ।

ॐ योगिध्येयपदद्वन्द्वायै नमः ।

ॐ सुधामायै नमः ।

ॐ अमृतसारिण्यै नमः ।

ॐ लावण्यसिन्धवे नमः ।

ॐ सिन्दूरतिलकायै नमः ।

ॐ कुटिलालकायै नमः ।

ॐ साधुसिद्धायै नमः ।

ॐ सुबुद्धायै नमः ।

ॐ बुधायै नमः ।

ॐ वृन्दारकोदयायै नमः ।

ॐ बालार्ककिरणश्रेणीशोणायै नमः ।

ॐ श्रीप्रेमकामदुघे नमः ।

ॐ रसगम्भीरसरस्यै नमः ।

ॐ पद्मिन्यै नमः । 300

ॐ रससारसायै नमः ।

ॐ प्रसन्नायै नमः ।

ॐ आसन्नवरदायै नमः ।

ॐ शारदायै नमः ।

ॐ सुभाग्यदायै नमः ।

ॐ नटराजप्रियायै नमः ।

ॐ विश्वनाट्यायै नमः ।

ॐ नर्तकनर्तक्यै नमः ।

ॐ विचित्रयन्त्रायै नमः ।

ॐ चित्तन्त्रायै नमः ।

ॐ विद्यावल्ल्यै नमः ।

ॐ शुभायै गत्यै नमः ।

ॐ कूटारकुटायै नमः ।

ॐ कूटस्थायै नमः ।

ॐ पञ्चकूटायै नमः ।

ॐ पञ्चम्यै नमः ।

ॐ चतुष्कूटायै नमः ।

ॐ त्रिकूटाद्यायै नमः ।

ॐ षट्कूटायै नमः ।

ॐ वेदपूजितायै नमः । 320

ॐ कूटषोडशसम्पन्नायै नमः ।

ॐ तुरीयायै नमः ।

ॐ परमायै कलायै नमः ।

ॐ षोडश्यै नमः ।

ॐ मन्त्रयन्त्राणामीश्वर्यै नमः ।

ॐ मेरुमण्डलायै नमः ।

ॐ षोडशार्णायै नमः ।

ॐ त्रिवर्णायै नमः ।

ॐ बिन्दुनादस्वरूपिण्यै नमः ।

ॐ वर्णातीतायै नमः ।

ॐ वर्णमात्रे नमः ।

ॐ शब्दब्रह्मणे नमः ।

ॐ महासुखायै नमः ।

ॐ चैतन्यवल्ल्यै नमः ।

ॐ कूटात्मने नमः ।

ॐ कामेश्यै नमः ।

ॐ स्वप्नदृश्यगायै नमः ।

ॐ स्वप्नावत्यै नमः ।

ॐ बोधकर्यै नमः ।

ॐ जागृतये नमः । 340

ॐ जागराश्रयायै नमः ।

ॐ स्वप्नाश्रयायै नमः ।

ॐ सुषुप्त्यै नमः ।

ॐ तन्द्रामुक्तायै नमः ।

ॐ माधव्यै नमः ।

ॐ लोपामुद्रायै नमः ।

ॐ कामराज्यै नमः ।

ॐ मानव्यै नमः ।

ॐ वित्तपार्चितायै नमः ।

ॐ शाकम्भर्यै नमः ।

ॐ नन्दिविद्यायै नमः ।

ॐ भस्वद्विद्द्योतमालिन्यै नमः ।

ॐ माहेन्द्र्यै नमः ।

ॐ स्वर्गसम्पत्तये नमः ।

ॐ दुर्वासःसेवितायै नमः ।

ॐ श्रुत्यै नमः ।

ॐ साधकेन्द्रगतये नमः ।

ॐ साध्व्यै नमः ।

ॐ सुलभायै नमः ।

ॐ सिद्धिकन्दरायै नमः । 360

ॐ पुरत्रयेश्यै नमः ।
ॐ पुरजिदर्चितायै नमः ।
ॐ पुरदेवतायै नमः ।
ॐ पुष्ट्यै नमः ।
ॐ विघ्नहर्यै नमः ।
ॐ भूत्यै नमः ।
ॐ विगुणायै नमः ।
ॐ पूज्यकामदुहे नमः ।
ॐ हिरण्यमात्रे नमः ।
ॐ गणपायै नमः ।
ॐ गुहमात्रे नमः ।
ॐ नितम्बिन्यै नमः ।
ॐ सर्वसीमन्तिन्यै नमः ।
ॐ मोक्षायै नमः ।
ॐ दीक्षायै नमः ।
ॐ दीक्षितमातृकायै नमः ।
ॐ साधकाम्बायै नमः ।
ॐ सिद्धमात्रे नमः ।
ॐ साधकेन्द्रायै नमः ।
ॐ मनोरमायै नमः । 380

ॐ यौवनोन्मादिन्यै नमः ।
ॐ तुङ्गायै नमः ।
ॐ सुश्रोण्यै नमः ।
ॐ मदमन्थरायै नमः ।
ॐ पद्मरक्तोत्पलवत्यै नमः ।
ॐ रक्तमाल्यानुलेपनायै नमः ।
ॐ रक्तमालारुचये नमः ।
ॐ शिखाशिखण्डिन्यै नमः ।
ॐ अतिसुन्दर्यै नमः ।

ॐ शिखण्डिनृत्तसन्तुष्टायै नमः ।
ॐ सौरभेय्यै नमः ।
ॐ वसुन्धरायै नमः ।
ॐ सुरभ्यै नमः ।
ॐ कामदायै नमः ।
ॐ काम्यायै नमः ।
ॐ कमनीयार्थकामदायै नमः ।
ॐ नन्दिन्यै नमः ।
ॐ लक्षणवत्यै नमः ।
ॐ वसिष्ठालयदेवतायै नमः ।
ॐ गोलोकदेव्यै नमः । 400

ॐ लोकश्रियै नमः ।
ॐ गोलोकपरिपालिकायै नमः ।
ॐ हविर्धान्यै नमः ।
ॐ देवमात्रे नमः ।
ॐ वृन्दारकवरानुयुजे नमः ।
ॐ रुद्रपत्न्यै नमः ।
ॐ भद्रमात्रे नमः ।
ॐ सुधाधारायै नमः ।
ॐ अम्बुविक्षतये नमः ।
ॐ दक्षिणायै नमः ।
ॐ यज्ञसम्मूर्तये नमः ।
ॐ सुबालायै नमः ।
ॐ धीरनन्दिन्यै नमः ।
ॐ क्षीरपूर्णायै नमः ।
ॐ अर्णवगतये नमः ।
ॐ सुधायोनये नमः ।
ॐ सुलोचनायै नमः ।
ॐ रामानुगायै नमः ।
ॐ सुसेव्यायै नमः ।
ॐ सुगन्धालयवासगायै नमः । 420

ॐ सुचारित्रायै नमः ।

ॐ सुत्रिपुरायै नमः ।

ॐ सुस्तन्यै नमः ।

ॐ स्तनवत्सलायै नमः ।

ॐ रजस्वलायै नमः ।

ॐ रजोयुक्तायै नमः ।

ॐ रञ्जिकायै नमः ।

ॐ रङ्गमालिकायै नमः ।

ॐ रक्तप्रियायै नमः ।

ॐ सुरक्तायै नमः ।

ॐ रतिरङ्गस्वरूपिण्यै नमः ।

ॐ रजःशुक्राम्बिकायै नमः ।

ॐ निष्ठायै नमः ।

ॐ रतिनिष्ठायै नमः ।

ॐ रतिस्पृहायै नमः ।

ॐ हावभावायै नमः ।

ॐ कामकेलिसर्वस्वायै नमः ।

ॐ सुरजीविकायै नमः ।

ॐ स्वयम्भूकुसुमानन्दायै नमः ।

ॐ स्वयम्भूकुसुमप्रियायै नमः । 440

ॐ स्वयम्भूप्रीतिसन्तुष्टायै नमः ।

ॐ स्वयम्भूनिन्दकान्तकृते नमः ।

ॐ स्वयम्भूस्थायै नमः ।

ॐ शक्तिपुट्यै नमः ।

ॐ रतिसर्वस्वपीठिकायै नमः ।

ॐ अत्यन्तसभिकायै नमः ।

ॐ दूत्यै नमः ।

ॐ विदग्धायै नमः ।

ॐ प्रीतिपूजितायै नमः ।

ॐ कुल्लिकायै नमः ।

ॐ यन्त्रनिलयायै नमः ।

ॐ योगपीठाधिवासिन्यै नमः ।

ॐ सुलक्षणायै नमः ।

ॐ रसरूपायै नमः ।

ॐ सर्वलक्षणललक्षितायै नमः ।

ॐ नानालङ्कारसुभगायै नमः ।

ॐ पञ्चबाणसमर्चितायै नमः ।

ॐ ऊर्ध्वत्रिकोणनिलयायै नमः ।

ॐ बालायै नमः ।

ॐ कामेश्वर्यै नमः । 460

ॐ गणाध्यक्षायै नमः ।

ॐ कुलाध्यक्षायै नमः ।

ॐ लक्ष्म्यै नमः ।

ॐ सरस्वत्यै नमः ।

ॐ वसन्तसमयप्रीतायै नमः ।

ॐ प्रीत्यै नमः ।

ॐ कुचभरानतायै नमः ।

ॐ कलाधरमुखायै नमः ।

ॐ अमूर्धायै नमः ।

ॐ पादवृद्धये नमः ।

ॐ कलावत्यै नमः ।

ॐ पुष्पप्रियायै नमः ।

ॐ धृत्यै नमः ।

ॐ रतिकण्ठ्यै नमः ।

ॐ मनोरमायै नमः ।

ॐ मदनोन्मादिन्यै नमः ।

ॐ मोहिन्यै नमः ।

ॐ पार्वण्यै कलायै नमः ।

ॐ शोषिण्यै नमः ।

ॐ वशिन्यै नमः । 480

ॐ राजिन्यै नमः ।

ॐ अत्यन्तसुभगायै नमः ।
ॐ भगायै नमः ।
ॐ पूषायै(ष्णे) नमः ।
ॐ वशायै नमः ।
ॐ सुमनायै (नसे) नमः ।
ॐ रत्यै नमः ।
ॐ प्रीत्यै नमः ।
ॐ धृत्यै नमः ।
ॐ ऋद्ध्यै नमः ।
ॐ सौम्यायै नमः ।
ॐ मरीच्यंशुमालायै नमः ।
ॐ प्रत्यङ्गिरायै नमः ।
ॐ शशिन्यै नमः ।
ॐ सुच्छायायै नमः ।
ॐ सम्पूर्णमण्डलोदयायै नमः ।
ॐ तुष्टायै नमः ।
ॐ अमृतपूर्णायै नमः ।
ॐ भगयन्त्रनिवासिन्यै नमः ।
ॐ लिङ्गयन्त्रालयायै नमः । 500

ॐ शम्भुरूपायै नमः ।
ॐ संयोगयोगिन्यै नमः ।
ॐ द्राविण्यै नमः ।
ॐ बीजरूपायै नमः ।
ॐ अक्षुब्धायै नमः ।
ॐ साधकप्रियायै नमः ।
ॐ राजबीजमय्यै नमः ।
ॐ राज्यसुखदायै नमः ।
ॐ वाञ्छितप्रदायै नमः ।
ॐ रजस्संवीर्यशक्तये नमः ।
ॐ शुक्रविदे नमः ।
ॐ शिवरूपिण्यै नमः ।

ॐ सर्वसारायै नमः ।
ॐ सारमयायै नमः ।
ॐ शिवशक्तिमय्यै नमः ।
ॐ प्रभायै नमः ।
ॐ संयोगानन्दनिलयायै नमः ।
ॐ संयोगप्रीतिमातृकायै नमः ।
ॐ संयोगकुसुमानन्दायै नमः ।
ॐ संयोगायै नमः । 520

ॐ योगवर्धिन्यै नमः ।
ॐ संयोगसुखदावस्थायै नमः ।
ॐ चिदानन्दैकसेवितायै नमः ।
ॐ अर्घ्यपूजकसम्पत्तये नमः ।
ॐ अर्घ्यद्रव्यस्वरूपिण्यै नमः ।
ॐ सामरस्यायै नमः ।
ॐ परायै नमः ।
ॐ प्रीतायै नमः ।
ॐ प्रियसङ्गमरूपिण्यै नमः ।
ॐ ज्ञानदूत्यै नमः ।
ॐ ज्ञानगम्यायै नमः ।
ॐ ज्ञानयोनये नमः ।
ॐ शिवालयायै नमः ।
ॐ चित्कलायै नमः ।
ॐ ज्ञानसकलायै नमः ।
ॐ सकुलायै नमः ।
ॐ सकुलात्मिकायै नमः ।
ॐ कलाचतुष्ट्यै नमः ।
ॐ पद्विन्यै नमः ।
ॐ अतिसूक्ष्मायै नमः । 540

ॐ परात्मिकायै नमः ।
ॐ हंसकेलस्थल्यै नमः ।

ॐ छायायै नमः ।

ॐ हंसद्वयविकासिन्यै नमः ।

ॐ विरागतायै नमः ।

ॐ मोक्षकलायै नमः ।

ॐ परमात्मकलावत्यै नमः ।

ॐ विद्याकलायै नमः ।

ॐ अन्तरात्मस्थायै नमः ।

ॐ चतुष्टयकलावत्यै नमः ।

ॐ विद्यासन्तोषिण्यै नमः ।

ॐ तृप्ये नमः ।

ॐ परब्रह्मप्रकाशिकायै नमः ।

ॐ परमात्मपरायै नमः ।

ॐ वस्तुलीन शक्तिचतुष्टय्यै नमः ।

ॐ शान्तये नमः ।

ॐ बोधकलायै नमः ।

ॐ अवाप्ये नमः ।

ॐ परज्ञानात्मिकायै कलायै नमः ।

ॐ पश्यन्त्यै नमः । 560

ॐ परमात्मस्थायै नमः ।

ॐ अन्तरात्मकलाकुलायै नमः ।

ॐ मध्यमायै नमः ।

ॐ वैखर्यै नमः ।

ॐ आत्मकलानन्दायै नमः ।

ॐ कलावतेयै नमः ।

ॐ तारिण्यै नमः ।

ॐ तरण्यै नमः ।

ॐ तारायै नमः ।

ॐ शिवलिङ्गालियायै नमः ।

ॐ आत्मविदे नमः ।

ॐ परस्परशुभाचारायै नमः ।

ॐ ब्रह्मानन्दविनोदिन्यै नमः ।

ॐ रसालसायै नमः ।

ॐ दूतारासायै नमः ।

ॐ सार्थायै नमः ।

ॐ सार्थप्रियायै नमः ।

ॐ उमायै नमः ।

ॐ जात्यादिरहितायै नमः ।

ॐ योगियोगिन्यै नमः । 580

ॐ आनन्दवर्धिन्यै नमः ।

ॐ वीरभावप्रदायै नमः ।

ॐ दिव्यायै नमः ।

ॐ वीरसुवे नमः ।

ॐ वीरभावदायै नमः ।

ॐ पशुत्वाभिवीरगतये नमः ।

ॐ वीरसङ्गमहोदयायै नमः ।

ॐ मूर्धाभिषिक्तायै नमः ।

ॐ राजश्रिये नमः ।

ॐ क्षत्रियायै नमः ।

ॐ उत्तममातृकायै नमः ।

ॐ शस्त्रास्त्रकुशलायै नमः ।

ॐ शोभायै नमः ।

ॐ रसस्थायै नमः ।

ॐ युद्धजीविकायै नमः ।

ॐ विजयायै नमः ।

ॐ योगिन्यै नमः ।

ॐ यात्रायै नमः ।

ॐ परसैन्यविमर्दिन्यै नमः ।

ॐ पूर्णायै नमः । 600

ॐ वित्तैषिण्यै नमः ।

ॐ वित्तायै नमः ।

ॐ वित्तसञ्चयशालिन्यै नमः ।

ॐ भाण्डागारस्थितायै नमः ।
ॐ रत्नायै नमः ।
ॐ रत्नश्रेण्यधिवासिन्यै नमः ।
ॐ महिष्यै नमः ।
ॐ राजभोग्यायै नमः ।
ॐ गणिकायै नमः ।
ॐ गणभोगभृते नमः ।
ॐ करिण्यै नमः ।
ॐ बडवायै नमः ।
ॐ योगयायै नमः ।
ॐ मल्लसेनायै नमः ।
ॐ पदातिगायै नमः ।
ॐ सैन्यश्रेण्यै नमः ।
ॐ शौर्यरतायै नमः ।
ॐ पताकायै नमः ।
ॐ ध्वजवासिन्यै नमः ।
ॐ सुच्छत्रायै नमः । 620

ॐ अम्बिकायै नमः ।
ॐ अम्बायै नमः ।
ॐ प्रजापालनसद्व्रतये नमः ।
ॐ सुरभ्यै नमः ।
ॐ पूजकाचारायै नमः ।
ॐ राजकार्यपरायणायै नमः ।
ॐ ब्रह्मक्षत्रमय्यै नमः ।
ॐ सोमसूर्यान्तर्यामिन्यै नमः ।
ॐ स्थित्यै नमः ।
ॐ पौरोहित्यप्रियायै नमः ।
ॐ साध्व्यै नमः ।
ॐ ब्रह्माण्यै नमः ।
ॐ यज्ञसन्तत्यै नमः ।
ॐ सोमपानरतायै नमः ।

ॐ प्रीतायै नमः ।
ॐ जनाद्यायै नमः ।
ॐ तपनायै नमः ।
ॐ क्षमायै नमः ।
ॐ प्रतिग्रहपरायै नमः ।
ॐ दात्र्यै नमः । 640

ॐ सृष्टायै नमः ।
ॐ जात्यै नमः ।
ॐ सताङ्गतये नमः ।
ॐ गायत्र्यै नमः ।
ॐ वेदलभ्यायै नमः ।
ॐ दीक्षायै नमः ।
ॐ सन्ध्यापरायणायै नमः ।
ॐ रत्नसद्दीधितये नमः ।
ॐ विश्ववासनायै नमः ।
ॐ विश्वजीविकायै नमः ।
ॐ कृषिवाणीज्यभूत्यै नमः ।
ॐ वृद्ध्ये नमः ।
ॐ धिये नमः ।
ॐ कुसीदिकायै नमः ।
ॐ कुलाधारायै नमः ।
ॐ सुप्रसारायै नमः ।
ॐ मनोन्मन्यै नमः ।
ॐ परायणायै नमः ।
ॐ शूद्रायै नमः ।
ॐ विप्रगतये ॥ 660

ॐ कर्मकर्यै नमः ।
ॐ कौतुकपूजितायै नमः ।
ॐ नानाविचारचतुरायै नमः ।
ॐ बालायै नमः ।

ॐ प्रोढायै नमः ।

ॐ कलामय्यै नमः ।

ॐ सुकर्णधारायै नमः ।

ॐ नावे नमः ।

ॐ पारायै नमः ।

ॐ सर्वाशायै नमः ।

ॐ दुर्मोचन्यै नमः ।

ॐ दुर्गायै नमः ।

ॐ विन्ध्यवनस्थायै नमः ।

ॐ कन्दर्पनयपूरण्यै नमः ।

ॐ भूभारशमन्यै नमः ।

ॐ कृष्णायै नमः ।

ॐ रक्षाराध्यायै नमः ।

ॐ रसोल्लसायै नमः ।

ॐ त्रिविधोत्पातशमन्यै नमः ।

ॐ समग्रसुखशेवधये नमः । 680

ॐ पञ्चावयववाक्यश्रिये नमः ।

ॐ प्रपञ्चोद्यानचन्द्रिकायै नमः ।

ॐ सिद्धसन्दोहसुखितायै नमः ।

ॐ योगिनीवृन्दवन्दितायै नमः ।

ॐ नित्याषोडशरूपायै नमः ।

ॐ कामेश्यै नमः ।

ॐ भगमालिन्यै नमः ।

ॐ नित्यक्लिन्नायै नमः ।

ॐ भी(भे)रुण्डायै नमः ।

ॐ वह्निमण्डलवासिन्यै नमः ।

ॐ महाविद्येश्वरीनित्यायै नमः ।

ॐ शिवदूतीति विश्रुतायै नमः ।

ॐ त्वरिताप्रथितायै नमः ।

ॐ ख्यातायै नमः ।

ॐ विख्यातायै कुलसुन्दर्यै नमः ।

ॐ नित्यायै नमः ।

ॐ नीलपताकायै नमः ।

ॐ विजयायै नमः ।

ॐ सर्वमङ्गलायै नमः ।

ॐ ज्वालामालायै नमः । 700

ॐ विचित्रायै नमः ।

ॐ महात्रिपुरसुन्दर्यै नमः ।

ॐ गुरुवृन्दायै नमः ।

ॐ पुरगुरवे नमः ।

ॐ प्रकाशानन्दनाथिन्यै नमः ।

ॐ शिवानन्दानाथरूपायै नमः ।

ॐ शक्त्यानन्दस्वरूपिण्यै नमः ।

ॐ देव्यानन्दानाथमय्यै नमः ।

ॐ कौलेशानन्दनाथिन्यै नमः ।

ॐ दिव्यौघगुरुरूपायै नमः ।

ॐ समयानन्दनाथिन्यै नमः ।

ॐ शुक्लदेव्यानन्दनाथायै नमः ।

ॐ कुलेशानन्दनाथिन्यै नमः ।

ॐ क्लिन्नाङ्गानन्दरूपायै नमः ।

ॐ समयानन्दनाथिन्यै नमः ।

ॐ वेदानन्दनाथमय्यै नमः ।

ॐ सहजानन्दनाथिन्यै नमः ।

ॐ सिद्धौघगुरुरूपायै नमः ।

ॐ अपरागुरुरूपिण्यै नमः ।

ॐ गगनानन्दनाथायै नमः । 720

ॐ विश्वानन्दस्वनाथिन्यै नमः ।

ॐ विमलानन्दनाथायै नमः ।

ॐ मदनानन्दनाथिन्यै नमः ।

ॐ भुवनाद्यायै नमः ।

ॐ लीलाद्यायै नमः ।

ॐ नन्दनानन्दनाथिन्यै नमः ।

ॐ स्वात्मानन्दानन्दरूपायै नमः ।

ॐ प्रियाद्यानन्दनाथिन्यै नमः ।

ॐ मानवौघगुरुश्रेष्ठायै नमः ।

ॐ परमेष्ठिगुरुप्रभायै नमः ।

ॐ परगुह्यायै नमः ।

ॐ गुरुशक्त्यै नमः ।

ॐ स्वगुरुकीर्तनप्रियायै नमः ।

ॐ त्रैलोक्यमोहनख्यातायै नमः ।

ॐ सर्वाशापरिपूरकायै नमः ।

ॐ सर्वसङ्क्षोभिण्यै नमः ।

ॐ पूर्वाम्नायप्रथितवैभवायै नमः ।

ॐ शिवायै शक्त्यै नमः ।

ॐ शिवशक्त्यै नमः ।

ॐ शिवचक्रत्रयालयायै नमः । 740

ॐ सर्वसौभाग्यदाख्यायै नमः ।

ॐ सर्वार्थसाधिकाह्वयायै नमः ।

ॐ सर्वरक्षाकराख्यायै नमः ।

ॐ दक्षिणाम्नायदेवतायै नमः ।

ॐ मध्यार्कचक्रनिलयायै नमः ।

ॐ कौबेराम्नाय देवतायै नमः ।

ॐ कुबेरपूज्यायै नमः ।

ॐ कुलजायै नमः ।

ॐ कुलाम्नायप्रवर्तिन्यै नमः ।

ॐ बिन्दुचक्रकृतावासायै नमः ।

ॐ मध्यसिंहासनेश्वर्यै नमः ।

ॐ श्रीविद्यायै नमः ।

ॐ महालक्ष्म्यै नमः ।

ॐ लक्ष्म्यै नमः ।

ॐ शक्तित्रयात्मिकायै नमः ।

ॐ सर्वसाम्राज्यलक्ष्म्यै नमः ।

ॐ पञ्चलक्ष्मीतिविश्रुतायै नमः ।

ॐ श्रीविद्यायै नमः । 760

ॐ परज्योतिषे नमः ।

ॐ परनिष्कलशाम्भव्यै नमः ।

ॐ मातृकायै नमः ।

ॐ पञ्चकोश्यै नमः ।

ॐ श्रीविद्यायै नमः ।

ॐ त्वरितायै नमः ।

ॐ पारिजातेश्वर्यै नमः ।

ॐ त्रिकूटायै नमः ।

ॐ पञ्चबाणगायै नमः ।

ॐ पञ्चकल्पलतायै नमः ।

ॐ पञ्चविद्यायै नमः ।

ॐ अमृतपीठिकायै नमः ।

ॐ सुधासुवे नमः ।

ॐ रमणायै नमः ।

ॐ ईशानायै नमः ।

ॐ अन्नपूर्णायै नमः ।

ॐ कामदुहे नमः ।

ॐ श्रीविद्यायै नमः ।

ॐ सिद्धलक्ष्म्यै नमः ।

ॐ मातङ्ग्यै नमः । 780

ॐ भुवनेश्वर्यै नमः ।

ॐ वाराह्यै नमः ।

ॐ पञ्चरत्नानामीश्वर्यै नमः ।

ॐ मातृवर्णगायै नमः ।

ॐ पराज्योतिषे नमः ।

ॐ कोशरूपायै नमः ।

ॐ ऐन्दवीकलया युतायै नमः ।

ॐ परितः स्वामिन्यै नमः ।

ॐ शक्तिदर्शनायै नमः ।

ॐ रविबिन्दुजे नमः ।

ॐ ब्रह्मदर्शनरूपायै नमः ।

ॐ शिवदर्शनरूपिण्यै नमः ।

ॐ विष्णुदर्शनरूपायै नमः ।

ॐ सृष्टिचक्रनिवासिन्यै नमः ।

ॐ सौरदर्शनरूपायै नमः ।

ॐ स्थितिचक्रकृतालयायै नमः ।

ॐ बौद्धदर्शनरूपायै नमः ।

ॐ महात्रिपुरसुन्दर्यै नमः ।

ॐ तत्त्वमुद्रास्वरूपायै नमः ।

ॐ प्रसन्नायै नमः । 800

ॐ ज्ञानमुद्रिकायै नमः ।

ॐ सर्वोपचारसन्तुष्टायै नमः ।

ॐ हृन्मय्यै नमः ।

ॐ शीर्षदेवतायै नमः ।

ॐ शिखास्थितायै नमः ।

ॐ ब्रह्ममय्यै नमः ।

ॐ नेत्रत्रयविलासिन्यै नमः ।

ॐ अस्त्रस्थायै नमः ।

ॐ चतुरस्त्रायै नमः ।

ॐ द्वारकायै नमः ।

ॐ द्वारवासिन्यै नमः ।

ॐ अणिमायै नमः ।

ॐ पश्चिमस्थायै नमः ।

ॐ लघिमायै नमः ।

ॐ उत्तरदेवतायै नमः ।

ॐ पूर्वस्थायै नमः ।

ॐ महिमायै नमः ।

ॐ ईशित्वायै नमः ।

ॐ दक्षिणद्वारदेवतायै नमः ।

ॐ वशित्वायै नमः । 820

ॐ वायुकोणस्थायै नमः ।

ॐ प्राकाम्यायै नमः ।

ॐ ईशानदेवतायै नमः ।

ॐ अग्निकोणस्थितायै नमः ।

ॐ भुक्तये नमः ।

ॐ इच्छायै नमः ।

ॐ नैरृतवासिन्यै नमः ।

ॐ प्राप्तिसिद्धये नमः ।

ॐ अवस्थायै नमः ।

ॐ प्राकाम्यार्धविलासिन्यै नमः ।

ॐ ब्राह्म्यै नमः ।

ॐ माहेश्वर्यै नमः ।

ॐ कौमार्यै नमः ।

ॐ वैष्णव्यै नमः ।

ॐ वाराह्यै नमः ।

ॐ ऐन्द्र्यै नमः ।

ॐ चामुण्डायै नमः ।

ॐ महालक्ष्म्यै नमः ।

ॐ दिशाङ्गतये नमः ।

ॐ क्षोभिण्यै नमः । 840

ॐ द्राविणीमुद्रायै नमः ।

ॐ आकर्षायै नमः ।

ॐ उन्मादनकारिण्यै नमः ।

ॐ महाङ्कुशायै नमः ।

ॐ खेचर्यै नमः ।

ॐ बीजाख्यायै नमः ।

ॐ योनिमुद्रिकायै नमः ।

ॐ सर्वाशापूरचक्रस्थायै नमः ।

ॐ कार्यसिद्धिकर्यै नमः ।

ॐ कामाकर्षणिकाशक्त्यै नमः ।

ॐ बुद्ध्याकर्षणरूपिण्यै नमः ।

ॐ अहङ्काराकर्षिण्यै नमः ।

ॐ शब्दाकर्षणरूपिण्यै नमः ।

ॐ स्पर्शाकर्षणरूपायै नमः ।

ॐ रूपाकर्षणरूपिण्यै नमः ।

ॐ रसाकर्षणरूपायै नमः ।

ॐ गन्धाकर्षणरूपिण्यै नमः ।

ॐ चित्ताकर्षणरूपायै नमः ।

ॐ धैर्याकर्षणरूपिण्यै नमः ।

ॐ स्मृत्याकर्षणरूपायै नमः । 860

ॐ बीजाकर्षणरूपिण्यै नमः ।

ॐ अमृताकर्षिण्यै नमः ।

ॐ नामाकर्षणरूपिण्यै नमः ।

ॐ शरीराकर्षिणीदेव्यै नमः ।

ॐ आत्माकर्षणरूपिण्यै नमः ।

ॐ षोडशस्वररूपायै नमः ।

ॐ स्रवत्पीयूषमन्दिरायै नमः ।

ॐ त्रिपुरेश्यै नमः ।

ॐ सिद्धरूपायै नमः ।

ॐ कलादलनिवासिन्यै नमः ।

ॐ सर्वसङ्क्षोभचक्रेश्यै नमः ।

ॐ शक्त्ये गुप्ततराभिधायै नमः ।

ॐ अनङ्गकुसुमाशक्त्ये नमः ।

ॐ अनङ्गकटिमेखलायै नमः ।

ॐ अनङ्गमदनायै नमः ।

ॐ अनङ्गमदनातुररूपिण्यै नमः ।

ॐ अनङ्गरेखायै नमः ।

ॐ अनङ्गवेगायै नमः ।

ॐ अनङ्गाङ्कुशाभिधायै नमः ।

ॐ अनङ्गमालिन्यै शक्तये नमः । 880

ॐ अष्ट वर्गदिगन्वितायै नमः ।

ॐ वसुपत्रकृतावासायै नमः ।

ॐ श्रीमत्त्रिपुरसुन्दर्यै नमः ।

ॐ सर्वसाम्राज्यसुखदायै नमः ।

ॐ सर्वसौभाग्यदेश्वर्यै नमः ।

ॐ सम्प्रदायेश्वर्यै नमः ।

ॐ सर्वसङ्क्षोभणकर्यै नमः ।

ॐ सर्वविद्राविण्यै नमः ।

ॐ सर्वाकर्षणाटोप कारिण्यै नमः ।

ॐ सर्वाह्लादनशक्तये नमः ।

ॐ सर्वजृम्भणकारिण्यै नमः ।

ॐ सर्वस्तम्भनशक्तये नमः ।

ॐ सर्वसम्मोहिन्यै नमः ।

ॐ सर्ववश्यकर्यै शक्त्यै नमः ।

ॐ सर्वसर्वानुरञ्जन्यै नमः ।

ॐ सर्वोन्मादनशक्तये नमः ।

ॐ सर्वार्थसिद्धिकारिण्यै नमः ।

ॐ सर्वसम्पत्तिदायै शक्तये नमः ।

ॐ सर्वमन्त्रमय्यै नमः ।

ॐ सर्वद्वन्द्वक्षयकर्यै नमः । 900

ॐ त्रिपुरवासिन्यै सिद्ध्यै नमः ।

ॐ सर्वार्थसाधकेश्यै नमः ।

ॐ सर्वकायार्थसिद्धिदायै नमः ।

ॐ चतुर्दशारचक्रेश्यै नमः ।

ॐ कलायोगसमन्वितायै नमः ।

ॐ सर्वसिद्धिप्रदायै देव्यै नमः ।

ॐ सर्वसम्पत्प्रदायै नमः ।

ॐ सर्वप्रियङ्कर्यै शक्तये नमः ।

ॐ सर्वमङ्गलकारिण्यै नमः ।

ॐ सर्वकामप्रपूर्णायै नमः ।

ॐ सर्वदुःखप्रमोचिन्यै नमः ।

ॐ सर्वमृत्युप्रशमन्यै नमः ।

ॐ सर्वविघ्नविनाशिन्यै नमः ।

ॐ सर्वाङ्गसुन्दर्यै देव्यै नमः ।

ॐ सर्वसौभाग्यदायिन्यै नमः ।

ॐ त्रिपुरेश्यै नमः ।

ॐ सर्वसिद्धिप्रदायै नमः ।

ॐ दशकोणगायै नमः ।

ॐ सर्वरक्षाकरेश्यै नमः ।

ॐ निगर्भायै योगिन्यै नमः । 920

ॐ सर्वज्ञायै नमः ।

ॐ सर्वशक्तये नमः ।

ॐ सर्वैश्वर्यप्रदायै नमः ।

ॐ सर्वज्ञानमय्यै देव्यै नमः ।

ॐ सर्वव्याधिविनाशिन्यै नमः ।

ॐ सर्वाधारस्वरूपायै नमः ।

ॐ सर्वपापहरायै नमः ।

ॐ सर्वानन्दमय्यै देव्यै नमः ।

ॐ सर्वरक्षास्वरूपिण्यै नमः ।

ॐ महिमाशक्तिदेव्यै नमः ।

ॐ देव्यै नमः ।

ॐ सर्वसमृद्धिदायै नमः ।

ॐ अन्तर्दशारचक्रेश्यै नमः ।

ॐ देव्यै त्रिपुरमालिन्यै नमः ।

ॐ सर्वरोगहरेश्यै नमः ।

ॐ रहस्यायै योगिन्यै नमः ।

ॐ वाग्देव्यै नमः ।

ॐ वशिन्यै नमः ।

ॐ देव्यै कामेश्वर्यै नमः ।

ॐ मोदिन्यै नमः ।

ॐ विमलायै नमः । 940

ॐ अरुणायै नमः ।

ॐ जयिन्यै नमः ।

ॐ सर्वेश्वर्यै नमः ।

ॐ कौलिन्यै नमः ।

ॐ अष्टारसर्वसिद्धिदायै नमः ।

ॐ सर्वकामप्रदेश्यै नमः ।

ॐ परापररहस्यविदे नमः ।

ॐ त्रिकोणचतुरश्रस्थायै नमः ।

ॐ सर्वैश्वर्यायै नमः ।

ॐ आयुधात्मिकायै नमः ।

ॐ कामेश्वरीबाणरूपायै नमः ।

ॐ कामेशीचापरूपिण्यै नमः ।

ॐ कामेशीपाशरूपायै नमः ।

ॐ कामेश्यङ्कुशरूपिण्यै नमः ।

ॐ कामेश्वर्यै नमः ।

ॐ इन्द्रशक्तये नमः ।

ॐ अग्निचक्रकृतालयायै नमः ।

ॐ कामगिर्यधिदेव्यै नमः ।

ॐ त्रिकोणस्थायै नमः ।

ॐ अग्रकोणगायै नमः । 960

ॐ दक्षकोणेश्वर्यै नमः ।

ॐ विष्णुशक्तये नमः ।

ॐ जालन्धराश्रयायै नमः ।

ॐ सूर्यचक्रालयायै नमः ।

ॐ रुद्रशक्तये नमः ।

ॐ वामाङ्गकोणगायै नमः ।

ॐ सोमचक्रायै नमः ।

ॐ ब्रह्मशक्तये नमः ।

ॐ पूर्णगिर्यनुरागिण्यै नमः।

ॐ श्रीमत्त्रिकोणभुवनायै नमः।

ॐ त्रिपुरात्मने नमः।

ॐ महेश्वर्यै नमः।

ॐ सर्वानन्दमयेश्यै नमः।

ॐ बिन्दुगायै नमः।

ॐ अतिरहस्यभृते नमः।

ॐ परब्रह्मस्वरूपायै नमः।

ॐ महात्रिपुरसुन्दर्यै नमः।

ॐ सर्वचक्रान्तरस्थायै नमः।

ॐ समस्तचक्रनायिकायै नमः।

ॐ सर्वचक्रेश्वर्यै नमः। 980

ॐ सर्वमन्त्राणामीश्वर्यै नमः।

ॐ सर्वविद्येश्वर्यै नमः।

ॐ सप्रपञ्चायै नमः।

ॐ सर्वविश्वोत्पत्तिधात्र्यै नमः।

ॐ सर्ववागीश्वर्यै नमः।

ॐ सर्वयोगीश्वर्यै नमः।

ॐ पीठेश्वर्यै नमः।

ॐ अखिलेश्वर्यै नमः।

ॐ सर्वकामेश्वर्यै नमः।

ॐ सर्वतत्त्वेश्वर्यै नमः।

ॐ आगमेश्वर्यै नमः।

ॐ शक्त्यै नमः।

ॐ शक्तिधृषे नमः।

ॐ उल्लासायै नमः।

ॐ निर्द्वन्द्वायै नमः।

ॐ द्वैतगर्भिण्यै नमः।

ॐ निष्प्रपञ्चायै नमः।

ॐ महामायायै नमः।

ॐ सुवासिन्यै नमः।

ॐ परमानन्दसुन्दर्यै नमः। 1000

इति श्रीरुद्रयामले तन्त्रे भैरवभैरवीसंवादे श्रीत्रिपुरसुन्दरीसहस्रनामावलिः समाप्ता।

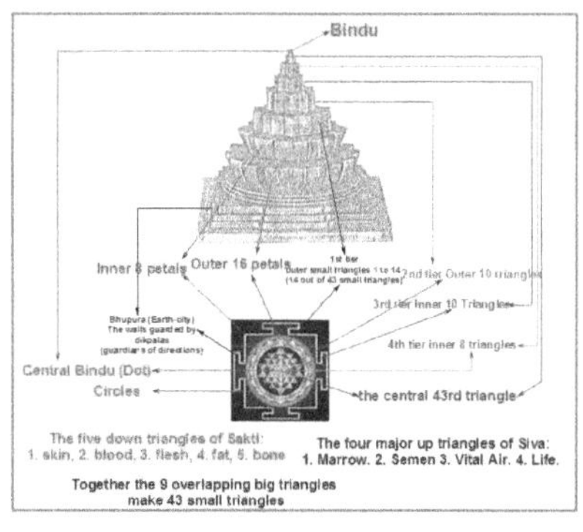

* * * * *

Śrī Tripura Sundary Aparādha Kṣamāpaṇa Stotram

This verse is to seek pardon with *Sri Devi* for any mistakes unknowingly happened during the worship.

Atha Stotraṃ Pravakṣyāmi Tripurārṇava Īritam |
Kiṃ Kiṃ Dvandvaṃ Danujadalini Kṣīyate Na Śrutāyāṃ
   Kā Kā Siddhiḥ Kulakamalini Prāpyate Nārcitāyām |
Kā Kā Kīrtiḥ Suravaranute Vyāpyate Na Stutāyāṃ
   Kaṃ Kaṃ Bhogaṃ Tvayi Na Cinute Cittamālambitāyām || 1

Sakusaṃ Sakusaṃ Rambha Svāritā Mokṣavibhrame |
Ciccandramaṇḍalāntaḥsthe Namaste Haravallabhe || 2

Jagaduddhāraṇodyogayogabhogaviyogini |
Sthitibhāvasthite Devi Namaḥ Sthāṇupriye'mbike || 3

Bhāvābhāvapṛthagbhāvānubhāve Vedakarmaṇi |
Caitanyapañcake Devi Namastubhyaṃ Harāṅgane || 4

Sṛṣṭisthityupasaṃhārapratyurjitapadadvaye |
Cidviśrāntimahāsattāmātre Mātarnamo'stu Te || 5

Vahnyarkaśītakiraṇabrahmacakrāntarodite |
Catuṣpīṭheśvari Śive Namaste Tripureśvari || 6

Carācaramidaṃ Viśvaṃ Prakāśayasi Tejasā |
Mātṛkārūpamāsthāya Tasyai Mātarnamo'stu Te || 7

Smṛtā Bhavabhayaṃ Haṃsi Pūjitā'si Śubhaṅkari |
Stutā Tvaṃ Vācchitaṃ Vastu Dadāsi Karuṇāvare || 8

Bhaktasya Nityapūjāyāṃ Ratasya Mama Sāmpratam |
Vāgbhavādimahāsiddhiṃ Dehi Tripurasundari || 9

Paramānandasandohapramodabharanirbhare |
Duḥkhatrayaparimlānavadanaṃ Pāhi Māṃ Śive || 10

Śabdabrahmamayi Yacca Devi Tripurasundari |
Yathāśakti Japaṃ Pūjāṃ Gṛhāṇa Madanugrahāt || 11

Ajñānādalpabuddhitvādālasyād Duṣṭabhāvataḥ |
Mamāparādhaṃ Kārpaṇyaṃ Kṣamasva Paradevate || 12

Ajñānāmasamarthānāmasvasthānanivāsinām |
Aśuddhaṃ Balamasmākaṃ Śiśūnāṃ Haravallabhe || 13

Kṛpāmayi Kṛpāṃ Bhadre Sakṛnmayi Niveśaya |
Tāvadahaṃ Kṛtārtho'smi Na Te Kiñcana Hīyate || 14

Yanmayā Kriyate Karma Jāgratsvapnasuṣuptiṣu |
Tat Sarvaṃ Tāvakī Pūjā Bhūyād Bhūtyai Rame Śive || 15

Dravyahīnaṃ Kriyāhīnaṃ Vidhihīnañca Yad Bhavet |
Tat Sarvaṃ Kṛpayā Devi Kṣamasva Paradevate || 16

Yanmayoktaṃ Mahājñānaṃ Tanmahat Svalpameva Vā |
Tāvat Sarvaṃ Jagaddhātri Kṣantavyamayamañjaliḥ || 17

Iti Śrī Tripura Sundarī Aparādha Kṣamāpaṇa Stotraṃ Sampūrṇam |

श्री त्रिपुर सुन्दर्यपराध क्षमापण स्तोत्रम्

अथ स्तोत्रं प्रवक्ष्यामि त्रिपुरार्णव ईरितम्।
किं किं द्वन्द्वं दनुजदलिनि क्षीयते न श्रुतायां
   का का सिद्धिः कुलकमलिनि प्राप्यते नार्चितायाम्।
का का कीर्तिः सुरवरनुते व्याप्यते न स्तुतायां
   कं कं भोगं त्वयि न चिनुते चित्तमालम्बितायाम्॥ १

सकुसं सकुसं रम्भ स्वारिता मोक्षविभ्रमे।
चिच्चन्द्रमण्डलान्तःस्थे नमस्ते हरवल्लभे ॥ २

जगदुद्धारणोद्योगयोगभोगवियोगिनि ।
स्थितिभावस्थिते देवि नमः स्थाणुप्रियेऽम्बिके॥ ३

भावाभावपृथग्भावानुभावे वेदकर्मणि ।
चैतन्यपञ्चके देवि नमस्तुभ्यं हराङ्गने॥ ४

सृष्टिस्थित्युपसंहारप्रत्युर्जितपदद्वये ।
चिद्विश्रान्तिमहासत्तामात्रे मातर्नमोऽस्तु ते॥ ५

वह्न्यर्कशीतकिरणब्रह्मचक्रान्तरोदिते ।
चतुष्पीठेश्वरि शिवे नमस्ते त्रिपुरेश्वरि॥ ६

चराचरमिदं विश्वं प्रकाशयसि तेजसा ।
मातृकारूपमास्थाय तस्यै मातर्नमोऽस्तु ते॥ ७

स्मृता भवभयं हंसि पूजिताऽसि शुभङ्करि ।
स्तुता त्वं वाञ्छितं वस्तु ददासि करुणावरे॥ ८

भक्तस्य नित्यपूजायां रतस्य मम साम्प्रतम् ।
वाग्भवादिमहासिद्धिं देहि त्रिपुरसुन्दरि॥ ९

परमानन्दसन्दोहप्रमोदभरनिर्भरे ।
दुःखत्रयपरिम्लानवदनं पाहि मां शिवे॥ १०

शब्दब्रह्ममयि यच्च देवि त्रिपुरसुन्दरि ।
यथाशक्ति जपं पूजां गृहाण मदनुग्रहात्॥ ११

अज्ञानादल्पबुद्धित्वादालस्याद् दुष्टभावतः ।
ममापराधं कार्पण्यं क्षमस्व परदेवते॥ १२

अज्ञानामसमर्थानामस्वस्थाननिवासिनाम् ।
अशुद्धं बलमस्माकं शिशूनां हरवल्लभे॥ १३

कृपामयि कृपां भद्रे सकृन्मयि निवेशय ।
तावदहं कृतार्थोऽस्मि न ते किञ्चन हीयते॥ १४

यन्मया क्रियते कर्म जाग्रत्स्वप्नसुषुप्तिषु ।
तत् सर्वं तावकी पूजा भूयाद् भूत्यै रमे शिवे॥ १५

द्रव्यहीनं क्रियाहीनं विधिहीनञ्च यद् भवेत् ।
तत् सर्वं कृपया देवि क्षमस्व परदेवते॥ १६

यन्मयोक्तं महाज्ञानं तन्महत् स्वल्पमेव वा ।
तावत् सर्वं जगद्धात्रि क्षन्तव्यमयमञ्जलिः॥ १७

इति श्री त्रिपुर सुन्दरी अपराध क्षमापण स्तोत्रं सम्पूर्णम् ।

*****

About the Author
(http://Ramamurthy.jaagruti.co.in)

Dr. Ramamurthy is a versatile personality having experience and expertise

in various areas of Banking, related IT solutions, Information Security, IT Audit, Vedas, Samskrutam and so on.

His thirst for continuous learning does not subside. Even at the age of late fifties, he did research on a unique topic "Information Technology and Samskrutam" and obtained Ph.D. – doctorate degree from University of Madras. He is into a project of developing a Samskrutam based compiler.

It is his passion to spread his knowledge and experience through conducting classes, training programmes and writing books.

He has already published books as detailed below. Further books are in pipe-line.

#	Title	Remarks	Pages
		Indology Related	
1.	*Shrī Lalita_Sahasranāmam*	English translation of Shrī *Bhāskararāya's Bhāṣyam*	750
2.	Power of *Shrī Vidyā*	The secrets demystified – with lucid English rendering and commentaries	80
3.	ஸ்ரீ வித்யையின் ஶக்தி	ஸ்ரீ வித்யா ரகசியங்கள்	100
4.	*Samatā – समता*	An exposition of Similarities in *Lalita_Sahasranāma* with *Soundaryalaharī*, *Saptaśatī*, *Viṣṇu Sahasranāma* and *Shrīmad Bhagavad Gīta*	172
5.	ஸமதா – समता	ஸ்ரீ லலிதா ஸஹஸ்ரநாமம் ஸௌந்தர்யலஹரீ, ஸப்தஶதீ, ஸ்ரீ விஷ்ணு ஸஹஸ்ரநாமம் மற்றும் ஸ்ரீமத் பகவத் கீதைகளில் ஒற்றுமையின் ஒரு வெளிப்பாடு	266
6.	*Advaita* in *Shākta*	Advaita Philosophy discussed in Shakta related Books	80
7.	*Shrī Lalitā Triśatī*	300 divine names of the celestial Mother – **English** translation of *Shrī Ādhi Śaṅkara's Bhāṣyam*	193
8.	ஸ்ரீ லலிதா த்ரிஶதி	300 divine names of the celestial Mother – Tamil translation of *Shrī Ādi Śaṅkara's Bhāṣyam*	234
9.	Secrets of *Mahāśakti*	Chandi demystified	78
10.	*Daśa Mahā Vidyā*	Ten cosmic forms of the Divine mother	60

#	Title	Remarks	Pages
11.	ஸ்ரீ வித்யா பேதங்கள்	ஸ்ரீவித்யா உபாசனையின் படிகள் - கோவை ஸ்ரீதச் சண்டி மலர்	51
12.	*Shrīvidya* Variances	Variances in Srividya Upasana	50
13.	ஸ்ரீ தேவீ ஸ்துதிகள்	பல முக்கிய அம்பாள் ஸ்தோத்ரங்கள்	133
14.	Śrī Devī Stutis – श्री देवी स्तुति:	Various important stotras of Sri Devi	223
15.	ஷண்மத மந்த்ரங்கள்	பொள்ளாச்சி ஸ்ரீ ஸஹஸ்ரசண்டி மஹாயாக நினைவு மலர்	145
16.	*Śanmata Mantras* – षण्मत मन्त्रा:	Important Mantras relating to Gods of six religions	87
17.	தேவதா மந்த்ரங்கள்	அக்கரைப்பட்டி ஸஹஸ்ரசண்டி மஹாயாக நினைவு மலர்	32
18.	ஆதி ஸங்கரரும் ஷண்மதமும்	ஷண்மதங்களைப் பற்றிய ஒரு அறிமுகம்	32
19.	ஸ்ரீ ஷண்மத தேவதா அர்ச்சனை	ஸ்ரீ மஹா கும்பாபிஷேக மலர்	64
20.	*Vaidhīka* Wedding	Typical Wedding process in English	56
21.	வைதீகத் திருமணம்	Typical Wedding process in Tamil	57
22.	ஸ்ரீகுரு பாத பூஜா விதானம்	சித்தகிரி ஸஹஸ்ரசண்டி மலர்	44
23.	குரு வார வழிபாடு		70
24.	ஸ்ரீவித்யா ஊடாம்னாய மந்த்ரங்கள்	சித்தகிரி ஸஹஸ்ரசண்டி மலர்	60
25.	*Ekatā*	Oneness among Shiva, Vishnu and Shakti	277
26.	ஏகதா - एकता	ஸிவபெருமான், விஷ்ணு மற்றும் ஸக்திக்குள் ஒற்றுமை	370
27.	*Vedas* – An Analytical Perspective	A description of Veda, Vedanta, Vedanga, Jyotisha, Shastra, etc.	240
28.	வேதங்கள் - ஒரு பகுப்பாய்வு	A description of Veda, Vedanta, Vedanga, Jyotisha, Shastra, etc.	280
29.	பரமாச்சார்யாள் நோக்கில் ஸ்ரீ லலிதாம்பிகா	The explanation given by Paramacharya on some of the names in Lalita Sahasranama	175
30.	*Ṣaṇṇavati Tarpaṇa*	Repaying Debts to Ancestors	42
31.	ஷண்ணவதி தர்பணம்	முன்னோர் கடன் தீர்த்தல்	48
32.	*Shrī Mahā Pratyangirā Devī*	Holy Divine mother in ferocious form	41
33.	ஸ்ரீ மஹா ப்ரத்யங்கிரா தேவீ	தெய்வீக அன்னையின் பயங்கர வடிவம்	51
34.	*Śrī Chakra Navāvarṇam*	Marvels of *Śrī Chakra*	115
35.	ஸ்ரீ சக்ர நவாவர்ணம்	ஸ்ரீ சக்ரத்தின் அதிசயங்கள்	130
36.	அம்பிகையின் (திரு) அவதாரங்கள்	ஸ்ரீ தேவியின் பல்வேறு அவதாரங்கள்	142

#	Title	Remarks	Pages
37.	Incarnations of Holy Mother	Different Incarnations of *Śrī Devī*	140
38.	ஸ்ரீ பிரணவானந்தர் - ஒரு சரிதம்	ஒரு அரிய ஸ்வாமிகளின் திவ்ய சரிதம்	121
39.	ஸன்யாஸம் - ஓர் அலசல்	ஹிந்து மத ஸன்யாஸ பேதங்கள் - ஒரு பகுப்பாய்வு	140
40.	Asceticism – an Analysis	A Study of Hindu *Sanyasam*	140
41.	ஶாந்தமும் ப்ரணவமும்	(**ஸ்ரீ** ஶாந்தானந்தரும் **ஸ்ரீ** ப்ரணவானந்தரும்) குரு சிஷ்யருக்கு உபதேசங்கள்	120
42.	ஸ்ரீ ஸஹஸ்ராக்ஷரீ வித்யா	2020 சாதுர்மாஸ்ய மலர்	84
43.	*Shakta Upanishats*	*Upanishats* about *Sri Devi*	385
44.	ஶாக்த உபநிஷதங்கள்	*Upanishats* about *Sri Devi*	400
45.	ஸ்ரீ **தேவீ கீதை**	Sri Devi Geeta	194
46.	*Śrī Devī Gīta*	Sri Devi Geeta	180
47.	*Śrī Gāyatrī Sahasranamam*	1,000 Divine Names of *Śrī Gāyatrī Mātā*	392
48.	ஸ்ரீ **காயத்ரீ** ஸஹஸ்ரநாமம்	ஸ்ரீ **காயத்ரி** மாதாவின் 1,000 திவ்ய நாமங்கள்	450
49.	ஸ்ரீ ஸெளந்தர்யலஹரீ	ஸெளந்தர்யலஹரீ ஒரு உள்-அறிவு	250
50.	*Śrī Soundaryalaharī*	*Soundaryalaharī* an Insight	200
51.	*Śrī Vārāhī Devī*	Holy Divine Mother with a hog face	96
52.	ஸ்ரீ வாராஹீ தேவீ	பன்றி முகத்துடன் கூடிய புனிதத் தெய்வீக அன்னை	106
53.	*Śrī Vijaya Bhairavar*	A Terrifying, Sacred, Divine form of Lord Shiva	164
54.	ஸ்ரீ விஜய பை4ரவர்	ஶிவபெருமானின் ஒரு திகிலூட்டும் புனித தெய்வீக உருவம்	188
55.	ஸ்ரீ ப4த்3ர காளீ	ஸ்ரீ தேவியின் ஒரு திகிலூட்டும் புனித தெய்வீக உருவம் — 1st Devi of Dasha Maha Vidya	226
56.	*Śrī Bhadra Kālī*	A Startling, Sacred and Divine form of *Śrī Devī* — 1st Devi of Dasha Maha Vidya	224
57.	ஸ்ரீ தாரா - நீல ஸரஸ்வதீ	2nd Devi of Dasha Maha Vidya	182
58.	*Śrī Tārā Devī* – Blue *Saraswatī*	2nd Devi of Dasha Maha Vidya	174
59.	*Śrī Tripura Sundarī Devī*	3rd Devi of Dasha Maha Vidya	182
60.	ஸ்ரீ த்ரிபுர சுந்தரீ தேவீ	3rd Devi of Dasha Maha Vidya	192
61.	*Chaṇḍī Homa Vidhānam*	Process of performing Chandi Homam	200
62.	சண்டி ஹோம விதானம்	Process of performing Chandi Homam	200
	Applied Samskrutam Based		
63.	*Paribhāṣā Stora–s*	An exploration of *Lalita Sahasranāmam*	96
64.	பரிபாஷா ஸ்தோத்ரங்கள்	ஸ்ரீ லலிதா ஸஹஸ்ரநாமம் - ஒரு ஆய்வு	135

#	Title	Remarks	Pages
65.	*Shrī Cakra*, An Esoteric Approach	Mathematical Construction to draw *Shrī Cakra*	64
66.	ஸ்ரீ சக்கரம் வரையும் முறை	ஸ்ரீ சக்கரம் வரைய கணித கட்டுமானம்	84
67.	Number System in Samskrutam	An overview of Mathematics based on Samskrutam	123
68.	ஸமஸ்க்ருதத்தில் எண்ணியல்	ஸமஸ்க்ருதத்தில் பொதிந்துள்ள எண் கணிதம்	140
69.	*Vedic* Mathematics	30 formulae elucidated	146
70.	Vedic IT	Information Technology and Samskrutam	162
	IT Based		
71.	Orthogonal Array	A Statistical Tool for Software Testing	180
	Banking Based		
72.	Retail Banking	A guide book for Novice	213
73.	Corporate Banking	A guide book for Novice	232
74.	Dictionary of Financial Terms	A Guide Book for all – Demystifying Myriad Global Financial Terms	215
75.	GRC in BFS Industry	(**G**overnance, **R**isk Management and **C**ompliance by Banking & Finance Industry)	200

*****